Praise for
Bold Ventures

"[A] gorgeous and roving debut…Van den Broeck's exploration extends beyond the lives and works of her subjects, turning into both a philosophical meditation on creativity and a brilliant character study of misunderstood artists."

—*Publishers Weekly* (starred review)

"A darkly comic meditation on the nature of creativity and the narrow margins between triumph and despair. Part memoir, part travelogue, and part reflection, this unique and hugely engaging book takes a fresh look at the tragicomic condition of being human."

—Carolyn Steel, author of *Sitopia*

"This book resembles the remarkable twisted steeple of the Church of Saint Omer, one of the buildings Charlotte Van den Broeck visits in *Bold Ventures: Thirteen Tales of Architectural Tragedy.* An award-winning poet, she brings an unexpected perspective, as did the green elm timbers that crooked and bowed the Calais spire into the shape of a battered witch hat. In her vivid prose, she examines dreams gone bad, immersing herself in a compelling counter-narrative in which events in her own life meld with both reveries and passing meetings with Goethe's young Werther, Borromini, and Sylvia Plath. Though Van den Broeck's subject here is failure—buildings disappoint, designers die by their own hand—her investigation into the fragility of creative hope has a genuine obsessive power."

—Hugh Howard, author of *Architects of an American Landscape: Henry Hobson Richardson, Frederick Law Olmsted, and the Reimagining of America's Public and Private Spaces*

"[*Bold Ventures*] dares to seek out a depth rarely encountered nowadays, one necessary for calling yourself an artist…this writer has something very special."

—*Low Countries*

"While going on essayistic quests that take her around the globe, Van den Broeck traces stories of self-complacency, fear of failure, and destiny. Indirectly, she researches the link between building and writing. Isn't every author bold by default, after all? In *Bold Ventures* she lives up to her ambition."

—*De Morgen*

"Van den Broeck has a very keen eye. But she also has a great mind, making transitions between philosophical contemplations and journalistic passages seem effortless."

—*De Standaard*

Bold Ventures

Also by Charlotte Van den Broeck

POETRY
Chameleon / Nachtroer

Bold Ventures

Thirteen Tales of Architectural Tragedy

CHARLOTTE VAN DEN BROECK

Translated from the Dutch by David McKay

Other Press
New York

Library of Congress Cataloging-in-Publication Data
Names: Broeck, Charlotte Van den, 1991- author. | McKay, David, translator. |
Broeck, Charlotte Van den, 1991- Waagstukken.
Title: Bold ventures : thirteen tales of architectural tragedy /
Charlotte Van den Broeck ; translated from the Dutch by David McKay.
Other titles: Waagstukken. English
Description: New York : Other Press, 2022.
Identifiers: LCCN 2022018765 (print) | LCCN 2022018766 (ebook) |
ISBN 9781635423174 (hardcover) | ISBN 9781635423181 (ebook)
Subjects: LCSH: Architects—Death. | Architecture—Miscellanea. |
Architects—Suicidal behavior. | Creation (Literary, artistic, etc.) |
Failure—Psychology.
Classification: LCC NA2543.D43 B7613 2022 (print) |
LCC NA2543.D43 (ebook) | DDC 720—dc23/eng/20220621
LC record available at https://lccn.loc.gov/2022018765
LC ebook record available at https://lccn.loc.gov/2022018766

"Today" is a word that only suicides ought to be allowed to use, it has no meaning for other people. It merely signifies a day like all the rest.

Ingeborg Bachmann, *Malina*, trans. Philip Boehm

Architecture is a hazardous mixture of omnipotence and impotence.

Rem Koolhaas & Bruce Mau, *S,M,L,XL*

But suicides have a special language.
Like carpenters they want to know *which tools*.
They never ask *why build*.

Anne Sexton, "Wanting to Die"

CONTENTS

I

MUNICIPAL SWIMMING POOL (2005–2011), CITY PARK, TURNHOUT

ARCHITECT ANONYMOUS

As luck would have it, she landed on her back and could keep her mouth above water. Two weeks before her sixteenth birthday, Nathalie was caught by her long ponytail in the filter of the paddling pool. The incident occurred on a busy Sunday afternoon, when the adult pool was too crowded for her to swim lengths. Nathalie's uncle had brought her to Turnhout from the neighboring town of Retie. While waiting for a 25-meter lane, she was playing with her uncle and young cousin in the shallow children's pool. She was seated with her back to the edge of the pool when she felt a sharp tug on her hair. The back of her head slammed into the tiled edge. Nathalie tried to scramble to her feet but was held down by a painful yanking sensation. She reached for her ponytail – by instinct, we cover the spots that hurt most with our hands – but where it should have been, she felt only the back of her head against the wall of the pool.

From the time her ponytail was caught in the suction outlet to the time of her rescue Nathalie was in no immediate danger of drowning, but throughout those tense minutes she was held in an extremely uncomfortable position.

Pool supervisor Bert was the first to rush to her aid. The obvious solution was to cut off the ponytail, but Nathalie was struggling with all her might. This made the trapped ponytail pull even harder; at any moment, the skin and hair might be torn away from her scalp. Her thrashing also made it very difficult for Bert to position the scissors for the liberating snip. The girl was screaming blue murder, perhaps in severe pain or perhaps in protest.

As a pool supervisor, Bert was used to thinking on his feet. Without pausing to interpret her screams, he ruthlessly cut off the ponytail. Nathalie's uncle and a few concerned bystanders grabbed her and calmed her down, wrapping the back of her head in a towel. Bert – scissors in one hand, lopped-off ponytail in the other – then saw what must have happened. In the exact spot where Nathalie's head had been held against the edge of the pool, the circulation system had a suction outlet, protected by a cover four millimeters thick. The cover turned out not to have been screwed on securely, so Nathalie's ponytail had ended up behind it, pulled into the circulation system.

As soon as Bert learned of this fact, he took several immediate steps. He drained the paddling pool and reattached the cover, making sure it was screwed firmly into place. Problem solved.

Nathalie emerged from the incident free of serious injuries, but very shaken. "It doesn't really hurt, but it *was* a shock," she told a roving reporter from the local TV news.

At her birthday party two weeks later, I saw she had covered the bald spot with a large artificial flower. It was hideous, but we mentioned it only behind her back.

*

Since the opening of the swimming pool in Turnhout city park, in October 2005, it has never stayed open for more than three months at a time. All sorts of peculiar defects keep leading to temporary closures: from subsidence and system malfunctions to biblical scenes of its water transformed into milk.

The exorbitant cost and flawed design of the new swimming pool soon caused a scandal in the region. Ten million euros had been spent on it, and it never seemed to be open. The regular swimmers were left with a lot of unanswered questions – above all, whether their annual membership fee would be refunded.

At the time, the whole controversy surrounding the swimming pool largely escaped my attention. Less than four years later in 2009, after repeated electrical failures and water leaks, it became painfully clear that the swimming pool would have to close its doors for good. But by then I was studying ninety-five kilometers away in Ghent and had other things on my mind, such as world literature and severing my ties with the past. I went swimming once a week in the sublime Art Deco pool by the Leie River in the heart of the city. The boggy terrain of my hometown, and all the forces pulling me back there, were gradually releasing their hold on me. But the Turnhout swimming pool was being sucked in, quite literally.

Below the swimming pool was the boiler room. At an imperceptible yet steady pace, the room was sinking deeper and deeper into the marshy ground. The electrical system's safety sensors, three-quarters of the way up the walls, were ultrasensitive but not in the most strategic position: they detected leaks from the pool above, but not the rising water from below. The sensors were too high up to be activated until the water had almost filled the room. Well before that, the boiler and the other machines could be waterlogged beyond repair, and the swimmers above could be electrocuted.

Of course, the pool regulars and other taxpayers had their theories about the closure, but the local authorities were savvy enough to keep the sinking boiler room out of the news. Instead, the public debate focused on a confusing multitude of ever-changing technical issues.

In October 2009, a banner was hung above the entrance to the pool:

TEMPORARILY PERMANENTLY CLOSED FOR MAINTENANCE

This unaccommodating announcement seemed designed to permit the authorities to say, "We told you so," no matter what the future might bring.

In the months that followed, all sorts of investigations took place into ways of improving the electrical system. There were visits from one expert after another. Cost estimates were made and remade, late-night meetings convened – all in the hope of finding a new reopening date. And sure enough, in January 2011 – after being closed for a year and a half – the swimming pool reopened.

The new era lasted only a few weeks. In April, the banner was retrieved from storage, with a slight adjustment:

~~TEMPORARILY~~ PERMANENTLY CLOSED FOR MAINTENANCE

How often did I swim there myself? Not often enough to justify the significance this *lieu de piscine* now holds for me. In my defense, you often don't know until after the fact what you should remember, and by then you're stuck with the things you would rather have forgotten. And vice versa, in this case. Nonetheless, my first sight of the new swimming pool is still etched in my mind.

It must have been the first summer after the opening, July 2006. I am only fourteen years old and venturing out unchaperoned for the first time. Through my red bikini bottoms, my swelling hips are starting to show. My top is an orange polyester triangle, the sharp end pointing down at my exposed navel. On the inside of my wrist is a tribal stick-on tattoo from a bag of chips. I want a new bikini like Eva's, with high-leg bottoms and two separate pockets on top, one for each of my nonexistent breasts. Eva is playing with Max in the water nearby – her bikini top is a size B with underwire. Max is a chubby ten-year-old boy from her neighborhood with a cute, freckled face and a mischievous smile. When he's bored, he tries to touch us in places that don't really interest him but that he knows embarrass us. Eva's breasts are currently his main target.

It's really too cold to swim outdoors, but the indoor pool is closed for technical reasons. Eva and Max are in the water; I'm lying on my towel on the grass nearby. *Gooseflesh, pasty, scrawny*, lists the cruel inner voice of a fourteen-year-old girl gazing at herself. It also tells me my belly's sticking out too much, so I stretch back on my elbows to flatten the imaginary bulge. No one is looking at me in particular, I'm practically invisible, yet I can feel all the eyes of the outdoor swimmers burning into my flesh. I thrust my flat chest out, just in case anyone wants a look after all.

"Don't do that, Max, stop it!" I hear Eva shouting. Propped up on my elbows near the edge of the grass beside the pool, I can see the lonesome weeping willow in the next field. It's an old hayfield, which grows up to knee level in July. From my perspective, the long stalks seem to brush the bottom of the willow's hanging branches, and wherever they touch, it's as if the image is zipped shut and loses depth – a painting by a pupil still struggling with perspective.

I'm reading a modern retelling of the medieval love story of Abelard and Héloïse, set in New York – Arthur and Lois, they're called in this version. In Latin class, we've just translated the myth of Hero and Leander. Tales of doomed romance go well with weeping willows: the combination ignites the pilot light in my fourteen-year-old heart.

I lie flat on my back and then bring my chin to my chest to

see the willow poking out just above the long stalks. From this angle, the stalks seem to be climbing the tree, slinging themselves around the branches like ropes. Dangling from the largest branch is a noose of grass.

*

Eternal afternoon. The colors are radiant. No one has to work. *Peter Getting Out of Nick's Pool* (1966). California sun on men's bare buttocks. David Hockney's paintings celebrate the backyard swimming pool as a temple of relaxation, good living and sexual license.

It is August 2017. I am visiting the temporary exhibition at the Centre Pompidou. Drove to Paris on impulse. I've spent the past weeks working manically on a commissioned series of poems. Before that came a busy year and the year before that was busy too. I can hardly remember a time when I wasn't busy. I'm the busy type. I'm probably worn out, but I won't admit it. Instead, I'm always losing my temper over nothing. The only remedy is looking at art. I try to draw new energy from Hockney's expanses of pink, blue and yellow. *A Bigger Splash* (1967): simple forms, a playful explosion, a cheerful palette. The sun is beyond the edge of the canvas, but it must be blazing to judge by the colors, which drip with heat. How distant it seems, a simple life with a swimming pool – too far away ever to reach.

In *Portrait of an Artist – Pool with Two Figures* (1972), a man, probably Hockney himself, is standing at the edge of a swimming pool. The backyard overlooks a scenic landscape, mountainous, green, deep breath. Yet the man at the side of the pool is not looking out at the view, but down at the nude figure glimpsed through the water's surface, swimming towards him. Refracted light marbles the water. The swimmer lies frozen in the pool of blue. It seems improbable that he will surface and look up at his observer. Is it the man's gaze that traps him underwater, or my own desire to see a cage in everything?

I wander through the exhibition, passing scenes and colors, collages and pencil drawings, pop art influences and rebellions against them, and portraits of the men in Hockney's life – again and again, the roguish buttocks, the recurring swimming pools, the years rushing by. A man's existence in his work. Sixty years of brushstrokes – one way to pass a life.

In the last gallery is Hockney's video installation, *The Four Seasons*. Four panels face each other to form a square of screened-off space. I slip through the opening between two. On the inside, each wall consists of nine separate screens, together displaying a single moving image. I install myself on the bench in front of the winter wall.

Woldgate Woods, Winter, 2010: the camera advances down a snow-covered road through the woods at the speed of a careful driver. An earlier vehicle has left tire tracks in the carpet of snow. Along the road are bare trees covered with snow and frost. I watch and the motion pulls me into the image, into the landscape, into the white, and I am the observer, I am the driver, and at the same time I am the slow camera following the road into the woods. Yet I seem not to gain any ground, because the landscape, as I move farther into it, does not change, or at least so I thought, because now, before I know it, the snow-covered road is not only on the screen in front of me but also behind me; I am on the bench in the museum and in the middle of the snow, moving still deeper into the white landscape – no, letting the forward pull, the mesmerizing image, draw me still deeper into the white. In sync with the slow movement of the camera, I feel – just as I am being drawn through the landscape – salt running through me, as if tears were following the very same snow-covered track through my body. My god, I'm so tired. The white is so pure.

*

Not long after the swimming pool's permanent closure in 2011, rumors began to circulate in the Turnhout cafés. Friends from the old days brought the story to Ghent. Or maybe not; maybe I heard the rumors when I was back in the Kempen, perched at the bar in Café Ranonkel. Had I heard about the architect of the swimming pool? The long litany of technical troubles was rumored to have driven him to suicide. Depending on whose turn it was to tell the story, the architect might even have hanged himself in the sinking boiler room, the scene of the failures. A pitch-black joke.

The question of whether the architect had really come to such a bitter end soon became secondary to the story's success. As the rumor gathered momentum, it was widely asked whether a person who caused a public fiasco on the scale of the Turnhout swimming pool, who showed incompetence in his profession and contempt for the public and their wallets – surely that type of person should pay the ultimate price? The storytellers believed, or wanted others to believe, that the construction faults could have led the architect to take his own life. For them, that belief was enough to justify passing on their version of the facts: an urban legend in the making, fictional but more convincing each time it was told. It was true because it was believed to be true, like the one about the killer in the back seat, which has terrified generation after generation by the glow of the campfire.

The cruelty of the reasoning behind the suicide story did not hit me, to be honest, until several years later. At first, I don't think I questioned the tale at all. Sometimes that's how it works here in Turnhout. Later, when I told the story myself, I spiced it up with a hint of dark romance, painting the architect as a tragic artist, desperately unable to make good on his ambitions.

The more sentimental versions of this fictional tale gave the architect a psychological backstory – not in the role of tragic artist, but as the underappreciated son of a well-known architect of the Turnhout School, a modernist movement that had put our town on the architectural map in the 1960s. The father was said to have arranged for the son to design the prestigious pool: a golden opportunity for him to make his own reputation instead of dining out on his father's success. In this version, what supposedly drove the son to the depths of despair was his failure in the eyes of his father and mentor. That's how cruel we can be to those we suspect of receiving unfair advantages.

Barroom gossip. Provincial rumors. A settling of scores. In any case, people were outraged about the swimming pool – and anger needs a target. Even though nothing had been proved, people thought it reasonable to point the finger at the architect. After all, *he* was the one who had designed the swimming pool with the boiler room below, in that marshy spot. Yes, perhaps it was too late to fix the mistake, prevent the failure, but at least in our narrative the person who had made the mistake had to pay with his life. The fictional underground suicide was confirmed and reconfirmed by every telling and each new twist. In any case, no one asked that the story provide any evidence for its own veracity. Therein lies the heartless verdict.

Of course in reality any number of individuals could have been responsible for the pool's endlessly multiplying failures; the link to the architect was an imagined one, but all the more powerful because of it.

*

Whenever I climb down the ladder into any swimming pool, I pass two phantoms from my memory. Him and me, sixteen years old forever. It's a Sunday afternoon, and we're interlaced against the wall of Turnhout's indoor pool. I am weightless in the water, my legs wrapped around his waist, his hands on my ass, his fingers reaching from there to explore the inside of my bikini bottoms. Between my legs, I can feel him getting hard in his orange nylon tent. Underwater there's less friction, but even so, he's thrusting against me so hard I'm scared he'll bruise me. We kiss without pausing for breath, like washing machines, with dramatic sweeps of the tongue. Between kisses, he tells me I'm "sexy," but I can't be sure, because he has his eyes closed when he says it. I want him to look at me.

Meanwhile, I don't dare look at him. I keep my eyes shut tight and remember a magazine article I recently read, by a girl who wrote about having sex with her boyfriend underwater. His penis got stuck inside her, vacuum sealed. It was really awkward. I consider our options if we find ourselves in a similar scenario. We could run off and join a traveling circus, as the stars of the sideshow "The Siamese Lovers." I'm crazy about him, I've just started the pill, and my body's pulsing with the promise of sex. The children we're scaring, the adults we're embarrassing – what do I care? The public swimming pool is an extension of my bedroom, where I have no privacy either: my mother makes me leave the door open when I'm sprawled on the bed with him.

Not until we hear screaming do I notice the world around us and push him off. On the other side of the pool, a small cluster of people has gathered around the lifeguard, who seems to have collapsed to the ground. There is blood on the nonslip floor. Two boys are running out into the corridor, towards the changing rooms. Not long afterwards, the lifeguard is loaded into an ambulance, and we all have to get out of the pool.

Since the corridor with the changing rooms is part of the scene of the crime, we have to change in the entrance hall, just inside the gates – almost a hundred swimmers, dripping all over the floor. The police interview all the witnesses.

Apparently, after the lifeguard had pulled a twelve-year-old troublemaker out of the pool, the boy returned with his older brother, a muscle-bound thug who beat the lifeguard senseless. Others claimed that the lifeguard was grabbing the boy to shut him up when his older brother came to his defense. The surveillance images reveal nothing more than the lifesaver standing with his back to the camera, in front of the boy, before being attacked from behind by the aggressor.

After waiting an hour and a half, we giggle as we tell the officer we didn't even see what happened; we were making out. They let us leave.

The incident leaves the lifeguard with a broken jaw and foot. The two boys remain unidentified. For the next few days, the swimming pool stays closed.

*

The architect who designed the pool is nameless; it has somehow proved possible to keep his identity out of the papers. This disappearing act only fuels the rumors of his suicide. Now and then someone claims to know who it is. Knowledge is power, even in café culture. Telling a good secret can earn you a free round, or at least persuade someone to hop on the barstool next to yours and keep you company. Rob V., a Ranonkel regular, says it wasn't the son of a well-known architect, but the nephew of a local councillor from an opposition party. René M. claims the architect wasn't even from Turnhout and certainly didn't die by his own hand, but the contractor disappeared without a trace when the building closed. Stan W., just as sure of himself, swears it was the contractor who took his own life after being unjustly accused.

By this stage, legal proceedings have been in progress for seven years. The city is claiming serious damages. The parties to the dispute have formally agreed not to give out any information about the case.

A former local councillor tells me the contractor saw the problem coming, but his advice went unheeded. The priority was to open the swimming pool fast, and in their haste, the local authorities overlooked the design flaws. Unwilling to waste any more words on the subject, he concludes, "The municipality pulled the wool over our eyes."

The mayor strictly observes the embargo on accurate information about the whole business. When I ask him exactly why the swimming pool was permanently closed, he parries the question with practiced ease: "Because of mechanical failures resulting from the issues at hand."

He is dismissive of the story about the architect but tells me he can't comment in view of the ongoing legal proceedings. Instead, he shows me a few photos of the new waterslide.

*

Danny lived on Driekuilenstraat, a minor one-way street that runs parallel to the street where my parents live. Whenever I order a Duvel, I think of him. Every day at noon, he went for a drink at the swimming pool cafeteria. He traveled the two kilometers to the city park in an electric wheelchair. He had managed to qualify for a free one from Social Services, because of his obesity and fatty liver. He perpetuated his suffering, and his benefits, by drinking twelve to fourteen Duvels a day. My father says it was actually twice that number, but facts don't always sound as credible as fiction.

In any case, while drinking he would sit at the window between the cafeteria and the indoor pool, placidly watching the swimmers, with no ulterior motives. He never made trouble or turned vulgar when drinking. He just drank himself into a stupor. By the end of his visit to the cafeteria, he would give off a sour smell, sometimes laced with urine. Apart from that, he was a polite customer and a reliable source of income for the cheerless cafeteria, where even the ham-and-cheese sandwiches were inedible.

When he drove home in his wheelchair at five, his wife would have a fried chicken ready for him, which he ate skin and all. After that, he would go to sleep and wouldn't rise again until just before noon the next day, when the whole routine would repeat itself. There was no money left for his wife to go out. His benefits and her pension covered the bills and the Duvels. She worked as a house cleaner, paid cash in hand, to meet unforeseen expenses. On Sundays, Danny would remain in the cafeteria longer than usual to watch the swimming club compete. The front crawl was his favorite event.

On this particular Sunday, the referee called a halt to the competition by order of the Sports and Recreation Service. Although Danny was fast approaching his fourteenth Duvel, he roused himself from his fog for the occasion. Through the window, he could see the members of the swimming club getting an earful from Bert the swimming pool supervisor. What Danny couldn't hear from the cafeteria, however, was that the swimmers had carelessly thrown down their towels and bags along the edge of the pool. In doing so, they had unintentionally covered most of the ventilation ducts (the club has three hundred members). In less than half an hour, this obstruction of the air supply drove the humidity up to 80 percent, causing light-headedness and making it hard to breathe.

The Sports and Recreation Service and the referee reprimanded the members of the swimming club, but it was Bert who gave it to them with both barrels, calling them filthy scum, treating them like delinquent children instead of grownup amateur swimmers who might benefit from a reminder to be more considerate of their surroundings. A few members mouthed off at him. The situation soon became tense. Yet despite the altercation, the swimming pool was evacuated in less than ten minutes.

Bert later acknowledged that he had responded "too impulsively" and said he hoped to work with the club on constructive ideas "going forwards": maybe he could station someone at the stairs full-time, to make sure no one brought in any bags or towels?

After the evacuation, the humidity quickly dropped back to 50 percent, but the swimming pool remained closed for the rest of the evening.

When the pool employees arrived the next morning to let in the early swimmers, they found the electric wheelchair at the entrance to the cafeteria, long before the usual opening time. Later that day, Danny's wife confirmed that he hadn't returned home the evening before. She had waited until the chicken was cold and then thought, *Ah, fuck it* . . .

*

On the blog *Old Times in Turnhout*, the mood is nostalgic. Under a sepia photograph of the outdoor swimming pools in the city park (three pools and a little fountain), I read the following response:

Whenever I think back to the outdoor swimming pool in the city park, I miss the good old days and can hardly believe it's not there anymore. My heart breaks whenever I go to the city park and think back to how it was then, how it is now, and how it never will be, ever again . . . (W.P. – 6/29/ 2012 – 6:17 p.m.)

Reply:

Dear W.P., There was no other choice. All the pools were connected to the same electrical system. The problems with the indoor pools also affected the outdoor pools. If the outdoor pools had stayed open, it would almost certainly have led to another breakdown. I'm glad at least they could prevent that. (D.V. – 7/17/2012 – 8:34 a.m.)

Reply:

Utter drivel. Where the local authorities failed completely was in thinking we had to have a fancy indoor pool. They never seriously considered the arguments for a large, no-frills outdoor pool. A proper Turnhouter shouldn't need any warm water. (M.V. – 4/2/2017 – 10:32 p.m.)

*

Quarter past seven, cold water, short circuit. Up for four hours already. Never gone to a public pool so early in the morning before. Last night my boyfriend left me. These are the first, desperate hours, and I've been swimming for an hour and a half. Arms and legs: heavy and hollow. Chest: breathless. Belly: in knots. Skin: saturated with chlorine. Mouth: not drowned, lips just above water level. No young lovers at poolside today.

On the bus home I fall asleep and miss my stop. But I wake up at home in bed and then fall straight back into deep sleep, all the way to the swimming pool floor. I'm back in the 25-meter lane. Stroke by stroke, I swim to the far end. Actual time and narrated time are identical in this dream, so I soon confuse it with my early-morning swim. Then moving becomes more difficult; the water feels thicker. As I reach the middle of the lane, I find I can't move any farther. The water has turned milky now. There are no other swimmers, no witnesses. The milk feels warm, warmer, I feel the milk-water around me warming up and sink down into it. Just for a second, I think, and I immerse myself in the thick, white warmth. That is, until I remember I need to breathe and my panic sends me swimming back up. When I reach the surface I collide with a moving membrane, elastic: it gives when I push, but it doesn't tear. There's no opening. I can't break through the skin on the warm milk.

"SWIMMING IN MILK" reads the headline a few days later, on Thursday June 11, 2009. On Wednesday afternoon, the water in the main pool in the Turnhout city park turned a milky white color. The swimming pool coordinator was not concerned at first. "When it's crowded, substances get into the water that can cause discoloration. That's most likely to happen in the summer," he said dismissively.

But among the swimmers, panic soon broke out. A child playing with his father at one end of the large pool swallowed a mouthful of the milky water and then vomited repeatedly. Several swimmers attested that the water had a suspicious chemical odor. An elderly lady was helped to the poolside just in time, before passing out; she thought the Spirit of God had moved upon the face of the waters and turned them to milk, like Christ turning water into wine.

When the last remaining swimmers decided to play it safe and leave the pool, a power failure disabled the scanning system for the membership badges, blocking their exit. At that, the management evacuated the site without further delay.

On Thursday morning, the water was still cloudy and whitish. This led to fears that maybe the pools had somehow been filled with the recycled gray water normally used for flushing the toilets and cleaning the showers. The coordinator responded, "Well, that's actually clean water, just not clean enough to swim in."

On Friday, the Provincial Hygiene Institute is expected to come and take water samples. The test results won't be available until at least forty-eight hours later. The expectation now is that the swimming pool will reopen on Tuesday at the earliest. Meanwhile, all they can do with that white water is rinse out the pool – rinse, rinse, rinse.

*

Good news: the new, custom-made filter expected to solve some of the swimming pool's recurring problems will arrive in Turnhout sooner than expected. As soon as it's here, they'll test it for a few days and try to predict how the water will look after thousands of people have swum in it. Depending on the results, the pool may reopen before the Christmas break.

But the 2009 Christmas break comes and goes, and in January 2010 the pool remains closed. The main pool is probably steadily leaking like a sieve, with water seeping down through the joints of the tiled floor and then through the concrete into the boiler room, where it drips onto the electrical wiring. No one is willing to admit that they'll have to pour fresh concrete.

"You say water is passing through the concrete; we say it's a leak. There are chinks, gaps and drill holes through which water could be leaking into the boiler room. Keep that in mind, and try to get beyond what you imagine is going on. Why do people in this bloody town always jump to conclusions before anything has even happened?" the spokesperson for the local authorities explains calmly.

*

In volume ten of the collected works of Charles Darwin, I find a passage about how humans and animals express emotion. It refers to the "grief-muscles" in the face, activated by encounters with death, sorrow and failure. Darwin describes this phenomenon, in the thoroughgoing rationalist spirit of the nineteenth century, not as the outward expression of inner life, but as a muscular contraction, a physical response.

The grief-muscles are interconnected. Pinching the eyebrows turns down the corners of the mouth and also influences the circulation of blood in the face: consequently, the complexion turns pale, the muscles go flaccid, the eyelids droop, and the head sinks towards the chest. The lips, cheeks and lower jaw are all pulled downwards by their own weight. According to Darwin, this is why the face of a person who hears bad news, or experiences failure, is said to "fall." Likewise, a perceived failure is said to result in "loss of face." Our face falls off. We lose it. We have no more identity.

It's just a metaphor. I don't have to make so much of it.

*

For want of their own swimming pool, the Turnhout schools sent their pupils to two nearby villages for swimming lessons throughout the 1990s and into the early 2000s. I once nearly drowned in the Arendonk pool, but no one took it seriously.

The last swimming class before the holidays was always reserved for "free play." Awaiting us in the water were colorful toys, some made of foam and others inflatable: pool noodles, floating mats, balls, kickboards and, across the whole length of the teaching pool, the belly slide. I was sitting on a red foam mat with the fat boy of the class when he told me he was in love with me and then, taken aback by his own confession, shoved me brusquely off the mat. The shove I had not seen coming. The boy didn't know his own strength; I flipped over twice and ended up under the mat. Instinctively, I pushed up on the mat, in the direction of the noisy air, but with the fat boy on top, it wouldn't budge. Immediate panic. Again, I tried to lift the mat. I was unsuccessful, and when I started to realize it wasn't working, I felt something take shape in my head, a thing I can only describe as a thin thread. A thin thread pulled taut across the diameter of my skull, my dwindling air supply all wound together, a thin thread of breath inside my head that I had to hold on to.

When I think back to those suffocating seconds under the mat, it frightens me to realize just how fast I gave up, how little survival instinct I showed in that instant.

The children at play and the wild, sloshing water all around me must have set the mat in motion. Once I noticed it could move horizontally, I realized I wasn't trapped at all; all I had to do was swim out from under the mat and I'd be free.

I gasped for air as I surfaced, pulled myself over to the ladder and, once I was safely out of the water, filled the place with the sound of my wailing. The lifeguard, who wore many hats – he was also my gym teacher and the after-school coordinator – came over to comfort me. When I told him I'd nearly drowned under the red mat, he said, "Of course you didn't."

*

On April 18, 2011 the swimming pool reopened after a closure of four hundred and forty-three days. By seven that morning, quite a crowd of swimmers had gathered at the door. Everyone who had been a member at the time of the closure back in 2009 had been invited to visit that day for an extension of their membership. They could swim for free for the same number of days that the pool had been closed. Around one hundred people queued up at the reception desk to add the missed days of swimming to their cards.

At twelve-fifteen, a traffic jam formed at the electronic gates that checked the armbands. Around forty swimmers could not pass through; the system was down.

It took twenty minutes to find the blown fuse, probably the result of unprecedented strain on the system that morning from renewing all the memberships. Ten minutes later, the first swimmers had changed. In the corridor from the changing rooms to the swimming pool, they were told to wait; the chlorine level was on the high side. Some became understandably angry and left.

After a brief technical inspection, the remaining swimmers were allowed to enter the water. Some still felt they were being played for fools; others were mainly relieved they could swim after all. Soon after the first splashes, the lights went out. A power failure. Since even the lockers needed electricity to open, the swimmers had to stand around in the dark in their swimsuits, while eighty excitable schoolchildren waited in the lobby for their turn in the pool.

Then the cause of the power failure was discovered. The swimmers weren't told what had gone wrong, but at least it was fixed. After the eighty children had changed, they queued up to jump from the diving boards into the three reserved lanes and start the 500-meter crawl.

Once the children were out of the water, the cafeteria closed, and the front desk employees decided enough was enough: in view of the unanticipated problems, it was better to close until the Sunday competition.

On Sunday, the competition was canceled. The swimming pool remained closed.

*

All adversity can be overcome. A few years later, the permanent closure became temporary once more. With a stubbornness I have not witnessed elsewhere, the Turnhout authorities made plans for a new swimming pool in the exact same place as the old one, despite the manifest likelihood that, like the old one, it would sink into the marshy ground. The aim was to reopen in the spring of 2014. This time, failure was not an option. It was no longer just about building a new swimming pool. More than that, it was an opportunity to set things right, to pick up Turnhout's fallen face from the ground and stick it back in place. The new pool was intended not only to appease the stranded swimmers, but also to signal a successful new beginning. The plans hinged on the transition to a new network that would make electrical failures and defective groundwater pumps a thing of the past. To this end, they included two new machine rooms, for rapid response to ventilation and water treatment issues.

The old waterslide was to be dismantled.

The boiler room that had caused so much trouble was to be replaced with a new, elevated machine room. On the same upper level would be three children's pools next to the cafeteria.

The 25-meter pool was to remain in place.

Instead of a wave machine, the new teaching pool would have a movable floor, and the new slide would have its own separate pool at the bottom.

This new slide would be 60 meters long and take snapshots of the swimmers as they whooshed past with a built-in camera halfway down – inspired by a popular log ride at a well-known theme park. The photographs would be for sale on key rings or printed in a choice of styles: regular, rum pirates, or dolphins.

The sauna and the Jacuzzi would still be there, but with an exciting new look.

The city authorities had chosen to build this new swimming pool instead of renovating the old one. The extra costs would be recouped in just five years, they said, and yes, the budget did make allowances for unforeseen costs and maintenance.

*

The new swimming pool did not open until February 2017. Less than a month later came the first temporary closure; during a children's swimming lesson, the water had given off suffocating chlorine fumes. Another three months later, a small band of evening regulars were confronted with a locked door, because it was "no longer financially feasible to keep the swimming pool open after 18:00."

*

Could a failed swimming pool really push someone to the point of tying a rope around a pipe on the boiler room ceiling and kicking the stepladder out from beneath their feet? When is a failure worth dying for? My real question is: What makes a mistake larger than life, so all-encompassing that your life itself becomes a failure? Where is the line between creator and creation?

I picked up the trail in Turnhout, on home turf, where most stories start, and it led me to twelve more works of architecture that had fateful consequences for their architects. In the span of three years, I visited these sites of failure. My goal was to rehabilitate those architects, to pick up their lost faces and stick them back in place, to do something to counter the pointlessness of their despair, the finality of their suicide. In moments of megalomania, I even imagined I might somehow reach into the past and stop them. At least, that was the kind of thing I told myself at first.

II

CHURCH OF SAINT OMER (1607–1676), VERCHIN

JEAN PORC (d. 1611)

Do I myself have the good fortune to live near a twisted church spire? As I reply, I try to sound suitably disappointed. After all, Madame Dupont is none other than the proud president of the Association des Clochers Tors d'Europe, the European Association for Twisted Spires. When the last president resigned four years ago, he put her forward as the most qualified successor. A complete surprise. The president serves a seven-year term, she tells me: not a decision to be taken lightly. But of course, she was honored to be chosen.

"What is more, she is the first woman president," her husband, Monsieur Dupont, breaks in. The two of them, a couple in their sixties, have driven two and a half hours to meet me at the church in Verchin, a village in Pas-de-Calais with barely two hundred inhabitants, nestled among country roads two kilometers from the source of the Leie River, known here as the Lys.

As I drove into the village, the twisted spire of the Church of Saint Omer was concealed by the bare November branches. Then it leapt into focus: that twisted spire wasn't sprouting from a tree, but sitting atop the church tower like a wizard's sagging hat.

The house across the street from the church is for sale. Next to it is a DIY shop with three parking spaces. Now and then a lorry passes, taking a shortcut down the main street. Other than that, there are no signs of life in the village. I presume the inhabitants are lurking behind the curtains and the lowered shutters.

The moment I arrived, Mme Dupont had me pegged as her curious visitor. She couldn't believe how young I was, not at all the way she'd imagined a *Belgian author*. But she said a friendly hello, and M. Dupont straightaway started scheming to lower the average age of the association's members.

So what does their association do exactly? Mostly media relations, exchange programs and research, they tell me. They explain the importance of gathering and sharing as much information as possible about the twisted spires. Of the eighty-two *clochers tors* in Europe, about half have now been described in Part I of the association's planned two-volume comprehensive survey. M. Dupont opens the boot of the car and takes out the book. They haven't yet seen all the spires it describes, but their dream is that one day they will. Each time they visit a new one they stamp their book, like devoted pilgrims.

M. Dupont has a favorite so far: the crooked spire in Chesterfield, covered entirely in lead, a very solid structure. Mme Dupont, in her role as president, prefers to remain impartial, but she does think the Verchin spire quite exceptional. "It's practically bowing to the passersby," she muses.

*

Because of building works, the village hall has moved temporarily to a shipping container behind the church. The toothy barking of a pair of German shepherds sends us scurrying down the sandy path in the right direction. The mayor of Verchin, M. Lamourette, is waiting for us in his makeshift office.

As we enter we are stifled by the tropical air blasting from a small electric heater, which keeps the container at a feverish temperature. Next to the heater are a filing cabinet and a coffee machine, opposite it six folding chairs and two simple tables. At one table, the secretary is screened off by a humming MacBook Pro, a strangely anachronistic sight in a village otherwise untouched by digital technology. At the other table, the mayor rises to his feet. His tabletop is practically empty, aside from an ink pad in the far right corner on which a rubber stamp waits to grant permission. Mayor Lamourette gives our hands a deft little squeeze that commands respect. He stresses how hard it was to clear this slot in his busy schedule for our amateur club of spire-lovers. And he hastens to add that we shouldn't expect to see the church interior; the building is on the verge of collapse.

A secretary serves us coffee; in the hot, stale air, it immediately brings on a dry headache. Then an unusually small man, perhaps close to eighty, comes sweeping into the container office. It's M. Beaufort, the association's local representative and Verchin specialist. He speaks to us in the regional Ch'ti dialect, with guttural sounds that make his French impossible to follow, as if pounding a nail deeper into his mouth with every word. I retreat into my own thoughts, noticing the missing tip of the index finger on his right hand. M. Beaufort ignores me; he seems fixated on the president, Mme Dupont, showering her with what I suspect are compliments. This flattery doesn't seem to make her husband jealous at all; on the contrary, M. Dupont receives the kind words to his wife as if they were intended for him. There must be a story behind that missing fingertip . . .

Only when Mme Dupont repeats M. Beaufort's words to me in polished French do I understand that my reason for visiting has upset him.

"This is a Catholic village with a famous church," M. Beaufort protests. "Everyone is proud of Saint Omer and its authentic, exceptional spire. By the standards of its time, it's a *very* fine piece of work. And now you've come to dig up some scandalous story?"

"No, I don't think so," I reply. "I've developed a personal interest in architectural failures – especially in failures that cost the architects their lives. Or, more precisely, led them to take their own lives. *Le suicide?*"

I can see that M. Beaufort would be delighted to thwack me on the head if it would send that word back down my throat. The look in his eyes is white-hot, but he reins himself in.

"The architect, whoever it was, did not jump from the church tower," M. Beaufort says with authority. "Why would he?"

His question sounds a little like a challenge; his certainty mocks me, with all my assumptions and romantic suspicions. No, that old story about the humiliated architect jumping from the crooked church spire is nothing but an old rumor, padded with shoddy research. What is more – as he, the local expert, makes clear – it was never *my* story to tell. He's sorry I had to travel 175 kilometers just to find out what I ought to have known beforehand.

My visit apparently feels like a personal affront to M. Beaufort, who has been researching the history and folklore of the church all his life. He could simply say I have no legitimate reason to be here, but he seems too crafty for that. Instead, he hopes to rectify my error, to debunk my preconceived ideas about his church, to improve my taste. In his eyes the spire, far from being a failure, is a vivid emblem of his otherwise color-less village, and by extension of himself.

Mayor Lamourette, familiar with M. Beaufort's stubborn pride, sees his conference table turning into a debating arena and takes on the role of referee. Lamourette confirms the existence of the story. Yes, according to legend, the architect leapt from the church tower after seeing that the spire was twisted. In Verchin, it's a kind of inside joke, but he doubts it has any actual historical foundation.

The church took about seventy years to build, Lamourette continues. It was the work of several generations: in those days, a grandfather would start building, and the grandson who inherited his trade would see the church to completion. It's not clear whether the design was the work of a single architect. Rome may have been teeming with Michelangelos, but here in Verchin, the builders probably belonged to the local masons' guild.

"Yes, it would have been the guild the first time round, but I must emphasize that the church as it is today dates from after the fire of 1860 and was built by the Verchin community," M. Beaufort interrupts, wresting back control of the conversation. "A distant cousin of mine, up the road in Teneur, is a genealogist. He draws up family trees and family histories for a very reasonable price. He's well informed about the latest dating methods and has examined the axe and the saw handed down to me by my grandfather, who received them from his grandfather. According to my cousin, and I have perfect faith in his judgment – did I mention he studied at a *grand école*? – both the axe and the saw are original tools from the period of the fire. In other words, my great-great-grandfather helped to rebuild the church with his own bare hands. All the people of Verchin, and of the neighboring villages, took up their tools of their own accord and without hesitation restored the building. Every brick that was laid was a paving stone on the road to paradise. Artisans were honored to take part in the restoration and did their very finest work. The spire was covered with twenty-two thousand pieces of Breton slate, each placed by hand. It's a kind of mosaic without color, a pious, understated work of art."

Growing tired of M. Beaufort's lecture, I let my eyes wander to the container's Plexiglas window, through which I can see the Saint Omer tower rising 28 meters into the sky. I must admit it has its charm. The vain spire wears its layer of Breton slate like a collar of dull jewels around its curved, slender neck. A hunchback doing its best to stand tall, it moves me with its mixture of imperfection and pride. M. Beaufort follows my gaze: "Magnificent, look how it soars!"

His boyish enthusiasm for the church spire, which isn't actually that tall, makes me wonder if he's ever left this place and been to a big city.

"Before the fire, the spire was much shorter," he continues. "Too short, in fact. Any church spire needs a weathercock high enough to spot the cocks in the neighboring villages – peekaboo! You see, a good weather vane teaches a moral lesson, reminding the villagers to live a righteous life. It sees everything, and I do mean everything! Just like the cock in the Bible story that crowed three times to unmask Judas, the traitor. At first, the Verchin weathercock was a few meters below the sight line of its neighbors. It was feared that this difference in height would devastate the village's morale. So after the church was destroyed, the villagers rebuilt it taller than ever, to strengthen our community, and so that our cock could look the others straight in the eye. But the frame of the church was not strong enough to hold up the 28-meter-tall tower. This lack of support, combined with the weight of the stone, caused the poorly anchored spire to twist."

So despite Verchin's efforts, the weathercock remained at half-mast, a full 140 centimeters or so below its original level. M. Dupont chuckles: "In other words, a monumental cock-up."

"Oh, you men and your crude jokes!" protests Mme Dupont, but she bursts into full-bodied laughter all the same. I stare out at the crooked spire again: three-quarters erect, drooping to the left, with the look of a lover who's starting to have second thoughts. M. Beaufort sticks out his right index finger significantly a couple of times, but his missing fingertip makes the gesture fall flat. The spire is not only bent under its own weight, but also twisted around its own axis.

"The whole plan went off at half cock!" M. Beaufort gleefully continues, enjoying the wordplay.

Mayor Lamourette steers us back into safer waters, telling us about the French architect and theorist Eugène Viollet-le-Duc, well known for restoring many churches damaged in the French Revolution. Viollet-le-Duc claimed that the peculiar phenomenon of the twisted spires had come about because the wood had not been dry enough. That was probably the case in Verchin: the frame of the spire was made of young elm. It would normally have been dried for four years before use, but the villagers were in a hurry to rebuild the tower. After a year of ceaseless, biblical rainfall, they went ahead and used the moist, green wood. Before long the spire started to warp, deforming the wooden frame.

"Why the rush? Why did they have to complete the spire so fast?" I ask.

Mme Dupont translates his answer to my question: "Lightning and tornadoes would be in a rush as well, if not for the church bells ringing all the time." Her expression suggests that she doesn't know quite what this means, any more than I do.

M. Beaufort takes advantage of the confusion to bring up a matter that's clearly been on his mind: "Young people don't know the meaning of contentment anymore. Today's society is so big and diseased and depressed. Young people go too far. They expect immediate gratification without lifting a finger, and on top of that they want to be the best. Ten out of ten for everyone. I drink beer every day, because in today's society, if you feel out of place ... well, that's the thing to do. It's all on account of the modern world that society got this way. I have nothing. Nothing. Only my sister who cleans the house. My parents worked as concierges and they were happy. We all slept in one room. I had to share everything, and today everyone lives in the lap of luxury and is miserable. People don't know how to live."

"You're a philosopher, M. Beaufort," Mme Dupont remarks.

He shakes his head to distance himself from every possible form of philosophy. He wants nothing to do with all that.

"Oh yes, you've got it all worked out in your head. But watch your words, M. Beaufort. There's a young person present who might imagine you're talking about her."

And at that moment, as they turn towards me, Mme Dupont's eyes shining with forgiveness and M. Beaufort's with spite, I sense that, in this place and at this moment, I stand for all the changes, flaws and technological advances that have crept into the world since they were my age. I see myself reflected in their eyes, the focal point of their disapproval, the object of their cultural pessimism. M. Beaufort seems to have seized on this occasion, my arrival in the village, where the average age is at least twice my own, to project everything he opposes onto one guilty young face, which happens to be present and happens to be mine. And is he really so wrong? As I passed under the bare branches of the horse chestnut trees on my way into Verchin, didn't they remind me of prison bars? As soon as I enter a sleepy village like this, I can't help but feel bogged down, trapped. In a reflex, I try to imagine how people can live their lives in these few monotonous streets – how they go about it, even purely in practical terms. How it is possible that a day passes here, and after that day the next one? It strains my imagination to breaking point. To be at the mercy of the knowable, morning, noon and night, caught in a microcosm you can fathom in a glance, to spend your whole life in a place that life never seems to reach. The suffocated feeling taking hold of me suggests that M. Beaufort's curmudgeonly ramblings have somehow trapped me in his image of who I am. Before I have a chance to correct that image, the door of the container swings open. A man trudges in and shouts, in a thunderous voice, "You ran off with my cousin!"

M. Beaufort springs to his feet, squaring up to the man. The two of them launch into a ferocious shouting match, hurling the rusty nails of their dialect in each other's faces. Mme Dupont follows their altercation with the intensity of my grandmother watching her soaps. She offers me a summary: "I believe this man is in love with M. Beaufort's cousin."

"He's my cousin himself, goddamn it! My own flesh and blood!" M. Beaufort cries.

Out in the open air, in the yard between the container and the church, the two cousins calm down. It appears it was all a misunderstanding. If I understand correctly, M. Beaufort did not so much steal his cousin's cousin as sabotage their wedding.

"She's a remarkable woman," the male cousin explains in a more subdued tone, breaking into a blush and taking off his cap. "If the spire clapped eyes on her, it would twist itself silly!"

He goes on to explain this reference to the well-known fairy tale of the virgins of Verchin. According to legend, the Saint Omer spire was first erected – straight and tall, like a proud phallus – to poke fun at the many girls who pretended to be virgins when they married. One day a beautiful girl, a pig farmer's daughter, came to church for her wedding. But unlike all the others, she was an actual virgin. The spire was so charmed that it leaned in for a better look at the unsullied creature. When it saw with its own eye that she was telling the truth, it twisted itself around its axis in surprise, vowing never to straighten itself out again until a second virgin came to the church to marry. But as you can see, he concludes, the spire is still waiting.

"That's sexist," Mme Dupont protests.

"Well, our cousin is twice as pure as the virgin of Verchin," the cousin explains. "On top of that, she's a pig farmer's daughter as well. It's fate. God must have wanted it that way, considering that the twist in our church spire looks exactly like a pig's prick. I want to marry her, here in church, before we get too old."

"We'll see what we can do," the mayor replies. He tells me the church isn't really in use anymore because the nave is on the verge of collapse. There have been no services for almost sixteen years. "And of course M. Beaufort will have to consent to the marriage. She's his cousin too," he adds, in the spirit of fairness.

M. Dupont has kept a low profile so far – hiding in Mme Dupont's shadow, so to speak. He must think that's his place as the husband of a powerful woman. But the folksy appeal of the tale of the virgins of Verchin seems to perk him up, and he asks me if I've heard the legend of the twisted church spire of Saint-Viâtre. No? *Magnifique!* Such a fantastic tale, it could hardly be made up.

Mme Dupont berates him: "Enough. If you go on like that, she won't take you seriously."

She means she's worried I won't take *her* seriously, now that her husband is openly letting his imagination run away with him. After a final stern glare, she joins the mayor and M. Beaufort's lovestruck cousin to negotiate for a peek inside the church. Once she's too far away to hear, M. Dupont steals up to me, his eyes wide with furtive excitement, eager to share his beloved folktale. Even M. Beaufort can't hide his curiosity. Hurriedly, like a child left unsupervised for a few precious moments, M. Dupont says, "In Saint-Viâtre, a village of strict

Catholics just south of Orléans, no meat is eaten at Lent. The
farm children who help their families in the fields have special
permission to eat fish on Fridays to build up their strength, but
only if they catch the fish themselves. So on Friday afternoons,
the boys roll up their trouser legs and the girls tie up the hems
of their skirts with their apron strings, and they go hand-fishing
in a shallow pond just outside the village. But oh, how grumpy
the Devil is! For the whole of Lent, there's no meat for him to
snatch. Envious of the children, who will soon be eating fish
fillet, he decides to catch a fish for himself. The only problem,
of course, is that the Devil doesn't have hands, but goat's hooves.
As you might imagine, hooves aren't all that handy for catching
fish. He stumbles and fumbles until he finally grabs hold of
one, but when he gets it out of the water – oh, no! – the slippery thing escapes his grasp. The Devil tries to grab it again,
but misses and bats it into the air with his hoof. The tasty mor-
sel lands on the Saint-Viâtre church spire with a smack! This
humiliating turn of events makes the Devil furious, and he
tries to shake the fish off the spire. All his pushing and pulling
tilts the spire to one side, but as hard as the Devil tries, his meal
remains out of reach ... Ever since then, the people of Saint-
Viâtre have made an annual tradition of pelting the spire with
fish fillets at the end of Lent – whoop, smack! – to mock the
Devil – smack, smack, smack!"

Mme Dupont summons her husband to her side. He obeys,
leaving me and M. Beaufort behind at the church tower. Now
that it's just the two of us, I notice a shift in his attitude. While
at first he gave the impression of being a self-taught member
of the local folklore society, now, with his object of study in full
view, he transforms into a scholar on the brink of a discovery.
While the Duponts are out of earshot, and the mayor and
M. Beaufort's cousin are preoccupied with the intricacies of a
marriage in the fourth degree of consanguinity, M. Beaufort

confides in me that he is conducting his own independent research. Although he acknowledges the fine work of the association, it is too preoccupied with publicity and photo ops, he explains. His own interest is in knowledge for its own sake. What keeps him going is selfless dedication. And his passion for his work, yes, that too.

I tell him I won't betray his confidence and wonder why this man, who jealously guards his hard-won expertise, has decided to let me in on his greatest secret: his arcane discoveries about the spire. Maybe he simply wants to demonstrate his genius. Before I know it he is leaning in, invading my personal space, trying to express himself as clearly as he can. He suddenly seems self-conscious about his dialect; instead of pounding a nail into his tongue with each word, he now spits out the nails, one by one, into my ear.

M. Beaufort's secret research focuses on the telluric influence of an underground river that flows through the region. Using a device of his own invention, he conducts measurements that reveal the movements of the earth and moon. The results are not yet definitive, but it is probable, highly probable, that since the construction of the spire, lunar radiation has exerted a slow, unrelenting pressure on the structure, and that this celestial force has contributed to its bent shape. Certain anomalous measurements initially seemed to imply that the spire's deviation might result from prolonged exposure to the heat of the sun. But his gut feeling – and what is science without feeling and intuition? – kept leading him back to lunar rays. If he can prove that the bend in the spire is caused by the moon, then it will be mere child's play to show that the twist results from the earth's rotation. He is becoming more and more convinced that if the Saint Omer spire had been erected south of the equator, it would have twisted in the opposite direction.

Now that M. Beaufort, red with excitement, has shared the provisional results of his research, I notice for the first time a resemblance between him and the spire. Both are spindly, weathered, twisted and impenetrable. He is the spire; the spire is part of him. I tell him his theory sounds very plausible.

Mayor Lamourette, the Duponts, and M. Beaufort's cousin reemerge from the container. The question of the marriage remains undecided, but the mayor has agreed – partly in honor of the special visit by the association president and the young Belgian writer – that he will make an exception and take us inside the church. He emphasizes that the village is not liable for any potential accidents.

M. Beaufort is hesitant to join us. At the same time, he can't bear to pass up this rare opportunity to visit the church. He brings up the rear of the group as we shuffle through the south portal, entering Saint Omer at our own risk. Inside, the reason for M. Beaufort's hesitation soon becomes clear. The layer of dust is so thick that even the artificial flowers on the altar are a uniform shade of gray. The scene in the large painting at the back of the church has been damaged beyond recognition by a coffee-like stain. But then the late afternoon sun comes pouring serenely through the glass windows, and the sculptures of Joan of Arc and St. Teresa bestow generous and indulgent smiles upon us. Decay and glory mingle into a gloomy, desolate sanctity. To the right, behind the pews, is a framed sheet of paper. In black calligraphy turned reddish-brown at the edges is the title *L'église de Verchin*, and below that, two quotations:

Rodière: "One of the most beautiful churches in the arrondissement!"

Lanfry: "The church deserves classification as a historic monument!"

The rest of the sheet is filled with a detailed timeline:

Verchin, part of the County of Artois from the 16th century

1607: Verchin, along the ancient Roman road from Thérouanne to Vieil-Hesdin, is granted its own fortified church to protect its exposed position along the main road. Its construction is authorized under the patronage of Antoine de Tramecourt and Louise de Saint-Venant.

Style: Flamboyant Gothic.

Westwork (the Church Militant): Massive, reinforced tower with multiple levels and arrow slits; the walls of the nave are 140 cm thick.

1611: Completion of the nave: five bays covered by large rib vaults.

16 January 1611: During work on the vaulting, chief mason Jean Porc falls to his death.

1630: Completion of the tower.

Façade: Masonry = a mixture of flint and sandstone. Most of it strategically covered with moss: camouflage effect!!!

Statues of saints: See list in folder.

The tray that must once have held the folders is empty and coated with dust.

"It's my sister's handwriting," M. Beaufort explains, "but I dictated the contents myself."

He stresses – though I didn't ask – that Jean Porc did not jump.

"He fell. Probably sheer bad luck. He was up at the top of a wobbly ladder, working on the ceiling vault, and he fell. That's all there is to it."

I nod as if perfectly satisfied with this explanation, but the story of the mason who fell and the architect who jumped are already merging in my mind.

Mme Dupont calls us over to the sacristy. She is standing in front of a long chest of drawers. Each drawer that she opens holds a richly embroidered robe – deep purple, grass green, yellowed white. The expensive fabrics are damp and mildewed, and covered with mouse droppings. Here and there, the wood of the drawers betrays the activity of termites. The last drawer slides open to reveal a cardboard sign with the word "Silence" written on it. We all laugh at this discovery, except M. Beaufort, who turns his back on us and leaves the church.

*

M. Dupont takes a photograph of the group clustered in front of the church. The cousin stands off to one side. M. Beaufort says goodbye with a quick handshake and hurries away down the sandy path without another word. The mayor withdraws into his container. As we walk to the car, I ask how Mme Dupont became so fascinated with twisted spires in the first place. The German shepherds have given up barking.

"Hmm, how did it happen? Well, our son was baptized in a church with a twisted spire, and then our friends were married in another church with a twisted spire. Such an original concept. But as president, I can't be influenced by personal sentiment. The thing is, my dear, I represent these churches, and that can be quite stressful at times."

Yet Mme Dupont's responsibilities seem to weigh heaviest of all on her husband's shoulders. Outside the car, as he ostentatiously dons his black beret with the association logo, he informs me that T-shirts are available and announces their plan to visit Belgium for a week to work on a video report.

Standing in front of the DIY shop, I wave goodbye to them and climb into my own car. After leaving the village, you follow the river to the hamlet of Lugy, where the Traxenne flows into the Lys. The hub of the street system there is a seventeenth-century redbrick church with a straight, slender spire.

III

POST OFFICE/TELEGRAPH AND TELEPHONE BUILDING (1947–1953), OSTEND

GASTON EYSSELINCK (1907–1953)

Two petrified feet underwater on the steps into the swimming pool. That's as far as I'm allowed to go. I'm six years old and haven't learned to swim yet. My father had promised to carry me into the sea, but we haven't had good weather all week. Seven days by the seaside, seven days of rain.

We've spent most of the trip – the only one I will take as a child – in a ninth-floor apartment on the Ostend promenade. Today, out of pure desperation, we are swimming in the indoor pool on Koninginnelaan. Here my brother will lose a large patch of skin from his right knee to a protruding corner of the waterslide. He is eight years old and, according to the warning sign, tall enough for the ride. I choose a strategic position at the edge of the pool so that I can watch my brother tumble out of the tube. Tense and focused, I wait for him to appear. At the top of the slide, a light switches from red to green when it's time for the next child to drop down the pipeline. As the children shoot out of the bottom at regular intervals, I divide them into two categories: brother and not-brother. I'm still unaware that what I'll recall about this moment is not his heroic splash, but the scrap of skin bobbing on the water in front of me, like a piece of shortbread. On his way down, he scrapes against the orange plastic of the slide. Those few square centimeters of tissue in chlorinated water will form a permanent obstacle to

my memory of the day. Whenever the event drifts to the surface, I'll believe for a few seconds that it happened to me. Even
now that I've returned to Ostend, walked by the Royal Galleries, and am passing the swimming pool on my way down
Koninginnelaan to the town center, I can see myself shooting
through the tube and, the next instant, sitting at the edge of the
pool with my feet on the underwater steps, my skinned knee,
chlorine stinging the wound, the torn patch floating on the water
in front of me, and my cries reverberating through the swimming
pool. As usual, the event soon falls into place, but even so, I always
feel guilty towards my brother. It's his injury. I have no right to it,
or to the scar. A confusion of wounds.

*

In the Leopold Hotel in Ostend, I'm meeting up with three
men named Koen: a writer, a painter and an architect. They
like reenactments. For example, they've already slept in the
modernist poet Paul van Ostaijen's bed and spent a day in the
Middle Ages. They're used to walking in the footsteps of dead
souls – apparently it brings you closer to your subject. When I
told the Koens about my quest for the tragic story of the architect Gaston Eysselinck, I found out they were doing their own
research into the city of Ostend. They invited me to join them
on their own quest.

The Leopold Hotel is about halfway between Eysselinck's
last place of residence, in Kemmelbergstraat, and his last project, the post office. We drink an aperitif with a herbal flavor.
Koen asks about the plans for my book. I tell him about the
Verchin church spire and its phallic twist, and then about the
Turnhout swimming pool. Excited by these tragedies, Koen
asks if I know that a murder of passion took place in this very
hotel.

"The Ostend Horror," Koen adds.

"Well, actually, he was acquitted," Koen breaks in. "They ruled that his wife had committed suicide."

"Anyway, there was something shady about the whole affair," Koen opines.

Five years ago, the wife of a Walloon politician was found dead in one of the rooms here. She had gone to the sea to be alone and write her debut novel. The politician followed her anyway. They had a couple of glasses of amaretto at the bar. Witnesses said they seemed like a respectable couple. While she was taking a shower before bed, there was a phone call from her therapist, who was also her lover, with whom she'd been involved right up to the time she married the politician. The politician picked up the phone. The therapist apologized and hung up, but it was too late. The politician could see in her call history that his wife and the therapist had talked on the phone thirty times over the past few days. That same night she lay dead in her bed.

"Do you think he killed her?" I ask.

"They had only been married for a year," Koen reflected – as if, generally speaking, it takes more than one year of marriage to find enough reasons to murder your wife.

*

The Koens and I stroll along the edge of Leopoldpark to the former post office building, adapted several years ago into a cultural center. On the middle of the low, protruding front section, a figure spreads her wings. From a distance, the shape of the sculpture suggests a crab. Coming closer you see, in the soft central part of the crab, a goddess with her knees drawn towards her chest. Growing from her flanks are four floating, recumbent women, who form the crab's pincers. Copper on a metal frame. The sculpture as a whole is a playful tangle of arms, wings and long manes of hair, and expresses a utopian message: the postal service will connect and perhaps even unify the world.

From his earliest drawings of the new post office in 1945, Gaston Eysselinck's design included a prominent sculpture. In a sense, this sculpture determines the effect of the rest of the architectural form. The large rear section of the building, for offices and service areas, had to be in the right proportion to the sculpture – and not vice versa. This was not some low-relief sculpture meant to prettify an otherwise featureless building front, but an autonomous work of art conceived as a fully-fledged and congruent part of the building.

Eysselinck, a committed socialist, saw his profession as a means of democratization and a vehicle for his ideology. He believed architecture should be accessible to all and foster a society where art and culture thrive. The confluence of archi-tecture and the visual arts became central to his architectural style, and finds expression in various parts of the post office building. For the entrance Eysselinck used hard bluish-gray Belgian limestone, a poetic choice of material: just 500 meters from the coast, the visible clumps of calcified shells and skeletal sea creatures evoke an ancient sea.

He also designed the furnishings for the interior. Two ceramic relief sculptures by Jo Maes flank the counters in the main lobby. Fourteen sandblasted scenes on glass by the same artist present an allegory of the development of the telephone and telegraph systems. The central work, the winged crab-goddess on the building front, sculpted by Eysselinck's friend Jozef Cantré, was given the ambitious title *The Communications Media*, or *Unity of the World through Telephony, Telegraphy and Postal Traffic*.

It was this sculpture, so well-intentioned, seeking the reconciliation of all social and political differences in the simple act of posting a letter, that would prove to be a fatal source of frustration and disillusionment for Eysselinck.

*

The post office is the only public building that Eysselinck ever designed. Its public role made the project an opportunity for him to express his political and architectural vision. By tying architectural form to social engagement, he made it an expression of his personality. Eysselinck was never willing to compromise, not in his work and not with himself – in so far as there was any meaningful difference between the two. The architect's stubbornness led to ongoing conflict and disagreements with the contractors, the clients, the directors of the telephone and telegraph service and the local authorities in Ostend. The newspapers reported "heated discussions." Whatever actually happened, the funding for the project came under threat at several stages. The greatest controversy was over the decoration of the building, especially Jozef Cantré's sculpture. To Eysselinck, this was an indispensable part of the design; to his clients, it was a large and unwarranted expense. The disagreement escalated to such a point that Eysselinck threatened to sue if the sculpture was not included. The tension also led him to quarrel with his friend Cantré. Eysselinck is said to have flown into a rage at the opening of Cantré's exhibition in Brussels, because the sculptor had placed an earlier version of his goddess on a pedestal, which Eysselinck deemed to be far too elitist.

Eysselinck's threats, his unyielding nature and his insistence on having his own way resulted, in June 1953, after repeated incidents, in his expulsion and permanent ban from entering the building site. Six months later, Eysselinck committed suicide in his apartment in Kemmelbergstraat. A few years after this, Cantré died too. Neither one lived to see the sculpture installed in 1963.

*

The Koens and I climb the stairs of the post office to access the roof through the employee canteen on the first floor. The roof-top terrace affords a view of Cantré's goddess from above. The perspective doesn't add much, but it feels important to see it from here. To pay tribute to the significance of this effort, we stand wordless for a while, staring at the goddess's back, until Koen breaks the silence.

"It's the eighth of December today."

"Sixty-four years and two days ago," I reply.

*

On December 6, 1953, there was a strong wind coming in from the east. The wind speed approached forty to fifty miles an hour. It was a cold day, with an average temperature of four degrees Celsius. With a windchill of minus two, it must have felt a little colder than today. The sun refused to show itself. It never rained, but the whole day was overcast. Eysselinck wouldn't have gone outside, since he loathed that kind of weather; when the wind roared tyrannically over the empty beach, he couldn't stand it. He had written his letter to Roger De Kinder the previous night; little sense in rereading it now that his mind was made up. Still, the whole day was unsettled and disordered. That is, until the foghorn sounded at nightfall: his chosen signal, which would relieve him of his life forever.

*

Eysselinck's suicide was explicitly linked to his work on the post office, which had met with resistance from the very first draft of his design. It received little attention from other architects at first. Too exclusively industrial, too functional, they said. Not until ten years after his death, in 1963, did it begin to garner more appreciation. Today, the post office is a listed historic building, recognized as a highlight of postwar modernist architecture in Belgium. Eysselinck's only work of public architecture has brought him posthumous fame.

But in his personal life, it was his downfall. He became so bound up with his work that every sign of incomprehension or dismissal must have piled up into one great existential rejection. Going on after that would arguably have felt like a betrayal of himself. In the end, his sense of failure must have become a destructive, unyielding behemoth.

"What about you, Charlotte? What do you think happened?" Koen asks.

I don't know if I should voice my thoughts.

"They say he was harassed. Towards the end they were openly undermining his work," Koen tells us. "He wasn't even allowed to enter the building site. Neither was his engineer, Mallebrancke."

"On top of that, he was in deep financial trouble," Koen adds.

"His whole world was coming apart before his eyes," Koen confirms.

"A typical life in architecture: one long string of miseries," Koen says from experience.

"Just a minute, Koen. Those were external factors. You have to remember he was also an incredibly stubborn bloke."

"Sure, it's hard to make compromises, especially for architects."

"And then he chose death, after seeing so many of his designs end in disaster," Koen speculates.

"How did he do it, Charlotte? Did he hang himself in his home in Kemmelbergstraat?" Koen probes.

"No," I say, "he closed the kitchen door, blocked the window with a rolled-up towel and turned on all the hobs."

I can see Koen is shaken. "Doesn't matter how he did it," he says. "Taking your own life is always an act of extreme violence."

I nod, because I don't want the Koens to become suspicious of the motives behind my project. Nor would I like them to think I'm too young to be truly interested in death. Two Koens wander over to the far end of the roof terrace. I say to the remaining Koen, "Most suicides never actually kill themselves." It's as if I'm trying to reassure him. After all, he's an architect too, and I wouldn't want him to feel insulted or unnerved by my choice of subject.

"Herman Hesse," he says. "*Steppenwolf.*"

"Right."

"Sometimes I wish I had chosen a different medium – language, for instance, like you. The days when architecture reflected our ideals or tamed our fears are long gone. And it's a good thing we no longer expect it to serve such trivial human purposes. Have you read the poet Bashō? I dream of a long-distance walk through Japan on the trail of his lines, a quest on a suitably human scale."

"Lines of poetry, or sentences, are often just as tame. Architecture has a more definite impact on the world. Besides, buildings have at least a shot at eternity. I don't have any illusions about my poems."

"Is that what you care about, 'eternity'?" I can hear the disapproval in Koen's voice.

I couldn't care less about eternity – and to be honest, I'm starting to feel the same way about the present, which can be so self-congratulatory and ruthless – but instead of telling him that, I say, "Maybe there's more at risk in architecture? It's on a larger scale, that's what I mean."

"You shouldn't put yourself at risk on any scale. Those architects of yours could have made different choices."

As a kind of illustration, Koen offers me a tale of the American architect Richard Buckminster Fuller. He too wrestled with thoughts of suicide. One day in 1927, discouraged by irregular earnings and after being dismissed from his job, he decided to drown himself in Lake Michigan. He reasoned that if he died at least his life insurance would provide for his wife and daughter. But far out into the lake, with water up to his lips and exhausted limbs, Buckminster Fuller realized he had no right to drown. It wasn't up to him to give or deny meaning to his existence, to stand in judgment over life and death. His suicide attempt proved to be a transformative experience, which throughout his career he described as a revelation. After the incident he became all kinds of things – for one, a poet.

"Then he wasn't much better off," I say, sounding more serious than I intended.

The other Koens rejoin us. As if they had planned their next question together, Koen asks me, "That foghorn you mentioned? The sound made Eysselinck sick to his core, you said?"

"It wasn't just the post office. There was also a love affair," I confess. Then I tell the Koens the story of Georgette Troy, a woman I know from the correspondence between her cousin Loulou De Geyter and Roger De Kinder, then the Ostend alderman responsible for public works. Georgette herself remains voiceless. What I know so far is that she was loved and that she died, nothing more. Maybe those are the most important things you can know about a person.

*

January 1954

Would the aldermen be so kind as to allow Mr. De Kinder to

visit the grave with her? The letter is typed. Thick ink, a fresh ribbon. In her condition, Loulou De Geyter is not capable of writing by hand – too shaky. At a quarter past eleven, the train from Antwerp is scheduled to arrive at platform 1. She asks him to meet her there so that they can go to the cemetery together. A minor wartime injury makes walking hard for her. Mr. De Kinder arrives as planned and recognizes Miss De Geyter on the platform from her jar of crumpled chrysanthemums in a plastic bag and her slight limp. Although this is their first meeting, they are already well acquainted. They were brought into contact by the same event that has brought them here today.

It's a short trip from the station to Stuiverstraat. The cemetery is just outside the town center, along the main road, but when they get there it's spacious and seems to extend from the entrance gate to a vast horizon. The bony frames of old American oaks rise over the outer wall. One quarter of the land is populated with austere white crosses. Mr. De Kinder pulls a slip of paper out of his pocket. Section 16, row 18, grave 15.

At Gaston's grave, Miss De Geyter can no longer control her trembling. Mr. De Kinder takes hold of the chrysanthemums, but she forbids him to leave the jar there. Gaston didn't want flowers, she tells him; the mums are for Georgette.

"Who found him?" Miss De Geyter asks. It was his son, Mr. De Kinder answers, when it was too late for anything to be done. His skin had already broken out in those unmistakable red blotches. He holds out his arm for Miss De Geyter, since he can tell she's struggling with her nerves. Arms linked together, they walk on to the grave of her cousin, Georgette Troy. She was buried near the guard's hut on the west side of section 22, the victim of a merciless disease, two months before the suicide of the man who loved her, Gaston Eysselinck.

The Socialist Party lost two hard workers, both deeply committed to the cause. They were also sorely missed by their friends. Despite Miss De Geyter's fervent hopes, Georgette and Gaston were not laid side by side.

*

November 1953

Loulou De Geyter writes a letter to Roger De Kinder, taking him into her confidence about a disturbing incident involving their mutual friend Gaston Eysselinck. A few weeks earlier, on a Tuesday, Gaston paid an unexpected visit to her place of work in Antwerp. He seemed confused and absentminded, wearing only a thin overcoat despite the cold. He walked straight past the front desk, to the surprise of the receptionist, who had never laid eyes on him before. And out of nowhere, he stepped up to Loulou's desk. In his right hand, he held a dip pen, as if he'd been working on a letter and, inspired by his writerly musings, had risen to his feet to finish his thought. He had nothing else with him. He put the pen down on her desk, saying only that Georgette had wanted her to have it. Loulou was astonished. Had he really come all the way from Ostend for that? Why hadn't he let her know beforehand?

At this, Gaston lost his composure and broke into a frenzy that shook him head to toe. He was furious with grief. It took the combined effort of several office workers to bring him to his senses. Just as he seemed to have recovered, he flung his arms around her neck, crying out, "Don't abandon me, don't leave me alone, I can't go on!"

He repeated it over and over again. Loulou offered to look after Gaston for a while at her place in Antwerp. She forbade him to return to the apartment in Kemmelbergstraat – too many memories there. Was he thinking of picking up his work again? Now would be a good time to have something to keep him busy. At first, Gaston seemed to be listening, but then he shrugged off her suggestions and boarded the train back to Ostend. Soon afterwards, he informed Loulou that he'd be spending some time on his own in the Ardennes. She wrote to him several times during the few weeks that he stayed there to ask how he was doing. His reply was always the same: a curt, polite "Thank you."

In her letter to Roger De Kinder, Loulou tells him she's worried about Gaston, partly because of what happened in her office. She asks whether Mr. De Kinder has heard from Gaston and knows whether he has returned to Ostend. Would he write back and let her know? She is the late Georgette's cousin and Gaston's friend, she tells him; he can trust her.

*

Gaston Eysselinck and Georgette Troy probably met in the socialist circles surrounding Emile Langui in Ghent. Immediately after the war, as plans began to be made for rebuilding the post office, they decided to move to Ostend together and start a new life. Gaston left behind two sons from his difficult first marriage. Georgette left her husband. It must have been the kind of affair that does serious damage to everyone involved. Their first apartment in Ostend was along the main boulevard, on the seventh floor. After a bitter quarrel with the manager, they moved to the apartment in Kemmelbergstraat, near the promenade. It was small, but there was room for his drafting table. The only nuisance was the monotonous moan of the foghorn, which sounded close when the window was open. Georgette laughed it off. He teased her, giving her the pet name "Pietje."

Eysselinck was thirty-eight years old, in love, stubborn and talented. Finally, he was able to settle down and be himself.

*

Even the smallest bacteria have a cell wall, a shield around the membrane that protects the nucleus. Shields can be made of all sorts of materials: cork, wood, carbohydrates – anything strong enough. We should pause more often to consider our cell walls, and our epidermis too, which is made of innumerable cells with walls that serve as our outermost shield. The cell wall protects us from intruders and external pressure. It encounters opposing forces but resists them through counterpressure of its own. Throughout each day, and the next, and every new one, our cell walls guard sleeplessly over our smallest, microscopic parts, so that we can form the grand total of all our cells, the integrated whole we think we are. When I was about fifteen years old, I began to distrust the workings of my body; most of the time it ran autonomously, without my conscious awareness. My distrust reared its head in particular situations, such as biology lessons, where I had to learn more about human bodily functions, and therefore couldn't help but reflect on my own body's potential dysfunctions. The same distrust took hold of me in situations with no clear script – for example, when staring out of a train window. In those unguarded moments, I was in danger of becoming conscious of my own breathing. This new consciousness came with the abrupt fear that I would have to keep consciously thinking about inhaling and exhaling, because if I forgot, if I let my attention slip for even a second, then my lungs might stop working. How could I just casually assume that my lungs would go on breathing? In theory, something could go wrong at any moment, and I would suffocate.

This distrust of mine also extended to other people's bodies. When I laid my head on my then boyfriend's chest, I would place my ear in the exact spot where his heartbeat was strongest. Not for sentimental reasons, but as a kind of human stethoscope. When he ejaculated, his heart would pump so hard, so hard, that I feared it might stop. Sometimes it took all night before I dared to break my contact with that heartbeat, to trust that even with no one listening that beat would persist in his body.

Microbiology lessons expanded the scope of this distrust to include the cell walls. Could I simply assume that they would continue to serve their mechanical purpose without being observed? As strong as cell walls are, if the opposing force is too great, or opposes them for too long, or puts up opposition they have no power to resist, then they may break. And once the cell wall breaks, the membrane is vulnerable. If the membrane, which is much weaker than the cell wall, breaks too, this is certain to lead to the death of the cell.

Cell walls, and consequently cells, break not only when they meet with opposition; they can also perish for lack of vital nutrients. Or what if my cells simply stop resisting?

*

In the summer of 1953, eight months after her diagnosis, Gaston and Georgette spend a few more days with Loulou De Geyter in Antwerp. Loulou expects the worst, but Georgette seems cheerful and, strangely enough, even optimistic. Before long she's persuaded even her cousin that she'll soon be making a full recovery. They have a brochure with them from the Stichting Wilhelmina, a charity in Amsterdam. On the cover is a red crab skewered on a saber. The brochure gives the impression that a cure is just around the corner.

Two months later, when Gaston calls to say he has brought Georgette to the Institut Bordet in Brussels, Loulou realizes that all their hope was in vain. The cancer has spread deep inside Georgette's cells. Gaston sat by her bedside day and night, and now, forced to part with her far too soon, he is suffering his own terrible inner pain, but you wouldn't know it to look at him. Loulou will remember Gaston from those days as a man who had reduced himself to a single function: supporting the woman he loves in the short time left to her. He is unswerving.

On October 4, 1953, after a severe illness, Pietje died of that merciless disease. Even Gaston's stubbornness could not fend it off.

On the way to the cemetery in Stuiverstraat, Koen stops off at Acacialaan 6, the De Wispelaere Residence. The house was designed by Eysselinck and dates from 1953. This house, and not the post office, was his final project. Among an ordinary string of houses, the De Wispelaere Residence stands out. It makes a slightly awkward impression, with its stairwell bulging from the top floor. This angular outgrowth makes it look as if the house is being propped up by its two neighbors. Aside from some small windows, the façade is mainly composed of brick and concrete. The house is sometimes called "the Bunker." The Koens send me up the crooked steps to the front door, while they wait in the car. They leave the engine running just in case I encounter some kind of resistance and need a getaway vehicle – they've seen it all before.

The doorbell's electric buzz goes straight to the midriffs of two little dogs, who start barking frantically when I press the button. The woman who opens the door wears a white sweater made of fabric resembling the hair of a Maltese. Although she wasn't expecting me, she doesn't send me packing just yet. Yes, she answers, Gaston Eysselinck did design the house. Her parents rented it in the 1970s. They were eventually given the chance to buy it for much less than the asking price; the owners were in a hurry to sell, because their son had large gambling debts. When her parents died, it seemed only natural to return to her childhood home. But it had been a gloomy place in the old days, she tells me, with brown paneling halfway up the wall and then black paint to the ceiling, and all those nooks and crannies – very dark and hard to decorate. She understands the importance of preserving the internal structure of the house, but even so, she's glad her parents had the original interior stripped out when they bought it. All those terrible built-in furnishings, too clever by half, not really comfortable, and dark, so dark, extremely oppressive.

I learn that, despite these differences of taste, she has taken it upon herself to restore the house in the spirit of the architect. She invites me to take a look inside; the kitchen's just been renovated. All new, with a central island, in spotless, glossy white marble.

"I like the modern look," she says. In front of the sliding doors that lead to the terrace and the garden below, there's a white plastic Christmas tree. The unwelcoming house front finds its antithesis in the large windows looking out on the garden. She sometimes wonders what Eysselinck would think of the changes she's made ... She hopes he'd be happy to have more light coming in. She has a few books about him, up in the attic. She doesn't know much about his suicide, except that he was probably the depressive type.

The original kitchen is now used as a pantry. She opens all her drawers and cupboards to show me how well stocked they are. It's hard, she says, always having to carry the groceries up those crooked stairs to the front door, and the wretched council won't even let her fix them – the house has been a listed historic building since 2009. So once in a while, she does groceries with a friend who is steadier on her feet. As I count the seventeen cans of tomato puree in the cupboard, I feel relieved that Eysselinck did not live to see these renovations.

*

In 1954, a year after Eysselinck's death, the post office was officially opened. The entrance is at the top of the grand staircase with bronze rails. Set into the monolithic blue limestone façade are three bronze revolving doors. The door on the left provides twenty-four-hour access to the telegraph and telephone division. During opening hours, the other two lead to the post office windows. Bronze offers the most resistance to the salty sea air.

From 1985 onwards, the door on the left was kept closed at night too. Late-night callers were welcome to use the telephone booths outside.

In 1995, the postal service moved out of the building to a new location on Slachthuiskaai, near the harbor and the station.

By the start of the year 1999, the old post office was largely vacant. Some rooms were used to store equipment, and a few telephone services were still housed around the corner.

*

Pitch-black. Yet in the open spaces of the sprawling cemetery, the blackness seems to dissipate into thinner darkness. So for a while, the Koens and I think we can spot each other, when in fact we are walking blind. We proceed down the main axis to the central pavilion, from which four paths extend in a cross. Without any strategy, we all wander off into the murk in different directions. We are searching for the grave of Georgette Troy, but before long I give up and start looking out for the silhouettes of my companions instead. Finding the tomb becomes less important than hearing a footstep or the rustle of a jacket, less important than the fear that the darkness will swallow me up. Koen's voice rescues me. He calls the group over to the guard's hut on the west side, section 22.

1:00 p.m., December 5, 1953

Instructions:
– H. has the finished stone for Georgette.
– V. knows what to do with it.
– B. will arrange for the stone to be taken to the cemetery.

Debts:
– 10,000 fr. to W.
– 22,000 fr. to Van M.
– To Mir: exact sum unknown. Was planning to give a case of good cigars in payment – the ones from the corner shop in the post office building. The first coffin has already been ordered. The receipt is in my wallet.
– 0 fr. to the tax administration.
– To H.: M.B. must decide.
– The bill for G. is in the bank book.
– To my friend M.B.: a trip to the Vosges and a trip to Marseille.
– My son W. gets the drafting table. I forgive my first wife nothing.

Will spare no thought for the judgment that will follow this act. Never did from the start, and won't now. Grown too cold.

Want to be buried on a patch of wasteland. No flowers – because they won't be from Georgette.

I grew up with Georgette – with her I would perhaps have become a very great man. It was not to be.

Georgette, Pietje, I miss you too much.

She is no longer there to give me courage, and so . . . because I see the impossibility of replacing her, I surrender . . .

Farewell to my friends, love to my mother, the guilt I assign to the people who know they are guilty, and I know who they are.

Gaston Eysselinck

In the sixty-three days between the death of Georgette Troy and his own suicide, Gaston Eysselinck completed his final work. It is neither a public building nor a private home. His final work rose from the stillness of his heart. He designed the gravestone for Georgette, the woman he loved and had lost too soon: an austere blue limestone memorial on a conical pedestal, the same type of stone he had used for the post office entrance. A mastaba for an Egyptian deity. As you gaze at the sculpted stone, her name seems to rise to the surface. Because they had lived together as an unmarried couple, they could not be buried side by side. But by designing her tombstone, he could sign his name beside hers for eternity. "Architect G. Eysselinck," he carved into stone formed over millions of years by the slow, slow deposition of layers of sediment – which over time collected the shells and skeletons of sea creatures millions of years old themselves – at the bottom of the warm, prehistoric sea that flooded our region millions of years ago and now encloses that teeming, petrified life in its depths.

IV
VIENNA STATE OPERA
(1861–1869), VIENNA

EDUARD VAN DER NÜLL (1812–1868)
AND AUGUST SICARD VON
SICARDSBURG (1813–1868)

In September 2015, soon after Angela Merkel's historic state-
ment *"Wir schaffen das"* ("We will manage this"), I go to Vienna
for a few days for a public reading, my first job outside Belgium. The European Union pays for my flight. I shake hands
with the Belgian and Dutch ambassadors and am presented
with business cards, lots of them, including one from a man who
the day before made small talk with Tom Cruise on the first
balcony of the Vienna State Opera. In the German program, my
name is followed by the words *flämische Schriftstellerin*, "Flemish
writer." I read four poems, accompanied by jazz musicians
under the crystal chandeliers of Café Westend, where you're
still allowed to smoke indoors. It takes me back to the era of
the salons. There's an Edvard Munch exhibition in the Albertina: love, death and loneliness in woodcut and lithography. To
counter the soothing effect of the half darkness, the walls of the
galleries have been painted royal blue and emerald green, elec-
troshock colors. Apart from the champagne breakfast at the
hotel, I don't eat a thing for the duration of my visit, because
I've never been able to eat alone. In my hotel room, I take a
long, worried look in the mirror, in search of anything that
might be used to unmask me as a liar. Someone made a poor
choice, and now I'm here under false pretenses, conditions I
cannot meet. I am an impostor. Meanwhile, in the newspapers,

Europe is cleaving itself into right and left wings. The news is
in thrall to the word "borders." Hungary is closing its borders.
Austria is sending the army to the border crossings from Hungary. Slovakia is intensifying its border controls to keep out the
flow of people. Yet I seem to pass through these borders as if
they were nothing.

After the reading in Café Westend, the musicians take me to
a karaoke night to raise funds for the refugee crisis. I make my
contribution, drinking White Russians from a shot glass and
singing Bruce Springsteen's "Dancing in the Dark." I don't
have to read the lyrics; I know the song by heart. "I get up in
the evening and I ain't got nothing to say. I come home in the
morning, I go to bed feeling the same way."

As I stand at the microphone in the green glow of the stage,
the audience seem to believe what I'm telling them. A little
off-key, but with conviction, I move on to the bridge: "I'm
dying for some action. I'm sick of sitting around here trying to
write this book. I need a love reaction. Come on, baby, give me
just one look."

Bruce's hip motions from the video seem to appeal to the
crowd too, so I surrender to the music: "You can't start a fire,
you can't start a fire without a spark."

Applause. Someone whoops. My performance brings in
twelve euros and eighty-three cents for the cause. I order
another shot; after all, the bar takings go to the same charity. At
the bar I run into Hausensteiner, the guitarist who accompanied my reading.

"I'm getting drunk and helping humanity at the same time,"
I say.

"So cynical! That's bad for a writer. People love karaoke. We
can use the money to buy food and bedding. You're a terrible
singer, but an OK performer."

I smile. "You know, I once wanted to be a classical guitarist, but I didn't make it. I played for eight years, until I came to this one piece," I tell him, and I try to hum the melody.

"Leo Brouwer," Hausensteiner says. " 'Un día de noviembre.' "

Now that he's named the composer and the piece, I'm sorry I brought it up. It feels as if he's caught me red-handed, as if he was there when the melancholy incident took place, years ago, in that unheated room in the Turnhout music school.

My guitar teacher had chosen the Brouwer piece for my intermediate exam and played it for me in all its underrated genius. *Andante cantabile*, 3/4 time. A great and impossible southern happiness, expressed and then lamented. The piece tells the story of something lost, *something* that must have been unfailingly beautiful, and when the music revealed to me that whatever it was, it really was gone forever, I could feel the water closing over my head. By the time he returned to the opening theme, there was no way back: the music had become the score to my happiness and my sorrow. A first approximation of what happened might be that, for the duration of those notes, I was larger than my gawky sixteen-year-old body – a physical sensation, as if my body were too small for the great shift that was underway inside me. When my teacher let the final note, a high E, die away gently in a long fermata, my first thought was *Again*. For weeks, I immersed myself in the music's melancholy, practicing until little calluses formed on my fingertips. The melody echoed all night in my sleep. The more I practiced, the less it sounded like that first, heightened experience. Soon there was no resemblance at all. In the end, I didn't take that exam, and I haven't played since then.

Hausensteiner thinks the story is melodramatic and tells me to take up the guitar again. "Or does that offend you?" he asks. "Where in Belgium are you from?"

"I come from the Kempen, but I escaped."

Hausensteiner frowns at my bad joke.

"It's a marshy area, boggy, get it? It's a metaphor. Everything sinks there. Our swimming pool literally sank into the earth."

"Like the Staatsoper here in Vienna. *Die versunkene Kiste*, they call it, the sunken chest," Hausensteiner says. "The architect hanged himself. I don't know why – it's a totally amazing building."

*

The sunken chest. The Königgrätz of architecture. A mishmash of styles. Even before it was completed, Vienna's opera house had dozens of disparaging nicknames. It was said not to achieve the requisite grandeur, because the base on which it rested was not far enough above street level – "It looks like a sunken ship," passersby whispered. A comparison was made to the Battle of Königgrätz, one of the bloodiest defeats in Austrian history. The "eclectic" combination of stylistic elements was described as a "shambles." In all the taverns of Vienna, the mocking rhyme was heard:

Der Sicardsburg und Van der Nüll, die haben beide keinen Styl,
Griechisch, gotisch, Renaissance, das ist ihnen alles ans!

[Sicardsburg and van der Nüll, neither one has any style,
Greek, Gothic, Renaissance, it's all the same to them!]

The architects of the opera house, August Sicard von Sicardsburg and Eduard van der Nüll, were slaughtered in the press and ground to dust in the rumor mill.

No style and no taste. In nineteenth-century Vienna, that verdict was damning. A large readership turned to newspapers, magazines and tabloids to find out what was *in* and what was *out*, which way the winds of fashion were blowing. Money and status were no longer the only social weapons; public opinion, as shaped by the press, became just as powerful. Even before they began their work, Sicard and van der Nüll found the critics arrayed against them. In the face of mounting pressure from the newspapers, they were expected to design a building that would be worthy of its central role in the city's life: the first structure in the ambitious Ringstrasse project.

*

Ten years earlier in 1857 Emperor Franz Joseph I decrees the demolition of the old city walls. The new policy of *Stadterweiterung*, urban expansion, sets Vienna on a transformative path from a fortified medieval city to a teeming metropolis. Thirty-four nearby towns are swallowed up. The razing of the walls and the annexation of the surrounding communities leaves the state with large swathes of new land, which it sells to private owners. The emperor uses the revenue from these sales to erect a series of majestic buildings along the new Ringstrasse, which becomes the main artery connecting the old city center to the new districts.

The wealthy, liberal middle class is growing rapidly and demanding greater political influence in the city's life. By investing in the Ringstrasse project – a political land grab – this group can cement its social status. The decision to build the opera house first is a symbolic one: cultural buildings have become the meeting grounds of the new middle class. The old opera house has too few seats for the growing numbers who can now afford tickets, and its architecture is embarrassingly outdated. The new paymasters want a building befitting the opulence of the nouveaux riches.

Building work begins in haste. The pressure is high; the

foundations for the opera house have to be laid before the Ringstrasse itself is put in place. In the end, the ring road is raised a little higher than expected, so the opera does not tower as high above the street as its architects intended. To the status-obsessed Viennese middle class, the opera's position so close to street level looks like an expression of impotence – as if the building, instead of standing tall, is sinking into the earth.

And yet, standing at the bustling intersection of Kärtner Ring and Opernring today, you cannot help but be moved by the opera house's stupendous beauty. Tickets sell out months in advance. Hundreds of tourists crowd the grand staircase for photographs. Being seen in one of the good seats heightens your reputation overnight. Today, the Vienna State Opera is one of the most prestigious opera houses in the world.

*

The first lie that came out of my mouth is still fresh in my mind. Since I had been raised with just one golden rule – "Do whatever you like, except lie" – it was a landmark event. I remember the ease with which I twisted the truth, and then the feeling of power that came from breaking the rule and getting away with it. I was seven years old and thought I had cracked life's code. No matter what trials awaited me, I could always count on lies to save my skin.

The school bell announces the afternoon break. We queue up, two by two. Stephanie lives across the street from the school and eats lunch at home. Her mother is never late to pick her up. I sense a kind of silent feud between our mothers, based on little else but a clash of personalities. That excludes the possibility of Stephanie and me ever becoming friends. With her bare belly and clunky Buffalo shoes, Stephanie looks more like a precocious fourteen-year-old than a girl of seven. Her mother dresses the same way, and looks fourteen years old too.

This afternoon, Stephanie's mother is wearing snakeskin boots. I nudge the girl next to me in the queue and point at her feet: *so ugly I could puke!* Stephanie's mother notices my pointing finger and marches up to me.

"It's rude to point," she hisses.

Without the least hesitation, as if simply repeating what I just said, I tell her, "I was pointing because I really love your boots."

And just like that, I've escaped. Stephanie's mother gives me a sweeter smile than ever before, pats me on the head and is gone. The success of the lie makes me tingle. If anyone asked when I knew I wanted to be a writer, I would say I wasn't sure, but in fact I've known ever since that afternoon on the playground that I wanted to be a liar when I grew up. Writing is the most credible lie I've talked myself into so far. If other people believe it, it's hardly a lie at all.

*

In retrospect, given my proclivity for twisting the truth, it's no surprise I fell in love with other liars. Two spirits with a shared obsession can achieve an intimacy so intense that at first it feels like destiny. A false destiny: the complete dedication required by your craft leaves little space in your life for another whole person. Still, they've produced some very compelling moments, those encounters between two writers with a knack for elevating an encounter above the everyday, giving a kiss the narrative gravity of inevitability and transforming real-life attraction into a fateful paragraph of sacred erotica. The curse of our craft is that we idealize the object of love.

Although he never used the name, I was one writer's Sylvia

Plath. I dubbed him my Count Vronsky. There was also a Heathcliff – he played along, and for a brief spell we even imagined ourselves Beyoncé and Jay-Z. (Minus the money.)

Fortunately, love remembered has a purpose: it provides us with material for our poems and novels. Even before it's alchemized into writing, an author's love is often already literary. But that kind of love is unsustainable. And utterly exhausting. The breakup rescues the writer and yields the best stories.

Except when the communion of souls is not a lie. When two people are propelled beyond their narrative by the same fire, when they truly exist side by side in reality, in a love that completes them, then the writer is relegated to the sidelines.

*

Eduard van der Null and August Sicard von Sicardsburg both study architecture at Vienna's Polytechnic Institute. The two are classmates and roam the same halls, but aside from a few polite exchanges, they never really have much to do with each other. Van der Null is a loner, serious and withdrawn. Other students avoid him because he's "no fun." He is always lost in some inner world, drafting in silence. Sicard is his antithesis: cheerful, enthusiastic, likable. He possesses a charm that transforms any room he enters. It would take him three lifetimes to see all his ideas through to completion, but he speaks so persuasively about the most incredible, megalomaniacal projects that he ignites a kindred passion in his listeners. His talents are noticed even beyond the corridors of the institute. In 1833, Pietro Nobile, court architect and professor at the Vienna art academy, offers the promising young man a part-time position as his assistant. This eventually allows Sicard to go on to the academy for further architectural studies.

Two years later, after an apprenticeship in the regional

building department, van der Nüll joins him there. Their paths cross again, and this time, their individual talents bring them together. Both win a series of academic prizes. Without meaning to, they attract each other's attention. Sicard becomes intrigued by the mysterious van der Nüll, who says little but reveals his genius at the drafting table. At the same time, the magnetic glow of Sicard's charisma makes even the disciplined Eduard glance up from his papers with growing frequency.

In 1838, Sicard and van der Nüll each submit a design for the prestigious Goldener Hofpreis Award. They win a shared gold medal and a three-year scholarship to travel Europe for their studies. From 1839 to 1843 they are on the road: Italy, Germany, Spain, France. The buildings they've read so much about appear before their eyes, three dimensional at last. They observe, sketch, draw, redraw, discuss, demolish and reconstruct with their pencils. It soon becomes clear to the two travelers that though they were thrown together by chance, they share not only a formal vocabulary but also a common quest. They dream of a style freed from the shackles of history, an alternative kind of architecture. This joint artistic project inevitably leads to a closer personal bond between them.

Venice. Thanks to their shared passion for Palladio's architecture, van der Nüll finds a safe opportunity to explain his complex personality. His silences, his moods – he can't do a thing about them. He tells Sicard about the shadow that hung over his childhood. His parents divorced when he was just three years old. It never mattered to him what anyone said; he has only one father. No, the reason for his sorrow is that his father started to believe the tales about a different father and became tangled up in them. When van der Nüll was thirteen years old, his father brought an end to a series of severe depressions by committing suicide. Eduard had no choice but to spend the rest of his childhood with his mother and the marshal, whom he addressed by his surname until the day he left home. Hearing that detail, Sicard lets out one of his hearty laughs.

Granada. In the gardens of the Alhambra, Sicard describes his childhood in Budapest: the horses, the canings. As the eldest of three sons in an aristocratic military dynasty, Sicard met with little understanding when he decided to become an architect – breaking with family tradition. After completing his studies at the Polytechnic Institute, he gave in to pressure from his father and joined the Ulans, the imperial cavalry. A year later, in a fit of rebelliousness, he pulled the feathers out of his tall cap and joined the art academy against his family's wishes. Van der Null says cautiously that he's glad Sicard kept up the struggle.

Notre Dame, Paris. A meeting of minds, once and for all. In the French capital they revel in their liberty and anonymity. They offer up their entire selves to each other, trim their mustaches in the same style and stay up talking the whole night in the cafés of Saint-Germain. They pass their lives together, without interruption, bonded by their shared calling and their deep friendship.

Despite this merging of spirits, their personalities remain polar opposites, but that dichotomy proves to be productive: their contrasting temperaments combust and their art continues to flourish. What might have driven two other people apart instead makes them inseparable.

But almost immediately after their three-year tour of Europe, Sicard puts an end to their symbiosis. He receives a dispensation for a marriage in the fourth degree of consanguinity, to his cousin Aloysia Janschky. They lose a son to cot death and have a daughter, Valentine. Meanwhile, van der Null throws himself into a new project: the interior of the Altlerchenfeld Church.

*

Although I pass Lerchenfelderstrasse every day of my stay in Vienna as I walk to the Architekturzentrum, I have never noticed the church before. Only after I read that Eduard van der Nüll designed the interior does it rise before me in light pink stone in the middle of the street.

I realize it's the first time I've ever been alone in a church. The only light enters through the windows of the north transept, settling like a thin layer of dust over the pews, the walls, the pillars and the floor. The same melancholy grips me here as when I saw David Hockney's winter landscape *Woldgate Woods* months ago at the Centre Pompidou. I feel the snow sweep through me again, but this time, laid bare beneath it is a circle of stone. The earth moves. The fall is harder this time. The barrel vaults over the apses have painted ceilings of desolate blue starry sky. To look up is to be godforsaken, alone in the depth of that color. Looking around, I find myself amid a violence of patterns on the walls, the columns, the carpets, everywhere. Flowers. Curlicues. Leafy forms. Gold. Arabesques. Every corner, every niche, the whole surface of the interior is decorated, the sheer abundance so inviting that I feel I'm dissolving into it.

Rage and rapture; no other combination could have driven van der Nüll to this ecstatic work. It was just after his grand tour and his break with Sicard that he turned to the interior of the Altlerchenfeld Church. Brilliant, manic, feverish and in godlike control, he seized the opportunity to convert his impressions from his travels into a visual form all his own. Out of a panoply of preexisting styles, he created something shockingly new. In the classicist city of Vienna, this was a revolutionary aesthetic. The interior of the Altlerchenfeld Church is now seen as the idiosyncratic height of romantic historicism.

An exorcism of old demons. A deluge of the soul. Grief over their lost intimacy, back in Vienna, destroyed by Sicard's marriage. The pressure of work, perhaps. Money. Whatever possessed him during his work on the church, it still animates the place today. In broad daylight, it blazes through me.

*

After a visit to the Altlerchenfeld Church – it proves too enticing – Sicard is no longer capable of keeping away from van der Nüll. How isolated his wife must have felt, left alone in their cage-like marriage. The two architects appear in public together and organize their lives around their complementary relationship. Sicard, the engineer and charmer, takes on the technical and managerial side of the projects, while van der Nüll draws the ornamentation in perfect solitude. Whenever they disagree, they soon arrive at an understanding. In fact, they never do disagree about the essentials, because both are faithful to the key principle of their shared approach: to serve architecture itself in its purest form. United by this perspective, the two cannot be conceived as separate entities in any meaningful sense. They form the conditions of each other's existence, as architects, as artists and as men.

This unique collaboration between Sicard and van der Nüll might almost be called an uncoupling of the architect's persona, which normally combines two roles: the artist *and* the professional. For an architectural design to come to life, it requires both creative genius and technical proficiency. These two working methods tug in different directions, creating a natural division of labor between the two men.

*

In 1843, Sicard and van der Nüll are each awarded a professorship at the city's architectural academy. This provides a degree of job security, but in the mid-nineteenth century professors were not paid well. Their constant search for architectural assignments continued unabated. The two partners opened a studio together, where they could usually be found when not at the academy. At first, their only jobs were for private patrons; they designed homes, a private school and an exclusive bathhouse. In time, however, they also began to receive major public commissions. The breakthrough came in 1848, when they were invited to design the complex for the Vienna Arsenal. It was whispered that the job had been sent van der Nüll's way by his alleged father, the marshal, "Herr Feld-Franz." The rumors flattened van der Nüll into mournful silence, triggering another bout of depression. Sicard continued as their public face, taking care of business with his usual good cheer.

As part of the city's expansion and the Ringstrasse project, an international competition was held in 1860 to design a new opera house, intended as the pivotal site on the redrawn map of Vienna. The competition emphasised creativity. The choice of styles was left wide open. The only condition was that the building should have enough seating for the beloved operagoers. Out of thirty-five designs, the emperor himself selected the work of Sicard and van der Nüll. By that time, it had been six years since their last assignment, and the two architects were in deep financial trouble. The prestigious opera commission assured them of not only income and artistic freedom, but also of a commodity still more essential in Viennese high society: prestige. For Sicard and van der Nüll, it was all or nothing.

On August 24, 1867, the wooden barriers around the construction site were removed and the public could witness the work in progress. The first newspaper reviews, published the next morning, were litanies of failure.

"WILL THE OPERA BE COMPLETED ON TIME?" The critics fretted about the daunting technical challenges. The project required meticulous management; were the two architects really up to the job? Looking at the results so far, the reviewers doubted the building would be completed on schedule. To reach the stage, they wrote, the scenery would have to learn to slither. From the outside, there might seem to be plenty of space for the audience, but that was deceptive, they warned – the interior was sure to be far too cramped. Only half the stage would be visible to the audience, and its placement would surely be terrible for the acoustics. Considering the many research trips taken by the two architects, Eduard van der Null and August Sicard von Sicardsburg, you might have expected a world-class opera house. But the result was disappointing, the press reported: their supposed wealth of experience was nowhere to be seen in their design for the Vienna State Opera. They were said to have forgotten the chimneys and stupidly planned just one boiler for the whole building. Operagoers will come down with pneumonia before the second act even starts, the critics moaned. And when it rains, water from the streets will wash into the building and flood the orchestra pit before you know it! The grand entrance was said to be so pathetic that even Sicard and van der Null preferred the back door. In short, the architecture of the new opera house was frankly poor and lacking in formal unity. Van der Null's elaborate ornamentation was no more than a fig leaf for inept design.

*

A climbing rope, that's how I would describe it. I can't see what it's attached to at the top, but the rope itself is sturdy, taut, strong enough to hold me. I can climb it, and the work is worthwhile, because the higher I climb, the more I see. There are days when the rope seems frayed, worn by the action of dirt, moisture and light. There are days when I'm tired, too done in to climb, and even on those days, the rope is present. There are days when I climb because I think I must, but it's heavy going, and each time I slide back down, the rope burns my hands, my inner thighs. There are days when the rope goes on and on, up into the sky like Jack's beanstalk, and I reach the heights with ease. There are days when the dangling rope mocks me like a noose. There are days when it writhes like a tentacle. But I am never too heavy for the rope's tensile strength; the rope is durable, a firm connecting cord. It stretches between me and writing. The rope has blood running through it and a heartbeat. Others might call the rope "intuition," but that sounds so tame, so easy – as if, once you learn to trust it, all you have to do is follow, whereas the rope offers resistance, demanding a countermove. I try harder to do my best. When my upward progress falters, I sooner or later become distrustful, despondent, because the rope never reveals what it's attached to – where is all this climbing taking me? I start to wonder whether the rope ever ends.

I think of the twentieth-century English writer and reviewer Cyril Connolly, who published only one novel, a book condemned by many critics. He then published a work of non-fiction exploring why he had failed to write the masterpiece he should have written. His third book, *The Unquiet Grave*, was a collection of aphorisms and quotes from authors he admired, published under the pseudonym of Palinurus. It opens with this passage:

> The more books we read, the clearer it becomes that the true function of a writer is to produce a masterpiece and that no other task is of any consequence. Obvious though this should be, how few writers will admit it, or having drawn the conclusion, will be prepared to lay aside the piece of mediocrity on which they have embarked.

To claim you have produced a masterpiece is utter hubris, but the opposite seems, if possible, even more inconceivable. At what point do you acknowledge your mediocrity?

Mediocrity, crueler than mere failure. In failure there lies a certain greatness, often tied to a kind of torment that might drive you on to some new pursuit. Mediocrity, in contrast, is a state that cannot be transcended; it leads to stillborn work. The remoteness of the masterpiece and the peril of mediocrity make it impossible, most days, to put anything down on paper. I don't usually get past the observation that I can't do it, that I've forgotten how, that if I ever could do it to begin with, it was no more than a fluke. Sometimes I take my life in my hands and write anyway, because what's even harder than getting started is the thought of admitting it won't amount to anything. If I ever come to that conclusion, I hope I will be brave enough to stop.

*

And when there was no jeering, there was silence. While some newspapers chose ridicule, others practiced the worst form of criticism: disregard. The first overviews of the architecture of the new Ringstrasse did not say a word about the opera house, even though it was the project's most important building. Instead, they went on at length about the competing architect Theophil Hansen, the darling of the bourgeoisie and the press, who many believed should have been awarded the commission for the opera. Hansen was the standard-bearer of neoclassical Vienna. He had taken the time-honored route of learning his profession in Athens, and his ideas about architecture were never too controversial. By emulating the classical paradigm, he bowed to the predictable tastes of Vienna's ostentatious bourgeoisie.

The contrast with Sicard and van der Nüll could not have been starker. They saw imitation as idiocy; their aim was a new architecture, a formal language that was rooted in the past yet wholly original. To them a building was a human growth, developing from a single point into two dimensions and then up through the air, the way a human develops.

The alleged blunders reported by the critics are not to be found anywhere in the building itself. Instead, the whole affair appears to have been a hatchet job in the service of the outraged Theophil Hansen.

*

In 1866, the fifty-five-year-old Eduard van der Nüll married Maria Killer, thirty years his junior. Until then he had always refused to marry anyone. It was Sicard who suggested that van der Nüll take a bride, since he himself was bedridden following a nervous breakdown. The harsh reviews of the opera, the tabloids, the fabrications, the lies, the pressure of their work – it all became too much even for the stalwart optimist Sicard. Having lost confidence in his personal judgment, he allowed the verdict of the outside world to crush his spirit. Everyone was trying to unmask him as a fraud. Maybe they were right, he must have thought. Maybe he'd always been bluffing. Maybe his only real talent, from the start, had been for pretending.

Besides, there were money troubles. A boycott of the project made it harder to get things done. They had applied for and received permission to work with wild Istrian stone from a quarry in Croatia. Yet at the last minute, higher authorities had decided that the opera had to be built of Austrian *Kelheimerstein*, which was cheaper and easier to transport across the Danube. But the quarry was exhausted before the façades were complete, so the courtyards had to be finished with plaster. Van der Nüll had seemed to take these setbacks on the chin, but Sicard knew that his friend – the aesthete – was breaking down inside. Then came Sicard's own breakdown. *Nervenspannung.* Whenever anyone mentioned the opera house in his presence, it would bring on a psychosomatic attack of fever. Sicard's illness upset the duo's careful balance, leaving the introverted, reclusive van der Nüll to manage their business and defend them in the press. A lonely fight. For a man like him, the psychological burden must have been severe.

In the depths of this despair, van der Nüll found the angelic young woman Maria Killer. Drawn to his mild nature and quiet talents, she agreed to marry him despite his lack of money. By then van der Nüll was destitute, reduced to penury by the delays in the opera project. For months he'd been sleeping on the floor of his studio or keeping watch all night by Sicard's bed. Maybe marriage is a lie, but Maria Killer's naive adoration gave him at least the hope of one day receiving due recognition. The penniless couple took up residence in the home of van der Nüll's friend, the court sculptor August La Vigne. A few months later, the Sicard family moved into the same house.

Eduard van der Nüll hanged himself from the hat rack in his bedroom with a blue handkerchief. At six thirty in the morning on April 3, 1868, the chambermaid discovered the corpse, dangling blue and waxen.

Her shriek woke up everyone else in the La Vigne household. Maria Killer, who was sleeping lightly in the final months of her pregnancy, leapt out of bed in the next room and was the first to reach the scream. She found her husband in the arms of the hysterical maid, who was trying to pull him down from the hat rack. The maid was not strong enough to lift him and slip the knot up off the hook; her helpless fumbling seemed only to pull the handkerchief tighter around his throat. Maria

Killer grasped at her unborn child with her right hand and steadied herself against the doorframe with her left. Sicard came up the stairs from the lower floor. Before he'd had time to fully comprehend the situation, he shouted to his wife, Aloysia, to call the doctors. Then, pushing away the maid, he threw his arms around his partner's body, unhooked him, lowered him to the floor, shook, tugged, shook harder and roared at that lifeless body that would no longer listen.

The doctors arrived too late, but in time to catch Maria Killer when she fainted. She was carried to her bed, wailing, "The child, the child."

Her screams of despair were drowned out by Sicard's from the next room.

*

In the reports of van der Nüll's suicide, I hear hints of excitement as the press goes hunting for his exact motives. One popular explanation is the increasing pressure to move forward with the project. The newspapers also make tentative reference to the smear campaign, suggesting that the unrelenting criticism and derision drove the architect to "misjudge himself" to the point of madness. The most cynical of his opponents saw his deed as further evidence of his weak character. Barely a day after his death, the mythmaking commenced: "A sinister demon, killing heart and mind, hovers over the construction of this opera house" (*Neues Wiener Tagblatt*, April 5, 1868).

*

Ten weeks later, on June 11, 1868, August Sicard von Sicardsburg died, his strength sapped by the death of his friend.

I don't mean to accuse them of sentimentality, but it seems

they couldn't live without each other. That is a medical observation. The cord could not be severed. They died each other's
death. Neither architect made it to the official opening of the
opera on May 25, 1869.

Shortly after his death, or maybe because of it, van der Nüll
came to be seen in a different light. The newspapers began to
portray him as a tragic genius. Sicard's death gave rise to nothing but more mudslinging. He was said to have enjoyed
attending balls, where he drank to excess and subjected women
to unwanted attention, while swearing at the men in the crud-
est conceivable way.

Less than fifty years later, the winds of fashion had changed.
In 1907, the same newspapers that had gunned down the two
architects were showering superlatives on the Vienna State
Opera; on the brilliant, miraculous stairway to the boxes; on
the boxes themselves, the size of cozy, intimate apartments; on
the galleries, which extend a warm welcome to all who would
come, look and listen; and on the spacious auditorium, which
renders each tone still more tender, more poignant – for such
is its sacred and serious task. And to think that the two master
builders took their own lives, fearing they had created an
imperfect work. When in fact it was perfect, perfect.

V

SAN CARLO ALLE QUATTRO FONTANE (1634–1677), ROME

FRANCESCO BORROMINI (1599–1667)

I study the blue of the sky through the window to choose the exact shade of colored pencil. Maybe it starts here. I am six years old. On the kitchen table in front of me is my first school assignment: a biblical comic strip to be colored in. A sheet of paper with scenes of shepherds in a hilly pasture, a children's version of the story of Abraham (leaving out the human sacrifice). From the moment the blue pencil meets the paper, I take my responsibility seriously. From that first blue line, I am a person with homework to do, with a job to perform – or, to be more exact, with a job to complete to perfection. I press hard on the pencils to make the areas of color as rich as I can, because that's how the sky is, dense and deep and blue, not outside the lines, let alone the borders. It's not until my mother turns on the light and rouses me from my diligent trance that I feel the cramp in my right hand, the pinched blood in my fingertips. Outside, the blue of sky has turned three pencil shades darker. The TV is playing the closing credits to *The Simpsons*. My mother says it's beautiful but adds that I didn't have to work so hard – it's just a drawing. We put the comic strip up on the fridge with letter magnets until I take it to school the next day. Before going to bed, I take another look. I have misgivings, though I'm not sure what about.

Two years later, I embark on a brief career as a visual artist at

the drawing academy in Arendonk, a small village on the border between Belgium and the Netherlands. A retrospective
exhibition of my work from the period would reveal that at the
age of eight I had vague cosmopolitan yearnings. Following the
dictates of the Muse, I molded a series of figures out of clay: an
Arab with a turban, the Hindu god Vishnu, a warrior from the
terra-cotta army, an Asian sage, an Indian tepee, a Greek
amphora and a Western family around the television set – with
the daughter in complete control of the Croky chips.

My last clay creation can in retrospect be described as
visionary: a year before the film came out, I made a small figure
of an anthropomorphic chicken that bears a striking resemblance to Ginger from the animated film *Chicken Run* – except
that my chicken is wearing a red scarf instead of Ginger's floral
print. After the chicken, I was removed from the drawing academy. Art historians would conclude that my career was cut
short in its prime, just before my commercial period began,
but what did I know about art history or commerce? I had to
stop. After the chicken incident, my parents decided it was for
the best. The problem was that the chicken had become a
source of tension in our household.

While most of my clay figurines were dedicated to both my
parents, I had made the chicken for my father alone. He took
care of our real chickens in the garden, so it seemed only fair.
My father wanted to put the clay chicken on prominent display at his workplace, but the thought of exposing my creation
to strangers' eyes gave me second thoughts about the whole
thing, to the point where – after molding it, firing it, painting
it and adding a final layer of varnish – I wanted nothing more
to do with the chicken. It wasn't good enough. My father tried
to reassure me, telling me over and over again what a beautiful
chicken it was, but I cried, begged, refused, insisted and cried
again, harder. Please, Daddy, I said, please smash the figurine.

Or else throw it in the bin. I said he could put it in our chicken coop if he had to, for the real chickens to destroy, or at least befoul beyond recognition with smears of chicken shit. I went on insisting until, in time, the figurine vanished. The next Saturday morning, when I heard I'd been pulled out of the drawing academy, I accepted the decision with equanimity. Getting my way was preferable to facing my failure.

Soon afterwards came the millennium. When I think back to the apocalyptic stories going round at the time, the chicken incident starts to make more sense. If the world really was going to end at the dawn of the year 2000, I didn't want to be remembered for that stupid, meaningless clay bird. I needed to leave a superior kind of debris.

That New Year's Eve, my parents, my brother and I watched a musical show with kids' champagne and chips. A few minutes before midnight, the D-Devils took the stage. Two men dressed as devils began preaching, to repetitive house beats, that the six gates of hell were open and the time had come to dance with the Devil. My brother went wild – it was his favorite song.

"And dance with the Devil!" he sang along, shaking and twitching with delight. I kept my eyes squeezed shut all the way through. When it was over and the clock struck twelve, the two cannons let out loud bangs that burst into clouds of silver confetti. We hadn't exploded. Nothing had changed.

After the Apocalypse failed to materialise, my brother snapped his D-Devils single in two. I made a list of things that could win me eternal fame:

- breaking records in the *Guinness Book of Records*
- singing really really well
- inventing world peace
- becoming Jane Goodall and spending my whole life studying apes

You see, I was not the child with a death wish. I had plans.

*

There are no shades of gray. There is completion and there is failure. That's how it's always felt: a rigid bar at the level of my midriff, impossible to move up or down. Yet that bar can swing a long way backwards and forwards, to alarming heights, a trapeze from which an acrobat prepares to leap.

Perfectionists are said to strive for perfection because they cannot love themselves, because they look for the admiration of others to confirm their value, but that hunger can never be satisfied. When I *am* admired, it means little to me. Isn't that more like a surplus of self-love? Eyes fixed on my own protruding belly button. Narcissus, chained to his reflection. And despite my desire for perfection, I fear few things as much as I do completion. I feel incapable of ever taking responsibility for a finished thing. It's much safer to imagine that a thing is perpetually striving towards completion, because that striving leaves room for improvement. It could always be better.

*

When I saw a picture of the Church of San Carlo alle Quattro Fontane in Rome, I knew almost for certain that the brazen and sensuous façade, its concave and convex undulations, must have been designed by a restless spirit. A simple Google search confirmed my suspicion. The architect, baroque master Francesco Borromini, is thought to have suffered from a manic-depressive disorder. Combined with his obvious perfectionism, this must have been the generative force behind his large oeuvre of superhuman designs. But the creative ferment of his genius had a dark side: he went through pitch-black periods of utter dejection.

In a sense, Borromini's entire career was dominated by that church, San Carlo, whose small footprint has given it the nickname San Carlino. Along with the adjacent monastery and sleeping quarters, it was Borromini's first solo architectural commission – though anything but a routine job. The parcel of land on which the church was to be built was small and inconvenient: an asymmetrical corner plot at the intersection of Via del Quirinale and Via delle Quattro Fontane, at the very summit of the Quirinal Hill in Rome. That same intersection contained four fountains placed by order of the pope, which had to be taken into account in designing the church. Borromini inserted San Carlino among all those pre-existing elements with such mastery that you might think the street, the fountains and the hill were all made to fit the church, and not the other way round.

The floor plan is complex and invites several different readings. The clearest interpretation may be as a diamond with elliptical sides, or more precisely as two equilateral triangles with one shared side, around which an oval can be drawn – a deformation of the traditional central plan, which can be pictured as a stretched Greek cross.

Tutto il suo sapere. Borromini was instructed to display all his knowledge and skill in the church. His brilliant design brought him greatness and despair. Lack of money kept him from starting work on the façade until the end of his life.

*

Any creation is, to some degree, tainted with its maker; how could it be otherwise? The creative act gives form and expression to something from within the self. It is a movement from inside to outside, from the fathomless inner world to the tangible. An outdated, nineteenth-century image, I know: the artist as an autonomous creative genius. It's probably closer to the truth to see it as a dialectical process, a movement going from outside to inside and back. The world makes impressions on the inner world of the maker, which take new forms in the outside world through the permeable wall of artistic composition. However I describe it, it is a give and take that binds the artist tight to his creation. Applied to my own work, this tells me that my writing is mine and mine only. Or at least, it makes me feel as if that's true. The only thing I have is writing. It shapes who I am, and that is reassuring. It rescues me from thinking too much about myself. In matters of identity, I can fall back on certain prevailing assumptions about the writer's life, or on the opacity of my professional practice to outsiders. In most cases, I am not expected to go into detail. Another advantage is that most people have no interest in my writing whatsoever. Sheltered by their indifference, I almost never have to explain myself. If I wish, I can withdraw into my shell completely. Another writer once suggested to me that there may be something temporary about it, saying, "Maybe you'll only write two books and then it will be over, and you'll do something else."

"Yeah, you never know," I replied, because I wanted to sound noncommittal, but when I imagine stopping I can only picture a void.

*

In Ovid's *Metamorphoses*, the Cypriot prince and sculptor Pygmalion confuses this close tie, this mutual contamination of artist and work, with self-love. He gives the impression of being a perfectionist in search of supreme beauty, a standard he also applies to others. That may be why he cannot find a wife; for Pygmalion believes all women are steeped in sin. This conviction dashes his hopes for marriage but also gives him the space to devote himself entirely to his art. Since women of flesh are too flawed for him, he sets out to sculpt the perfect woman.

His efforts are successful. One day, Pygmalion puts the finishing touches to the ivory sculpture of a woman of perfect beauty, Galatea. He falls head over heels in love with her – he can't help it, having made her so lifelike, as if she's just asking to be adored. And adore her he does, with a passion. Pygmalion dresses his ivory wife in fine fabrics and jewelry, flattering her and caressing her like a lover. But the stone remains cold; Galatea is lifeless and unable to return his adoration. Pygmalion's love for the sculpture is not only unrequited, but also narcissistic; his love object is merely the outward manifestation of his inner ideal, of his own desires. In fact, through the sculpture he is in love with himself. And this form of self-love, this complete and perfect form, is unsatisfactory. Pygmalion's wishes will remain unfulfilled until he is willing to allow for flaws. He pleads with the love goddess Aphrodite to relieve his heartache, pleads with her to give him a woman who looks like his creation, too ashamed to ask for the ivory woman herself. Fortunately, Aphrodite has experience of men who fear their true desires will be condemned, and sees straight through his wish.

One night when Pygmalion comes home and kisses his stone Galatea on the lips, as he has done so many times before, the statue turns into a flesh-and-blood woman. Perfection has proved too frigid; imperfection transforms into love.

In the BBC documentary *Guys and Dolls*, several men, modern-day Pygmalions, speak openly about their "synthetic love" for their "real dolls," life-size mannequins that bear a startling resemblance to real women, right down to their soft skin and tongues. At first, these dolls were marketed as sex objects, but the neo-Pygmalions in the documentary have developed deep emotional relationships with theirs. They see their dolls as life partners in the fullest sense. The most interesting subject is DaveCat, a man in his thirties who was also featured in an episode of the American program *My Strange Addiction*. For years, DaveCat has had a monogamous relationship with Sidore, a doll tailored to his desires. He has put himself forward as an advocate of synthetic love and makes frequent television appearances. Since he is prone to become overstimulated and prefers seclusion, he feels his synthetic partner is simply a much better match for him than a human – or, as he puts it, an "organic partner."

"A synthetic will never lie to you, cheat on you, criticize you, or be otherwise disagreeable," DaveCat says. "It's rare enough to find organics who don't have something going on with them, and being able to make a partner of one is rarer still."

DaveCat's life leaves no room for character flaws or imperfections. He is pleased that Sidore has no will of her own and no personality beyond his preferences. He dresses her in latex, because she's sexy. He buys her glasses, because he's drawn to her intellect. Depending on his mood, he changes her wig. Sidore is a creature of his own making; DaveCat calls her a way of being "creative."

Like Pygmalion's carved block of ivory, the silicon-based Sidore has no inherent personal qualities, only those her creator has endowed her with. Yet unlike Pygmalion, DaveCat does not find fulfilment.

One evening a strange incident occurs. The local police receive a report of domestic violence and go to investigate. Entering the home in question, they find a scene of havoc, as if a whirlwind had swept through every room in the house. In one corner of the living room crouches a man with what appears to be a life-size doll in his lap. To smother his own wailing, he is pressing his face into a purple wig.

"I'm sorry, I'm sorry," the police make out through the sobs.

The doll is naked and damp. Her silicon face is torn in several places.

"I lost control, officer, I'm sorry, but she gets so jealous, I couldn't take it anymore ...," DaveCat explains for the police report, as he clings to the tear-soaked wig.

Shortly after this event, DaveCat gives an interview in which he introduces his new doll, the Russian Lenka, to the public. Lenka is his mistress; Sidore knows all about it and puts up with her presence.

*

A few days before his suicide, some time in late July 1667, Francesco Borromini knocks the maquettes off his table in one furious, well-aimed sweep. The clay hits the floor with a dull crack, very different from the sound of the glass in the display cases when he shatters them and stamps on the skeletal frames, smashing and snapping the fragile woodwork underfoot, and before long the whole floor of his workshop is littered with splintered wood, cracked clay and shards of glass, all pocked with bits of red wax and drops of blood, and he overturns the many crates and boxes and hurls them across the room in a shower of antique medals, twelve compasses, shells, hundreds of shells, followed by rare, clattering metalwork, lamps and spoons, and then, inflamed by the ear-splitting rattle, he pulls the horse's head off the wall and flings it at the large stuffed ostrich, which tumbles to the floor, taking down the eagle's head, which rolls into a corner, and, as his destructive frenzy comes to a boil, he thrusts his hand between the shards of glass in the case, grabbing the snakeskins from the display and ripping them to pieces, first with his hands and then with his teeth, and with the torn skin still in his mouth – his insanity now at its peak – he pushes over the plaster bust of Seneca (leaving Michelangelo in place) and seizes with still greater violence on his book collection, which he pulls off the shelves spine by spine, one book after another hitting the ground with a bang that dislodges its backbone, the pages defenseless against his rage, crumpling and tearing as he charges like a roaring bull through the chaos to the far end of the room, where, as he stands at his drawing table, his madness draws back for a few pensive seconds of hesitation, and then he tears up his drawings after all, his blueprints, sketches and studies, his hundreds of papers, into thousands and thousands of pieces, confetti blowing around the room like snowflakes, mourning the massacre. Amid this paper snowfall a servant finds Borromini, close to calm, contemplative.

*

A few days before the destruction of his workshop, Borromini had lost his friend and admirer, the antiquarian Fioravante Martinelli, whose death appears to have been the proximate cause of his own suicide. Martinelli had planned to write a detailed monograph about the Church of Sant'Ivo alla Sapienza; Borromini had furnished him with his original drawings for the project. Maybe after Martinelli's death Borromini had no more use for his drawings, and knew he could not keep his own demons at bay much longer.

But the destruction of his entire archive and his whole life's work – was that necessary? And if it was necessary, wasn't that enough? Did he wish he could bring down the stones themselves? In that last, dark episode of his life in architecture, Borromini, if he could have, might well have torn down his buildings with his own hands. The maker retains the right of destruction.

Various sources describe his difficult personality and volcanic temper. He clashed with his patrons more than once. It
is said that Borromini could not tolerate any intervention in
his work. To him, the architect's artistic intention was sacred,
and he would brook no compromise. His unflagging quest
for perfection, which seemed so close at hand in his pure and
intricate architectural forms, eventually drove him to despair.
He was only one man – how could he set an unshakable era
in motion?

*

Rome, late sixteenth to mid-seventeenth centuries. The city is
one vast building site. The Reformation has divided Europe,
and the Catholic Church is fighting back with its bombastic
baroque campaign: dynamic forms and dramatic effects,
designed to appeal to the inner world of emotion. Through art
and architecture, the Church hopes to regain its place in the
hearts of the people. Many buildings from this period reflect
the formal principles of classicism, because they were begun in
the Renaissance. But they were completed in the baroque
style.

Take, for example, the iconic St. Peter's Basilica in Rome. In
Michelangelo's original design, the floor plan was a Greek
cross with a broad ambulatory. When the architect Carlo Maderno was commissioned to complete St. Peter's in 1603, he
added a nave and narthex on the west side, changing the Greek
cross into a basilica plan. He also altered the design of the
façade, making it genuinely outward-looking. Half a century
later, in the spirit of the baroque idea that perfection is expressed
by rounded forms, Gian Lorenzo Bernini added impressive
elliptical colonnades that frame the approach to the basilica,
like motherly arms embracing the crowds of the faithful in St.

Peter's Square. In this sense, the colonnades' design embodies the baroque agenda.

The flood of investment in the new building campaign brought many professional opportunities for architects and artists. The two contemporaries Gian Lorenzo Bernini and Francesco Borromini were both put to work on the site of St. Peter's Basilica. Under the patronage of Pope Urban VIII, Bernini's career skyrocketed.

After the death of Carlo Maderno in 1629, Bernini, who had recently turned thirty, was appointed director of the entire building project. He took on the job of coordinating the ornamentation and sculpture in the interior. Driven by his ambition and self-taught genius, Bernini made choices that maintain a human scale in the church interior. His magnificent creations include the well-known *Baldacchino*, the canopy over the tomb of Peter the apostle.

In the shadow of Bernini's successes, Borromini carried out more modest assignments for St. Peter's, such as building the base for Michelangelo's *Pietà* and sculpting a vivacious but solitary cherub over the relief in the southwest corner. His skill and his powers of observation caught the attention of the chief architect, Maderno, who took an interest in the young Borromini and, in Maderno's final years, became almost a father figure to him.

While Maderno's death provided a stepping stone for Bernini, it left Borromini with a lifelong wound. Maderno's influence would remain in Borromini's thoughts to his dying day. Borromini's suffering was all the worse because he believed that he, as Maderno's protégé, should have been the one chosen to make his mentor's vision for St. Peter's Basilica a reality.

Here lies the germ of the enduring rivalry between the two future baroque masters. The feud between Bernini and Borromini was to become one of the best-known personal conflicts in the history of Western architecture. From that point on, their approaches to architecture branched in radically different directions. While Bernini was admired by the public for the dramatic simplicity of his compositions, Borromini took the experimental path, striving towards an extravagant complexity that met with resistance from the Church.

Bernini's architecture combined conventional forms with familiar elements in a manner that was safe and showed some continuity with classicism. His lavish interiors lent his buildings real artistic unity. Borromini's interiors, by contrast, were austere. He tended to use inexpensive materials, such as white stucco, and hardly any gold or marble. This emphasised the three-dimensional geometry of his designs, giving free rein to his complex patterns.

When Borromini was accused of desecrating the classical tradition, Bernini was, of course, among his most vocal detractors. After all, Bernini and his school believed architecture should reflect the proportions of the human body. Borromini's work is a distortion of the body, a lusty carnival of curves. Yet his designs never fail to intrigue. Despite Rome's reservations about Borromini's experiments, everyone acknowledged that nothing similar could be found anywhere in the world.

*

The eye finds no rest. Straight ahead of me is the frivolous mayhem of San Carlino, with nothing but the street between us, and I am going under. A tireless outpouring of bulges and hollows runs across the exhaust-blackened façade. Pressure and counterpressure in a high-intensity wrestling match. The façade of San Carlino is both firmly anchored and a jiggly pudding. The tilted tondo at the top, which serves as a pediment, seems to lean in for a better look at the passersby. Even the statues in the corners of the portal are on the move, one foot in front of the other, as if they might step out of the gable at any moment. The honking of traffic down the hill between the church and me mingles with the building's frenetic motion. It stirs me up, as if the surging stones represent the very essence of pursuit, reaching out of their joints towards some greater union with all that moves.

For Borromini, this was no easy project to complete. Not until thirty years after the church was built, in 1665, did he obtain the funding to continue his work. The struggle took half his life, and he seems to have given it his whole being. It devoured him, this unfinished thing, an open wound that gaped throughout his career, even after his later successes. With uncompromising dedication, he spent the last two years of his life working on the façade. But his perfectionism also returned, blocking his way forward. In this period, he was felled by a series of severe depressions. Maybe he had some presentiment of the historic influence of his creation and that was what sank his spirits. He saw something take shape beneath his fingers that could never be equaled. His San Carlino would go down in history as the icon of Roman baroque; no one would ever match that accomplishment, not even Borromini himself. You cannot win a fight with your own shadow. The thought of what comes afterwards is simply a void.

Inside the church, the outpouring continues. Above the niche of the main altar is the beginning of a dome in a cross-section, interrupted at the bottom by a triangle with curved sides – and as I struggle over this description, the very act of seeing resolves the formal complexity. The building is pure mathematics, so correct that it feels harmonious, light and perfectly natural. The columns draw the eyes of the visitors upwards, to the light. How much higher does the church seem than it really is, because of this heavenward motion? I find myself in a weightless space. To think that stone can be so spare, so light.

Dizzied, I wander out of the church – not into the street outside but into the street in memory. I am visiting Rome for the first time again, a few years earlier in July 2013. Not alone, as I am now, but with my first love and our best friend. In this triangular configuration, we have been taking the train across Italy for three weeks; Rome is our last stop. For years we have been inseparable. We've just graduated and we're completely broke; everything here is too expensive. We haven't booked tickets in advance, of course. The line for the Vatican winds back and forth through Bernini's whole colonnade. We spend those final days in Rome wandering aimlessly, straight past all the things we'd planned to see. The sense of traveling ends before our travels do. Yes, we're still moving through the scenery of our destination, but at the same time we are no longer really here, and it's hot – no, it's suffocating. A heat wave lingers over Europe this summer, and Rome is the focal point of the blazing sun, with temperatures above forty degrees Celsius. As I write this now I am seized in the same full-body stranglehold as then among the throngs of milling tourists, an unholy heat that chases the three of us out of the city center. Like exiles, we stagger up the Quirinal Hill, and in our craving for shade we go blindly past San Carlo alle Quattro Fontane. We simply do not see the church; it is just too hot. Around 100 meters farther on is the Giardino di Sant'Andrea – a "relaxing escape from heat," Tripadvisor calls it. We stay there all afternoon.

How could we have walked straight past the commanding spectacle of San Carlo? What *did* I see that day? The thick trunks of the trees in the garden, yes, and a view from that high place on the hill, of the city quivering in the intense midday light. The cover of the book our friend was reading: *A Philosophy of Boredom*, an essay by the Norwegian philosopher Lars

Svendsen. And the book my boyfriend was reading? I don't remember, but I can guess: a novel by Gabriel García Márquez. And now I see what else I saw: the pigeon, scruffy and half dead, under the tree that shaded us. Her tail bitten off, an injured wing drooping from one side, one eye crusted with pus; my heart breaks; the boys read, soaking up the shade of the tree, sinking into the afternoon's lethargy like Tityrus and Meliboeus, as if Virgil himself had dreamed up the two of them, there, lost in their books in the cool shade, and as long as they remain in that other realm, the realm of reading, I am the only one left to take pity on the half-dead pigeon. How can I make her better, find ways to fix her? I pour water into the cap of my bottle, crumble salty crisps near her beak; don't touch it, the boys say, it's probably sick. Of course it's sad, but there's nothing to be done. Yet I am doing something: I am acting by not taking action. I don't touch her. I watch. For almost two hours, I watch the pigeon suffer: Where is her tail? How did she end up with that damaged wing? Does the pigeon understand the pain she feels? Does the pigeon know she's dying? Could she be dead already? Is there any water left? And now? Is she dead now? Is it my job to put her out of her misery?

As the afternoon ends, we move on from the Giardino di Sant'Andrea in search of *aperitivi*. I leave the pigeon and her suffering behind. In silence, I drink to her certain death. No way of knowing how many more hours she had to wait for it.

That night, in the attic where we're staying, I can't get to sleep. The room is just below the roof and the heat of the day is still oppressive. The three of us are sharing a double bed. The rota we've drawn up gives us each one night on the side closest to the fan; tonight, it's my turn to be in the middle. One pair of legs feels familiar under the sheets; the other remains at a decent distance, on its side of the shared bed. In the middle of this triangle I lie, in near-mathematical harmony, at the fulcrum of the vital balance between my boyfriend and our best friend, nestled in the six years of intimacy that led to this night. My God, it seems to encompass my whole life. I am barely twenty-two years old, and I haven't the slightest sense of direction, I hardly even have any ambition to write, maybe that's why I can't sleep, why I can't help thinking of the pigeon, and then of the Etruscan haruspices, who could read good fortune and ill in animal entrails. What signs of my future lay hidden in that raggedy bird? What would the Roman augurs have made of her hobbled attempts to fly? Is this the unthinkable end of our intimacy? Must it expire?

I get out of bed, out of memory, and back to the present, strolling away from San Carlo towards the Giardino di Sant'Andrea. It's not hard even now, years later, to find that particular tree in the fenced garden, but there's no point in sitting there now as I did then.

*

The Giardino di Sant'Andrea is the garden of Sant'Andrea al Quirinale, a church built by Bernini. It was erected at the same time as San Carlino, and the sites are less than 200 meters apart. The rivals had to suffer each other's constant presence.

In Piazza Navona, Borromini worked on the church of Sant'Agnese, while Bernini, straight across the square, was carving the Fontana dei Quattro Fiumi out of travertine, a commission that would have gone to Borromini, had Bernini not charmed the pope's sister-in-law with a model of his design cast in silver. When the pope laid eyes on the silver miniature fountain, he was delighted and straightaway gave the job to Bernini, who with Borromini so close by could not resist rubbing his victory in his competitor's face and worked an insult into his design for the fountain. Over the basin, four river gods each look out in a different direction; the one facing the façade of Sant'Agnese covers his face with his hand, as if shielding his eyes from the sight of Borromini's church.

Borromini made an ironic gesture of his own by giving Sant'Agnese two monumental towers, the same height as its dome. This recalled the most embarrassing blunder of Bernini's career: the pair of bell towers he had built on either side of St. Peter's, which soon showed cracks and were hurriedly demolished.

Whose is bigger? In the middle of his fountain, Bernini placed a 16-meter-tall Egyptian obelisk, a match for Borromini's towers. Boyish pranks. But they were serious.

*

A perfectionist deserves a good enemy, preferably one a little more talented than he is, so that he can savor his victories. The rivalry between the two architects must at first have driven them to new heights, but in the end it made Borromini a bitter man. In the light of his artistic beliefs, the public's embrace of Bernini was incomprehensible and came to feel like a rejection of Borromini's own work.

In the summer of 1667, Borromini's nervous disorder came to a head. His high expectations of himself as he finished San Carlino, the death of his friend Martinelli, his envy of Bernini, his never-ending drive for perfection ... In retrospect, these were all signs that he had been drifting towards a cliff edge for years. Yet it was not until July 27, when he smashed up his workshop in a fit of anger and tore up all his drawings, that the people in his life intervened. If he had been capable of destroying the place where his whole life converged, then he was surely capable of worse. His cabinet of curiosities, his extensive art collections and the tools of his profession – all these had been sacred to him. Instead of asserting his status the way most architects did, with a pompous residence, he had surrounded himself with eccentric objects, from art to junk, and used them to build his own universe, a place where his imagination could roam freely.

The deliberate destruction of his studio was a spiritual suicide. A few days later, he escaped his minder's attention and from his arsenal – which included four swords, a halberd and a small handheld firearm – he selected a medium-sized saber on which to impale himself, so that his body could follow his spirit into oblivion.

The self-inflicted saber wounds did not kill him right away. He was patched up to the point where he could receive the final sacrament and make his will. Then Borromini died in solitude; he had never married. He left his property to a nephew, on the condition that he marry the niece of his mentor Carlo Maderno. After Borromini's death, his body was laid to rest in his mentor Maderno's tomb. At his own request, there was no inscription. A miserable last wish: the architect who begs for his name not to be immortalized in stone. With this act, Borromini distanced himself from his chosen material and thus made his obliteration complete.

Bernini outlived his rival by several years, spending his old age in complacent idleness. His son Domenico tells of Bernini's daily visits to the Giardino di Sant'Andrea in his final years; there, under the foliage, with a view of Borromini's San Carlino on one side and his own Sant'Andrea on the other, the elderly master felt a deep peace settle over him.

*

Then I do it after all. The past catches up with me and I find myself sitting under the tree where I found the ominous bird.

I stay there for a while. Memories well up. It suddenly pains me, all over again, that everything turned out so unlike how we'd planned it. The triangular form proved neither pure nor durable. The summer after our graduation trip, I pulled away, further and further, out of that triad, under the pretext of needing time to read, and I did read, without interruption, in a fever, striving to recover the sense of direction that had so suddenly given way to fatalism. The more I read, the more I realized that the future I'd had in mind was nobody's story; no masterpiece on earth has ever charted the happy results of pursuing a dutiful and risk-free life. Goethe was a particular master of accounting for his characters' inexpressibly poor choices. Faust's pact with the Devil's agent Mephistopheles was a bad idea in hindsight, of course, but his aim was to live as he desired, without limit, and what an enthralling, enviable life he led, up to the point when he had to pay the price. And yes, young Werther could have chosen not to visit Lotte in Walheim again after she married Albert; he knew it would put her reputation at risk, but she herself was disreputable enough to return Werther's love yet do nothing about it. If Werther had stayed out of that hopeless situation, he would never have been forced to conclude that one of the three must die to dispel the eternal pain of the love that bound them, and that perhaps he was the one. But he did visit her, of course, without a thought to the obvious, deadly consequences, because the only thing that really mattered was pursuing his heart's desire. To me as a young reader, the idea was beautiful and inescapable and deeply human, not to mention infectious.

Despite just having earned a degree in literature, I developed an adolescent weakness in my reading for human frailties and the stubborn defiance of fate. Around the same time I took a sudden interest, seemingly out of nowhere, in late-nineteenth-century realist novels on the theme of unhappy marriages, from the woman's perspective: Couperus's flighty Eline Vere with her fear of commitment and her wayward mind; Tolstoy's Anna Karenina, whose amorous nature triumphs over conventional morals; Flaubert's escapist Madame Bovary; Fontane's problem child Effi Briest ... women, one and all, who battled middle-class boredom by exploring and yielding to sexual curiosity. For their scant moments of freedom, the price they paid was suicide – all except Effi, who died of a nervous disorder. Given the broader undercurrent of social criticism in these books, we cannot be sure the authors meant us to see these women's suicides as their just deserts. Society, with its institutional oppression of female agency, was also responsible. In any case, the heroine's tragic fate was not the real point, but a price worth paying for the story. Shedding the critical apparatus I'd acquired in my four years of study, I plunged into a new, experiential mode of living.

I might add that I noticed other dying pigeons in those days. If I happened to look down while waiting for my train, I would find one at my feet. I often had to swerve on the bicycle path to avoid one that had already been run over. The day a pigeon crashed into a kitchen window of the house where the three of us lived, I saw the pattern: the dead pigeons portended the end of the harmony between us. That very day, I left the triangle. Soon afterwards, I started writing poetry. Now everything else must swerve.

VI

NATIONAL LIBRARY OF MALTA (1786–1796), VALLETTA

STEFANO ITTAR (1724–1790)

Għawdex. The Maltese name of the island of Gozo sounds like an evolved Pokémon. We rent a house there in low season. Once a year we meet for a quick getaway, four old friends from the Turnhout art academy who have flown the nest, accompanied by our partners. Through the open bedroom window, I can hear their voices ring out by the pool in the garden below. Now and then one of them splashes into the water. Their laughter is contagious. Even the mosaic dolphin on the floor of the pool giggles with them. Eternal afternoon. I pull the flannel cover up over my head, exhausted, hoping for a half hour of sleep before dinner. All day I look for half hours of sleep to snatch – never fully rested, never able to turn off my thoughts for thirty consecutive minutes. Even now, in this ready-made resort, surrounded by dear friends and free-flowing conversation, I find myself fretting. Have to look up *bizzilla*. Have to email the archivist about the death notice. Have to write up my notes while they're fresh. The cover smells of sleep, its stale odor floods the trench that my piercing headache has dug in my mind. My thoughts rattle on.

*

Valletta, two days earlier. I am looking up at the statue of Queen Victoria, who is showing clear marks of corrosion from acid rain. Despite her weathered state, the queen casts her chaste, imperial gaze – not over her empire of yore, but over the ironically small Piazza Regina, in front of the National Library. The white parasols of Eddy's Café and Caffe Cordina flank her stony presence. A cup of coffee here costs four euros twenty, a price that includes one wicker chair from which to watch the procession of tourists strolling past on the broad stage of Repubblika Street. The Maltese call Piazza Regina their *salott*, their public salon, better known these days as a place to see and be seen than it is for the unusual neoclassical building looming over the street cafés: the National Library of Malta, once known as St. John's Library.

This library is the last building commissioned by the Order of Malta before the island was taken by the British in 1800. The order had received the island as a gift from the Holy Roman Emperor Charles V three centuries earlier, as a place to store up the vast wealth they had accumulated as Knights Hospitaller in the Crusades.

The building projects their prosperity. Its almost academic composition is pure and austere, a model of careful proportion and symmetry. The façade possesses a classical grandeur, with its Doric, Ionic, and bas-relief columns, its loggia, arches and pediment, and its restrained, graceful ornamentation – I could check off the features in my architectural history textbook. A flawless expression of the Renaissance pursuit of harmony.

St. John's Library exemplifies the elegance of Valletta as it took shape under the rule of the Order of Malta. "But it's unfortunate," one survey tells me, "that the architect of this final building commissioned by the Knights was not Maltese, considering how many other buildings, just as refined, were designed by Maltese architects."

Stefano Ittar, the architect of St. John's, happened to be born in the town of Owrucz, now Ovruch in northern Ukraine.

His father belonged to the Italian aristocracy, but a dispute
with the grand duke of Tuscany forced his family off their
land. Growing up in exile, deprived of the advantages of his
surname, Ittar would go through his whole life with the vague
feeling of having to compensate for something. He studied
until he excelled. In Rome, he had the opportunity to learn
the architect's trade as a protégé of the Vatican librarian, Cardi-
nal Albani. The Vatican's material and spiritual wealth must
have dazzled the young Ittar. It was probably there that his
desire was sparked to win back his aristocratic title; his talent
opened a way for him to clear his father's name. And so he did,
following an illustrious path to Spain, Rome and Sicily, and
ending up in Malta, where the order expressed its profound
appreciation of his work by awarding him the prestigious commission for St. John's Library. But no, he was not Maltese.

*

For a pass with RESEARCHER in block letters, all you
need is some form of ID – so I qualify. The librarian squints,
narrowing his eyes to thin slits, but with the best will in the
world he cannot read the name on my identity card. He holds
it so close his eyebrows brush the surface.

"Can't make it out," he says at last, with a placid smile.

I spell my name for him so that he can type the letters into
his computer one by one. When I repeat them for confirma-
tion, he leans in towards his screen. The man is practically blind.
"A blind librarian," I jot in my notebook. A detail I would never
have come up with by myself. Feeling his way, he leads me past
the shoulder-height card catalogues to a monkish reading stand
on one of the small wooden tables in the center of the room.
Behind me, a young man is seated at a computer the size of a
steamer trunk. There are no other visitors in the library.

With RESEARCHER pinned to my chest, the reading stand in front of me inviting me to use it, and the book and document collection of the Knights Hospitaller all around me, I feel my insides churning in anticipation, as if I'm on the verge of some life-altering insight. This vortex of history, this breach in time, slowing into the sacred, silent hours of a monk bent over a manuscript – this is where all knowledge begins, this is where my quest for tragic architects will start to make sense, in this place, in this union of architecture and literature.

A glance upwards gives me vertigo. The bookcases along the walls are crammed full, all the way up to the high ceiling. The lowest shelves are sagging under the weight of heavy books with tall spines. From bottom to top, the shelves and the books grow gradually smaller, from folio to quarto to octavo format. The optical effect is to make the space look narrower towards the top, as if the ceiling were shrinking.

The sharp, musty odor of age-old paper. The books are in bad shape. They seem to have been tossed willy-nilly onto the shelves, like a load of remaindered copies instead of historical documents and valuable manuscripts. Some bindings are hanging loose from the sections inside; most others have been lost to an onslaught of woodworm. A treasure chamber of archives, a thousand years of documentation, all being gobbled up. Millions of minuscule worms – I reel at the image of them creeping, invisible, across the books, the bookcases, everything itching, the books longing to scratch themselves until they bleed, until their ink gushes out of the paper and leaves the pages blank. How long has it been since a hand selected one of their timeworn spines, laid the book on the stand, and spread it open cover to cover, perhaps caressing the pages one by one like the hand of an adoring lover, careful not to tear the paper, or perhaps devouring the book in impatient hunger? With no one to consult them, the books loiter on the shelves in useless silence. Something is in danger of collapse. Even before the librarian has time to explain the three different search systems and catalogues, I leave the room.

*

Looked it up: *bizzilla* is the word for traditional Maltese bobbin lace. It is said that in the days of the British Empire, Queen Victoria had lace gloves made for her in Malta: sixty-nine long pairs and sixty-nine short. This was her way of supporting the lace industry and the local economy. Some smart-arses have used the words "lace" and *bizzilla* to describe the books in St. John's Library.

*

Evening's come, and we're at the gates waiting for the ferry to Birgu. The Grand Harbour has been closed to traffic today because of the regatta. When the last rowers finish, around 7:00 p.m., the boats begin crossing back and forth again. The waterside is teeming with supporters, stands and bouncy castles. There are mothers with baby strollers puffing on cigarettes, trophies shining in the sun, girls with thick makeup slipping away into crevices in the rocks with broad-shouldered rowers. Their fathers are oblivious, the music is loud, they're eating mixed grill (sausage, bacon, chicken, leg of rabbit) out of burger boxes. Whenever a team of rowers reaches the finish, the crowd breaks into respectful applause. Afterwards, the party spreads out farther over the wharves. Elegant Valletta forgets its manners and loosens its belt.

In Birgu we dine in a little restaurant, Tal-Petut. "Prodott Lokali Frisk," table for eight. The interior looks like a vegetable garden; the shelves on the walls are overloaded with fragrant herbs and spices, artful baskets of vegetables and bottles of shimmering oil. From the half-open kitchen comes an irresistible medley of aromas. The meal itself is an immersion, a whole-some cornucopia of singular, distinct flavors. The starter, a selection of homemade antipasti, fills the table. Crushed garlic with fresh parsley, served with local water crackers, sea salt and olive oil. Olives from the garden, pickled in honey, with a stripe of chili paste. Puréed fava beans with cumin, sea salt and olive oil. *Bigilla*: fava bean dip with pepper paste, parsley, sea salt and fresh herbs. Local dried sausage with coriander and boiled summer figs. An assortment of seasonal vegetables and tradi-tional cheeses. We eat and eat.

"And to think that at one point we all hoped to become artists," Bart says, passing the olives.

"I wouldn't dream of it now – it's too insecure. I work for my wages." Nikki sounds resolute. She takes a piece of sausage and swipes on a dot of fig jam with the tip of her knife before tasting it. Her partner, Ben, nods. The two of them work for a government minister and are always exhausted. Although I still think of them as ambitious people, barely three years in the working world have left them utterly disillusioned with the civil service. Their only apparent aim in life now is to make their holidays as frequent and luxurious as possible. Their jobs suck them dry and give them nothing in return.

"The worst thing, as far as I'm concerned, is that no one ever pats me on the head and says, 'Well done, Nikki.' "

Ben puts a gentle hand on her head and, with a blend of irony and tenderness, compliments her: "Babe, when they look at you all they really see is a phantom at a desk. It's the same for me. I have a PhD, I made it through a brutal application pro-cedure, and now they expect us to fend for ourselves. I guess they think that with all our advanced degrees we can figure out the job without their help. It's all on us."

"Go on like that and I'll start to think I'm lucky to be self-employed." Bart seems relieved.

"Even worse. Self-employed just means *self*-exploiting," Anna says. "Back when me and Bart were living together, he had just set up shop as an independent speech therapist. He left the house at seven thirty every morning and got home at eight every night. By then I was usually cooking. When he walked in the door, the first thing he did was pour himself a glass of wine. Over dinner, he would go over all the things he had to do before the next day, and after dinner he would do them. By the time he was done, he was wiped out and ready for bed. Bart literally did not have the free time even to ask me what was going on in my life, or how my day had been."

Anna's boyfriend, Frank, takes a piece of cheese and jokes, "That's right, Bart, I got no help from you at all with this one."

"OK, that's how it was at first. But later it got better, right? Right?" Bart throws his arms around Anna in a theatrical gesture. "And anyway, what was I supposed to do? I was climbing a mountain of paperwork with no one to guide me and had to make sure the numbers added up at the end of every month."

Bart's boyfriend, Stan, sees his opportunity. "He's no different now. He gets home and the least little thing sets him off, he's so irritable, because he sees clients every half hour from eight-thirty to seven without even a lunch break. One glass of wine and he's snoring and sliding off his chair. Not exactly quality time for the two of us."

"Come on, Stan, don't be melodramatic."

"How often do we make love on weekdays? I can't remember the last time that wasn't on Sunday."

I become very interested in the three types of cheese so I don't have to get involved in this discussion. One is hard and salty. One is like brie. And one is blue, too strong for my taste.

"You come home from work tired too, Stan. Sex just takes a little planning right now."

"Good thing we both keep our appointments, then," Stan

replies, his voice dripping with sarcasm. Before the conversation can explode into mutual recriminations, the next course is served. Ravioli filled with *ġbejna* (goat cheese), a tapenade made from local olives, deep-fried capers, fresh tomatoes, basil pesto and a sun-dried tomato dip.

The waiter refills our wine glasses. I clink glasses with Walter, the man I love. We needed this holiday. We take a refreshing sip and exchange a meaningful glance.

Walter steers the table talk onto safer ground. "How's it going at the magazine, Stan? I saw you're about to come out with a new issue."

Six months ago, Stan made the leap from a well-paid job at an insurance office to become the editor-in-chief of a leading LGBTQ+ magazine. Five hundred euros a month less and twice the hassle. His working days frequently swell into night shifts. Stan sums up his duties: "Coordinating twenty-five volunteers, contributing content, taking final responsibility for all the editing, keeping the social media running, preparing for interviews, doing the interviews and then hopefully finding the time to write a few articles under my own byline."

A wave of admiration goes around the table for this raft of responsibilities. Stan is tired, but also proud he can handle it all.

"How was Rome, Charlotte?" Nikki asks. She refills my glass and passes the dish of ravioli.

I tell them everything I learned in Rome about Francesco Borromini. The sensuous façade, his rival Bernini, the way he fell on his sword. As I tell the story, I hear myself as if standing outside my own body, weaving a suspenseful plot, trying to entertain my friends, wanting them to be awestruck by my story, to applaud my plan to set it down on paper, to recognize the importance, the necessity of it.

"Fun that you get to go on so many trips for your book," Nikki says.

My heart sinks at this reply – though I'm sure she doesn't mean anything by it.

"Yeah, lots of fun," I reply.

"You won't let it reach that stage, will you? I can't imagine I'd ever commit suicide," Bart says decisively, biting into a heavily laden slice of bread.

"Me neither," Anna agrees.

"Never thought about it?" I ask.

Leg of cockerel stuffed with ground beef, sautéed in white wine and fresh local herbs, served with baby carrots rolled in dried coriander and fresh rosemary and a scoop of whipped potatoes with leeks and sea salt. Eating becomes an act of resistance against the topic of conversation; we're almost bursting, and then comes the three-part dessert: poached apple, nougat and crushed ice with rosewater. Anna gives up, unable to swallow another mouthful. The rest of us aren't hungry either, but not wanting to miss any part of the experience, we muster our courage and brandish our spoons. Bart gamely offers to eat Anna's portion. Frank also rushes to her aid.

Despite the heavy meal, the wine hits hard. We linger around the table in a sluggish daze. Walter tells his anecdote about the museum guard, which I've heard before; two years into our relationship, the stories are beginning to repeat themselves. This time, he tells the anecdote in the form of a riddle.

"A freelance museum attendant is hired to guard an empty room," he begins. "The room is not part of an art project about emptiness or the void. The room has no properties of mathematical interest. There's no art on display there, no plans to display any art in the near future. The walls are white, but they weren't painted recently, so there's no need for the attendant to warn the visitors to keep a safe distance from the wet paint. The room is as empty as you can imagine it being. From ten a.m. to six p.m., the attendant guards the room. He takes a short lunch break, half an hour. Meanwhile, the guard responsible for an adjacent security zone keeps his eye on the room. Most passersby glance at the guard, then glance into the room, but they don't go inside – why would they? The room is empty! At the end of the guard's working day, when he closes the double doors to the room as instructed, he notices a key in the lock …"

I give Walter a look of encouragement. I'm worried about him, as I have been so often recently. I know he identifies with the museum guard. He's writing a doctoral thesis about rhythm in Middle Dutch verse. He does it with dedication but sometimes finds it hard to explain what all that dedication is meant to achieve. More and more often, he's not really sure himself. He has dark circles under his eyes.

"What if I'm guarding an empty room, sweetheart?" he asks me late at night, his computer screen shedding its blue light over the bed. I'm tired too. It's hard to find a diplomatic response. Sometimes I pretend to be sleeping.

Before Walter can sink into the same state of despondency here in the restaurant, the digestif arrives: prickly pear gin. The full glasses cry out to be emptied. Eight overeducated, fatigued twenty-somethings drink a toast to each other, the meal and our brief five-day reprieve. We still haven't burst, not quite.

At midnight, when we take the ferry back, the winning regatta team is still celebrating. On the dance floor, some partygoers are waving the blue-and-white club flag. The supporters, family members and rowers, sporting blue-and-white wreaths, are doggedly dancing to Bryan Adams.

*

The banquets in the home of Don Ignazio, Principe of Biscari, must have been a marvel of abundance. Goethe and Lord Byron both mention him in the diaries of their travels in Italy, describing him as a philanthropist, a congenial man with an enlightened mind and a genuine passion for science and the arts. The principe devoted his life to rebuilding the Sicilian city of Catania, in the shadow of Mount Etna, after it was destroyed by an earthquake. The men he sent to excavate the rubble found ancient treasures: temples and thermae, altars and goddess figurines, amphorae and mosaics ... He did not let a shard or stone of these glorious classical relics slip through his fingers.

One evening in 1765, the principe invited the architect Stefano Ittar to dine with him. Intrigued by Ittar's glowing references and his excellent pencil studies of Francesco Borromini, he wanted to meet the rising baroque master from Rome. The other guests at the table were, not by chance, the architect and city planner Giovanni Battista Vaccarini, who was supervising the reconstruction of Catania, and the architect Francesco Battaglia, who had brought along his eligible daughter Rosario.

Was it the principe's exceptional character, the welcoming atmosphere of his Palazzo Biscari, or the strange magnetism that draws certain people together? In any case, the dinner would change Stefano Ittar's life completely. He forged an important tie to the principe, who became not only a faithful friend but also his patron, as well as a partnership with Battaglia that would endure for years. His acquaintance with Rosario led to a marriage that produced six sons and three daughters. That night, Ittar even made a strong impression on the great Vaccarini, who – on his deathbed a few years later – handed down the position of city planner and court architect to the younger man with the fullest confidence.

Under Battaglia's guidance, and with Vaccarini's approval, the principe's financial support and the inspiration of Borromini's work, Ittar rapidly grew into a master architect. Barely three years later, in 1768, he would complete his best-known building, the Basilica della Collegiata in Catania. The church is the flamboyant epitome of Sicilian baroque.

*

Even with the windows shut, the reading room is unbelievably drafty. The temperature outside is thirty degrees Celsius. While my friends spend the afternoon swimming in the bay near the St. Elmo Bridge, I am back in the library, shivering in a thin summer dress. Ever since it was built, the placement of the windows has led to problems with humidity. The cold drafts are caused mainly by the five large windows on the north side of the reading room. But the architect, Ittar, put those windows on the cold side of the building deliberately, to protect the glass from the diabolical sirocco wind from the south.

The sirocco visits Malta twice a year, bringing dry, blazing hot air from the Sahara that raises temperatures in the far south of Europe to forty-five degrees. Even the night offers little relief. The islands' inhabitants lie feverish in their beds, unable to sleep. With dry, heavy heads, racked by the savage migraine the sirocco brings, they wait for it to pass. Behind closed shutters, they pray for the wind not to do too much material damage as it passes through. The dust it carries wreaks destruction, damaging even stone, metal and iron; glass could never hold it back, and the fragile books would not stand a chance.

Ittar placed the windows on the north side so that the glass would be out of the path of the tyrannical sirocco but still admit sufficient daylight. The disadvantage is that the cold remains inside the walls. Even before the library officially opened, there were complaints of bronchitis, gout and pneumonia from people who had barely set foot in the reading room. These exaggerated claims soon cast a pall over the building. *You'd have to be tired of life to set foot in that drafty cave! If the sweet release of death is what you seek, then enter that library and come that much closer to your final breath!*

*

On this second visit, I'm no longer as shocked by the tattered state of the collection, but between the fifth and sixth shelves in the cases that line the walls, I notice something strange. Sticking out from between the books in each case at that level is a pipe with a tap attached. When I ask the librarian what the taps are for, he points to the ceiling. Above it are tanks that hold reserves of nitrogen. If a fire breaks out, the nitrogen will be released from the taps. If the fire is not extinguished right away, the system will switch to water, but only if the flames rise too high, and he has never seen that happen.

I think of the wrinkled pages of my copy of Ingeborg Bachmann's *Malina*, my favorite book, which I've read so often in the bath. The rising steam from the hot water has warped the paper. Looking at the decrepit books on the shelves, I can't help wondering whether a fire would really be worse than gradual consumption by woodworm. At least it would spare them the torment of their slow disintegration.

The chill of the reading room has crept inside me. I take a break from my stack of reference books to warm up in the sunlit square outside. As I leave, the librarian admonishes me for leaving my "researcher" pass pinned to my chest. Outside these walls I am not a researcher, it seems. I order coffee at a table outside Caffe Cordina. A German tour guide makes a stop at the Piazza Regina, bringing a clutch of pensioners in his wake. From my wicker chair, I overhear him describing the statue of Queen Victoria and telling the story of her sixty-nine pairs of long lace gloves and sixty-nine pairs of short ones. He recommends a store down the street that sells the very finest Maltese lace – the most beautiful tablecloths in the world. He waves a hand at the building: "And over there is the library."

That's all he has to say about Ittar's final creation before beckoning the group onwards to the next sight. As they walk away a figure comes into view behind them, holding a sign:

IELES IL-LIBRERIJA TAD-DEMONS LI JIEKLU L-INJAM!!
FREE THE LIBRARY OF WOOD-EATING DEMONS!!

Wearing a three-piece suit, a fisherman's cap and sandals, the man stands like a sentry at his post in the burning sun. Sweat pearls on his face; a drop trickles from under the small, round frame of his glasses and down into his collar. When I speak to him, his responses are clipped and brisk, as if my questions about his cause are distracting him from the important business of standing up for it.

"Have you been inside? Have you seen the damage?" he asks me, searchingly.

I tell him I'm doing research in the library, but that earns me no special treatment.

"This is our National Library, and it's wasting away, both the building and the collection. The books in there are absolutely priceless. And the shelves that support those books are crumbling like glaciers in the era of global warming. The bindings have been eaten away, or come loose, or been replaced with rubber. Yes, rubber. Any book conservator would wither away in shame to see those rubber bindings – the disrespect! – and the idiots who work here aren't doing a thing, not lifting a single finger, to improve the conditions in which these books are kept. Last year Prince William took a tour of Malta and they showed him round the library without even offering him a helmet! With all those deteriorating books and rotting shelves, a bookcase could easily have collapsed and sent a whole set of codices tumbling onto his head! A death trap."

Having found a willing audience, the man with the sign responds just like anyone who hasn't been listened to in a long time, by releasing a torrent of pent-up verbiage. Introducing himself as the bookbinder Mafalzon, he continues his tirade. Today he can remain silent no longer, he tells me; today he is protesting the state of decay into which the National Library has fallen. Until recently, Mafalzon worked at the Department of Library Studies at the University of Malta. Years ago, he wrote an open letter to the newspapers calling for action. After describing the neglect of the library in great detail, he demanded steps to rescue the books from utter oblivion. Otherwise, he warned, the consequences would be disastrous. The letter met with moderate interest, and Mafalzon became optimistic that it would have the desired effect. Since then, five years have passed. In the library, the woodworm infestation remains unchecked.

"I can imagine it would make a person lose hope, Mr. Mafalzon," I say.

This remark seems to touch a nerve; he flies into a rage. "I have not lost *hope*. Anyone can scream and shout, but I'm screaming and shouting because I have solutions. For one thing, they could hire qualified book conservators. There are two bookbinders working in the library. I know them person-ally; they have hands like builders. And the way they treat the books, tossing them around the way a crane moves rubble. You should see how they've patched together Diderot's *Encyclopédie*; it's a dog's breakfast! I'm not denying their passion. What they lack is *skill*. They have good intentions, but you know where those lead, don't you? And it starts at the front desk. The only thing they know how to do there is send you up the stairs, where you can have a library card made for you without any sort of screening. Just anyone can wander in and do as they please with the rarest of books – does that make sense to you?"

"Scandalous."

"First of all: it doesn't have to be this way. Second: I don't mean to belittle the people who work there. Look at the archives in Rabat or the notarial archives right here in Valletta. They're in moldering old buildings too, they have tiny budgets too, yet they've moved with the times. Why hasn't the National Library? We have all this," he gestures behind him, "the books and the structure around them, and we're letting it all rot away. That's what really pains me."

The passing tourists are now openly taking pictures of the eccentric-looking Mafalzon. They knot their brows at the strange slogan on his sign, without once glancing over to the far side of the square, at the library.

"Do you know anything about Stefano Ittar?" I ask.

"Who?"

"Stefano Ittar. Ittar, the architect of the library?"

"Yes, I believe so, Stefano Ittar . . ." and at that, Mafalzon the bookbinder wanders off to another corner of the Piazza Regina.

*

In 1783, Stefano Ittar makes a radical decision. By this time he has been working as an architect and city planner under the patronage of the Principe di Biscari for twenty years. His mastery of the baroque style has brought him great celebrity. In his own lifetime, he has won a place in Sicilian architectural history. He is working on the dome of the Benedictine monastery in Catania when he receives the prestigious invitation from the Knights of Malta to design a library for the Order of St. John. Within twenty-four hours Ittar leaves everything behind, taking his family from Catania, the place that fostered his talent, to Valletta. In his pursuit of still greater fame, he breaks his ties to the principe and his mentor Battaglia.

We might suspect him of nostalgia: later in his career, perhaps he recalled the library where his love of architecture was ignited, thinking back to his studies with the Vatican librarian and reliving the grandeur of papal architecture. The feeling that had held him in its grip for so long, his sense of inadequacy because of his birth in exile, had at last been overcome. His name would reverberate from Rome to Malta!

The library of the powerful Order of St. John became a masterpiece for both personal and aesthetic reasons. Ittar's perfectionism drove him to new extremes: relentless purity of form, perfect symmetry and mastery of the classical idiom.

Yet Stefano Ittar is scarcely mentioned in the books about Maltese architecture stacked on the reading room desk in front of me. On the island where he planned to bring his body of work to its triumphant completion, he seems to have fallen into oblivion. While the design of St. John's Library is discussed here and there and included in reference books, I learn little more about the architect himself than his dates of birth and death. And rather than shedding light on his death, these sources muddy the waters. Stefano Ittar appears to have died in at least three different ways.

One death was natural, the result of old age. He was buried the very same day, after a mass celebrated by a Franciscan monk.

One death was due to complications from pneumonia, which he contracted because of poor working conditions. He received the last rites on his sickbed and died in communion with the Church.

One death was by choice, after a pileup of structural problems in building the library. The root of these difficulties was rumored to be poor architectural judgment.

But if the historical record leaves the nature of his death shrouded in uncertainty, it reports the date with precision. Stefano Ittar died on January 18, 1790, six years before the library was completed. Or at least, that's the date in the death records of the parish of Sancta Maria Portus Salutis. If he had really taken his own life, a church burial would have been unthinkable: suicide was a disruption of the divine order that held the world together and made it explicable; the self-murderer attempts to overthrow God's power over life and death. If Ittar had killed himself, his family would have had good reason to conceal the cause of his death, because his property could have been confiscated by law. That would have meant the end of their inheritance. Two of his six sons, Enrico and Sebastiano, had followed in his footsteps as architects. They are thought to have taken over his workshop and the library project, but there are also indications that they both fled Malta after his death. What were the two young architects running from? Money troubles? Their father's shadow? Napoleon Bonaparte, who had set his sights on the prosperous island of Malta?

By the time I leave the library, night is falling. I feel as if I've frittered away my time here. The streetlights cast a warm glow on the white sandstone of the building front. Its spare beauty is now more apparent than ever. Nothing distracts my gaze. The design's measured quality imparts a kind of serenity, briefly soothing me. The world's so exhausted we can't keep our eyes open, and we all dream of outdoing ourselves. Everyone is successful. Everyone is always looking for admiration. We hush up failure and call it a learning experience. It's all so petty, so self-absorbed ... Architects at least make grand gestures, playing for mortal stakes, on a massive scale, in the public eye, creating tangible surfaces and masses that impose proportion and outwit indifference. Architects who fail in public space fail in plain sight of thousands of onlookers, and their failure lives on for a long time. Their high-risk wager with history defies mortality. Their audacity must be too much for some people to bear.

*

And perhaps that's the key to Stefano Ittar's death, if I put my faith in one of the few recorded eyewitness accounts. Antonio Cachia, the Order of Malta's chief architect, reported an incident on the building site shortly before Ittar's death. Cachia claimed that the flat arches spanning between the columns of the ground floor arcade were starting to crack. The arches had to be shored up, he said, so that they could support the weight of the upper floor. The additions at crucial load-bearing points spoiled the taut, rhythmic pattern of Ittar's design for the façade. Cachia's accusation is said to have sickened the aging architect's soul.

Now, standing under the arcade, I see no evidence for those allegations. The extra support is nowhere to be found. The arches over the columns are unbroken, an integral part of the coffered vaulting.

Cachia probably had reasons of his own for trying to influence how Ittar would be remembered. When Ittar was brought to Malta to design the library, Cachia was passed over, even though as chief architect he had been the obvious candidate. You don't need a vindictive nature to want what's rightfully yours. Did Cachia believe that by virtue of his position, and as a native son of Malta, he was entitled to the commission?

A few years before Ittar's death, he snatched another job away from his rival. In 1787, the assembly of the Vénérable Langue de Provence, a division of the Order of Malta, ordered the construction of a number of homes for French residents of the island. Both Cachia and Ittar submitted designs. Cachia received a small fee for his troubles; Ittar was chosen as the architect.

When, not long afterwards, revolutionary developments in France made life difficult for the Langue de Provence, it must have been hard for Cachia to conceal his delight. The funds for Ittar's project soon dried up completely, and work ground to a halt. A new loan would have crippled both the architect and the builders. The project was still in progress when Ittar died.

By the time Ittar began work on the library, he was almost sixty years old. His inner life remains such an enigma, but after so many illustrious designs, did he still feel the need to prove himself – as a foreigner, or as an exile? Did he apply the same strict standards to himself as to his building: mastery, perfection and craftsmanship on the outside, but on the inside, a worm-ridden heart? Did he gnaw away at himself all his life with his self-imposed, insatiable ambition? Did the wood-eating demons devour Stefano Ittar?

*

The chairs outside the cafés in Piazza Regina have been cleared away, the parasols closed. Only now do I notice how many people are out in the streets. Gigantic red banners hang between the buildings, richly decorated with saints' portraits ringed in gold. The fronts of the churches are festooned with colorful lamps. Down the street, a brass band is playing a march.

Il-Festa I-Kbira makes its way down Republic Street to City Gate. A festival for the people of Valletta. Four sculptures of saints are paraded through the city center on wooden litters, each carried by twelve young men in white monks' habits. Their necks are fiery red, their faces contorted into painful grimaces. One, with a full black beard, looks me straight in the eyes with a dark expression as he shifts his shoulder to better support the weight.

"Lay worshippers paying the price for their good fortune, poor boys," says the man standing next to me, and he laughs. He has sealed his own good fortune with a tattoo of a saint on his upper arm. Under the portrait in ink is a banner reading "St. Paul." To judge by the resemblance, Paul is also the figure towering over the young men's shoulders. The statues will gather at City Gate and return from there to their respective churches for a late-night mass.

At City Gate, among the crowds, confetti, fireworks and plastic cups, I find my friends. The mood is exuberant. Walter kisses me on the lips, a promising sign. We drink beer and marvel at the Christian spectacle unfolding before us. The carnival churches with their lurid lights appeal to the lost souls we thought we were, fallen out of communion. The statues depart for home, followed by the marching band. For this occasion, two rival ensembles have merged: the La Vallette Band and the King's Own Band. It seems the brass band is the very thread of Malta and Gozo's social fabric. People join the procession, **waving flags** and pennants in exultation, singing along without error and with throaty conviction. Amid this euphoria, I'm struck by the pathos of the accompanying instruments. The cymbal player executes his two well-timed accents, then drops his arms and looks around, lost, for the remaining bars. He reminds me of Richard Sennett's words in *The Fall of Public Man*: "There is a brutal sense of isolation in public places, an isolation directly produced by one's visibility to others."

The object of scrutiny, the individual observed amid anonymous masses, suddenly becomes a unique instance, isolated, exposed to attention and therefore, inevitably, to judgment.

Yet even this pales in comparison to the intrusiveness with which a building – whose dimensions and public purpose expose it to so much attention – is besieged with judgments. In the midst of my friends and the high-spirited crowd, a heavy weight descends on me. I am surrounded but, at the same time, sidelined. Here in the thick of the experience, I am buffeted by it. There is no shelter.

*

The next day we travel from Valletta to Gozo, where we spend the last three days of our holiday. I will not return to the library again. My friends have ordered me to put the mysterious multiple deaths of Stefano Ittar out of my mind. I think about him as little as possible, which is not so hard, since I don't even know how he looks – I never unearthed a portrait. I feel as if, by contributing so little to his story, I, the very person who was searching for him, am now consigning him to oblivion more rigorously than he was ever forgotten before.

On the way to our holiday home we stop in Hondoq Bay. The beach is still deserted. We throw off our clothes as we scramble to the water's edge and then plunge shrieking into the still-cold Mediterranean waters. Stan takes a photo for Instagram. With the right filter, wearing our colorful bathing suits, we look like figures from a Hockney painting, captured in a carefree moment of relaxation. No one has to work.

That evening, a violent storm passes through the island. We take cover in our cottage, barricading the doors and windows, but the wooden shutters rattle noisily in their frames. The wind is cutting. The heavy wooden lawn chairs fly around outside. The storm toys with us like a juggler. In our bedroom, the blind beats out a rhythm against the windowsill. We hear the flowerpots shattering. Walter and I try to make love in the eye of this savagery, but I have a headache, a dry, splitting headache, and pull away from beneath him.

The next morning, the swimming pool is full of garden furniture and beer bottles. Slugs the size of fists sit around the edge; a bag of chips dangles from an upturned chair leg. The parasol lies flat. The barbecue has been dismantled.

Apocalyptic scene with holiday paraphernalia in the foreground. In the middle ground, the landscape extends from a low garden wall out into terraced fields. In the background is a hill with a flattened top. We stare dumbstruck out into the morning.

VII
VILLA EBE (1922), NAPLES

LAMONT YOUNG (1851−1929)

Ebe is in the kitchen, making a light salad. Late summer in Naples: the air lies thick on the skin in the evening's lingering heat. He's had no more than a snack today, but he lacks the appetite for a large meal. Lamont Young decides to go up to the tower room until his wife calls him down for dinner. The wide, dark wooden staircase, the fulcrum of Villa Ebe's design, spirals two storys up along the flank of the hillside precinct known as Pizzofalcone. Each step is a struggle for his weary legs. Yet today he doesn't stop at the first-floor study to peer out of the window at the upper garden. The bitter oranges do not require his supervision; they hang ripe and heavy on the tree.

In the tower, the arched windows along three sides frame a spectacular if all-too-familiar view: a triptych of the waterfront district of Santa Lucia. Through the windows on the south side of the tower, his gaze falls on the dome of the Chiesa della Concezione in the foreground. Then it crashes into the row of high-rises erected along the coastal road a few years ago. Behind them, the Tyrrhenian Sea laps against the rocks in the bay. Beyond the bay, he can picture the endless water, interrupted to the west by Cape Posillipo and brokenhearted Bagnoli. Naples could have drained its clogged arteries there, but the fantasy of a flourishing seaside resort was never realized.

Young looks away and moves on to the west side of the tower. A city view. Colorful housefronts climb stepwise up the top of the Vomero hill. Pink. Ochre. White. Terra-cotta. A tempting neighborhood in recent years. The pioneers put up a few glamorous palazzi, but they are gradually being followed by the middle class. It won't be long before the slopes are dense with buildings. The cable car line going up the hill has already proved its value.

On the east side, Vesuvius rises in the distance. For the past twenty years the volcano has stayed ominously silent. Beyond it lies the capricious coast of Sorrento, and bobbing not far from the sharpest point is Capri.

Ebe's smooth face, not yet ripe for the black veil of mourning for a few more years. The salt smell of the sea, one last time. The plane trees. The cypresses. The pines. What is the most beautiful sight he ever saw?

*

In 1929, at the age of seventy-eight, the Scottish-Neapolitan architect Lamont Young committed suicide in the tower of his last place of residence, a building of his own design: Villa Ebe, "the house of youth." His young wife Ebe Cazzani went on living there until her death. After that, there was no one left to take care of the house. In 1991, the villa became the property of the municipality of Naples.

*

Naples introduces itself as an odor, dominated in turn by petrol, bubbling kitchens, overbearing perfume and urine. As soon as I've wrested myself out of the historic center with its dark, narrow streets, the broad corsos running down to the bay have a smell more or less familiar from any sizable European city: exhaust fumes and rubbish bins. Not until I am down by the waterside does the odor open, letting go of its admixtures.

A forty-five minute walk from the apartment in Via Atri to Via Chiatamone. "Scusi, Villa Ebe? E-B-E?" I keep asking along the way, as I fumble with the city map. The few Neapolitans who stop seem somewhat offended that I'm asking about a place in their city they've never heard of, when each of them could point me to their own top five churches blindfolded.

Behind the Grand, New, Royal and Excelsior hotels on the panoramic road along the seafront, I eventually find the foot of Monte Echia. At the top of this hill, so I'm told, is Villa Ebe. Next to a run-down car park, I begin my ascent of the Rampe di Pizzofalcone, cutting past the wretched houses built into the slope, which zigzag upwards in seven equal stretches. The ramps meet in sharp corners like birds' beaks. This pattern illustrates the name "Pizzofalcone," a remnant of the days when falcons were hunted here.

There is no one on the Rampe. Most of the front doors are open, in the hope of a cool breath of wind in the midday heat. The entranceways, one after another, offer glimpses of what appears to be a single, standardized life, featuring a freezer and a baby stroller. Just outside the front doors, laundry is drying on crude racks drilled straight into the wall. One heavy, stained flannel sheet puts the screws to the test, brushing in slow motion towards the ground. In the places where no dwelling has been carved from the yellow tufa of the hillside, the rock walls are covered in graffiti.

"Pericolo di morte capite," I read in blue letters among the declarations of love and the cartoon penises – a sinister message that my brain leaps to connect to the story I'm working on. A few meters up, Lamont Young shot himself in the head. Is it possible his death is still remembered on the Rampe today?

On closer inspection, I see that the graffiti message consists of two parts. What it really says is, "Danger of beheading for anyone who parks here."

At the top, as sweat trickles from the backs of my knees down over my calves, the Rampe finally reward me with their prize:Villa Ebe, with its romantic crenellated tower.The brown volcanic stone has a dignified look among the yellow houses that surround it, yet just like them, the villa seems to sprout from the flank of Monte Echia, as if the flamboyant little castle were a natural outgrowth of the hill.

A second look reveals that the building is wounded. Windowsills of bare wood. Shattered panes. Overgrown weeds breaking up the stone of the terrace.A chain and padlock around the bars of the gate. Only the entrance remains intact, a misleading oasis. Inside the gate, through the low-hanging branches of a fig tree, the locked green door, painted not long ago, sags on its hinges. One little push would be enough to open it. Above it is a scene with colorful inlaid stones: a sun of golden tesserae sends beams like rope ladders down to a sea of blue pearls. Grasping the tail end of one of the rays is the half-moon, which is setting over the water. Carved into the stone are the words:

Lamont Young

Napoli 1851–1929

Utopista

Inventore

Ingegnere

di una Napoli moderna

He exists.

Then the Rampe swerve into their final stretch, along the garden of Villa Ebe. Unlike the ramshackle house, the garden is well maintained. Cacti, succulents, purple and fluorescent orange flowers, and even an orange tree in blossom. A beating organ salvaged from the corpse.

On the other side of Monte Echia, the bird's-beak road curves past withered grass strewn with abandoned mattresses and plastic bags, past the weathered front of the Archivio di Stato, past army barracks and all the way around to the office of the national police. From here, the other side of Villa Ebe should be visible. No entry for unauthorized persons.

*

On the wall of my host Giulia's apartment are two poorly enlarged photos, framed like a royal couple. She doesn't hold it against me that I've never heard of the Neapolitan singer Pino Daniele; the more fundamental problem is that I've never heard of Padre Pio.

"Are you a Catholic?" she asks, sounding skeptical.

I was confirmed, so it's not a lie when I say, "Yes."

"Padre Pio," Giulia explains, "is the holiest of men. He bled the blood of Christ from his own wounds. He could take confession hour after hour, sometimes day after day, without rest. He could bear so much of other people's troubles only because his heart was so pure. He also had the gift of being in two places at once."

Giulia, the concierge of the building, lives in the other part of the apartment on Via Atri, which has been split into two. The occupant travels a lot for work, and Giulia sublets his half while he's abroad. When I arrived yesterday, the marble table-top was heaped with tourist brochures and mini-maps. Giulia rambled on about all the attractions Naples has to offer –

without mentioning Villa Ebe – and showed me a ring binder containing her list of local restaurants, classified by her own five-star system. Sorbillo's? No, that was for American tourists; for real pizza, there was Del Grifo, and if I really wanted authentic, traditional Neapolitan cuisine, she would come and cook for me the next evening.

Giulia slips away into the kitchen, leaving me with the portraits. Pino Daniele looks about the same age as her, around fifty. He has a dark Vandyke beard and short, bleached hair. Under his guitar strap, he wears a garish T-shirt.

From the kitchen come the first notes of a sentimental tune. The dark voice of Pino Daniele sings a tribute to Guilia's beloved city in Neapolitan dialect:

> *Naples is a thousand colors, Naples is a thousand fears,*
> *Naples is the voice of children slowly waking, so you*
> *know you're not alone.*
> *Naples is a bitter sun, Naples is the smell of the sea,*
> *Naples is a dirty piece of toilet paper, and no one cares.*
> *And everyone just awaits their destiny.*
> *Naples is a stroll through the alleyways among the crowds.*
> *Naples is one big sleep, known throughout the world, but*
> *no one knows the truth.*
> *Naples is a thousand colors, Naples is a thousand fears,*
> *Naples is a bitter sun, Naples is the smell of the sea,*
> *Naples is a dirty piece of toilet paper and no one cares,*
> *Naples is a stroll through the alleyways among the crowds,*
> *Naples is one big sleep, known throughout the world,*
> *Naples is a thousand fears . . .*

Puparuoli mbuttunati! Peppers stuffed with *fior di latte*, ham and bread. *Ragù alla Napoletana!* Italian sausages, pork ribs and topside of beef, simmered in tomato sauce and poured over freshly rolled pasta. *Moscardini con pomodorini, olive e capperi!* A little octopus with cherry tomatoes, olives and capers. *Espresso con Vesuvio di cioccolata con crema gianduia!* Coffee with bonbons in the shape of Vesuvius, filled with hazelnut cream.

Giulia is giving this meal everything she's got. With every course she serves, she shines a little brighter with sweat and local pride. After serving each course, she rattles off the ingredients and retreats to the kitchen. I eat alone. Is it rude if I don't eat the little octopi? Giulia clears away my untouched main course in silence, but I suspect it takes all her self-control not to give me the tongue-lashing of my life. When she brings me the coffee, I ask her, "Giulia, have you ever heard of the Neapolitan architect Lamont Young?"

"Never heard of him, and anyway, I don't believe in ghosts. Could you pay me back for the groceries? The cooking is free – I did it just for you. But I need the money back for the groceries. Sixty euros. *Nun se fa niente pe' ssenza niente.*"

Nothing in life is free, or more precisely, You don't get nothin" for nothin."

*

The tourist guides that Giulia left for me refer in passing to Lamont Young as the architect of two eye-catching private homes in a pseudo-Victorian style: Villa Ebe and Castello Aselmeyer. Only rarely do they also mention his design for Parco Grifeo. Like Villa Ebe, which lies hidden on the west side of the hill, walled in by later buildings, Young himself has apparently been covered over by layers of deadening scholarship. The architecture professor Giancarlo Alisio at the University of Naples wrote a monograph about Young in 1978, which seems to be the only serious reference work about him. The available sources do not go into much detail, have never been translated and are primarily speculative in nature. They take sides either for or against Young. Either way, they describe him as a utopian. Most of his projects seem to have remained unbuilt.

The most fascinating of these projects is the Rione Venezia, Young's plan for upgrading the Bagnoli district near Posillipo into a romantic miniature Venice with all the beauty of Campania. He proposed to flood the unused countryside until it resembled an archipelago, connected to the city by a grid of canals. Visitors on tour boats and gondolas could have oohed and aahed at the lakes, the warm-water springs, the zoo and the Anglo-Italian landscape architecture. The beach would have offered plenty of space and some of the most beautiful sunsets in the world. He planned to build tasteful hotels there, and an art museum at the end of the pier. Rione Venezia would have unlocked the age-old potential of Naples to become an earthly paradise for flaneurs and tourists.

Another of his designs – the Progetto Metropolitana, 1872 – was a study for an ultramodern underground railway network. Young believed that this network, combined with cable cars on the hillsides, would solve the problem of traveling between the center and the lower-lying outer districts. Underground transport seemed like the ideal way to lure the people of Naples out of the crowded streets of the old town. The city had 450,000 inhabitants at the time, packed into homes intended for only 240,000. The cable cars would have spared them the steep uphill journey on foot. The plan was also an early example of sustainable development: Young wanted the material excavated for the metro to be used in construction elsewhere.

Both these proposals were rejected again and again, and remained no more than drawings. For years, a tangle of bureaucratic delays, economic difficulties and disagreements between various municipal councils made it impossible for Young to obtain financial support for his projects. In the end, both the Rione Venezia and the Progetto Metropolitana were dismissed with a sneer as "pointless and expensive."

*

A visionary in a blind age. In recent years, Young's work has been the subject of renewed interest. Most commentators now agree: he was simply born a century too early.

Young's designs sketched out a flourishing future for Naples, far removed from the problems confronting the city as he knew it. Poor sewerage and overcrowded dwellings encouraged the spread of cholera in the final quarter of the nineteenth century. The disease, which sailors had probably brought to the mainland from Sardinia, killed some eight thousand people in 1884.

Because the unchecked spread of cholera was so clearly exacerbated by the poor living conditions of most Neapolitans, the local authorities were forced to take measures to clean up the city. But they hoped for quick, pragmatic fixes. It was in this climate that Young's designs were laughed off as "utopian" thought experiments.

The urban cleanup project was soon embedded in a broader political agenda. A public institution, the Società pel Risanamento di Napoli, was founded to "restore the city to health." Whole districts were demolished and rebuilt as part of this policy of rehabilitation. And instead of the leisured middle-class visitors that Young had pictured in these outer districts, it was the working classes that the Risanamento drove out. The gap between the upper and lower cities widened.

There's nothing so remarkable about Young being passed over for the commission; after all, every competition has winners and losers. But the installation of a cable car by the Società pel Risanamento a few years later – along the exact route that

Young had proposed – raises the suspicion that his idea was filched. The city's first metro line would not begin operating until 1993, more than one hundred years after Young's Metropolitana design. And the very same place where Young had planned his Little Venice – the area around Posillipo, with the coastal village of Bagnoli as the main attraction – is now being transformed into a green tourist zone intended to fuel the city's economic recovery. There is talk of large public parks, hotels on the beach, restaurants, conference centers, spas . . . in short, the new Neapolitan Riviera, which shows remarkable similarities to Lamont Young's more-than-century-old vision of a Venice District in precisely the same spot.

A sour fruit in a sweet mouth. Throughout the twentieth century, Bagnoli was the heart not of Young's Little Venice but of the region's heavy industry. Until 1990, the Ilva company (formerly Italsider) had a steelworks there. What had once been the fertile ground of a rural village was poisoned through and through by a century of steel and asbestos production. The cleanup of the soil alone was estimated in a 1996 report to have cost five hundred million lire. By now, the industrial site has been completely dismantled. The landing stage for the steelworks is now a pier where tourists go for strolls, 900 meters out into the sea. To the left of the pier lies the island of Nisida, which is taken up almost completely by a detention center, an Alcatraz for adolescents.

When I arrive in Bagnoli, wearing my bathing suit under my clothes, I feel like an idiot. The air has a suffocated smell. The polyester-lycra blend is pinching my buttocks. The beach, strewn with garbage, is next to the old industrial site. A kindred spirit, another wandering twentysomething, seems startled to see me. What did I hope to find here?

*

I've noticed on Google Earth that the hotel opposite Villa Ebe has a luxurious rooftop pool. From that roof, the other side of Monte Echia must be visible. But in real life and at ground level, the Hotel New Continental strongly resembles its neighbor, the Hotel Royal Continental. This similarity makes me unsure of myself, but at least no one seems the least bit suspicious when I enter the marble lift. Ninth floor, then a staircase, which does in fact take me to the rooftop.

The pool has an unusual shape: a lower pentagonal part connected to an upper, kidney-shaped area. Two German women, also kidney-shaped, are dipping their feet in the upper section. No one else is using the pool. I cross the roof to the rear of the building, which offers me my first complete view of Villa Ebe. I count four stories embedded in the hillside. The west side of the villa, which wasn't visible from Monte Echia, has lost most of its tufa cladding and appears to be in worse shape than the part I could see from Echia. At the level of the tower, the villa has a terrace on this side across the whole breadth of the building. The parapet is crenellated, like the tower. There's an unexpected sign of life in the deserted building: a laundry line from which a child's Spider Man T-shirt, six colorful towels and a sheet are flapping in the breeze. Behind the laundry line, a wooden board seems to serve as a door. Zooming in with my camera, I search for an entrance, but it doesn't look as if the building is accessible from this side.

*

Killing yourself at the age of seventy-eight – is that a rejection of life or of death?

*

Lamont Young's buildings show no obvious design or construction flaws. There is a crack in the Victorian turret in Parco Grifo, yes, but I've read it was put there deliberately to create the gothic effect of a ruin, an anachronistic means of giving a new design an interesting past.

Young does not seem to have failed so much as simply been forgotten; the process began during his lifetime. He was never really admitted onto the public stage. That was punishment enough for an architect like him − if there's one thing I have learned about Lamont Young, it's how passionately he must have loved his city.

Young was progressive and pro-Naples. After the unification of Italy, his city stagnated into a provincial town; he hoped to reshape it into a metropolis to rival the London or Vienna of his day. He dreamed of less concrete, of botanical gardens, of ponds and fountains, of a smoother flow of traffic . . .

In all probability he *was* the utopian he was made out to be, a committed, practicing utopian. Villa Ebe and Castello Aselmeyer are evidence of that. This must have made it all the more agonizing for him not only to remain a lone dreamer, but also to see his dream disfigured, in his own lifetime, into something wretched. The construction of the steelworks could not have been further from his romantic dream of Little Venice. After all the years that Young had tried so hard to obtain permission and funding for his projects, the outcome must have filled him with despair.

"A world that can be explained even with bad reasons is a familiar world. But, on the other hand, in a universe suddenly divested of illusions and lights, man feels an alien, a stranger," Albert Camus says in *The Myth of Sisyphus*.

Young's dream did not resonate with his fellow Neapolitans in his day. Whether that was due to misunderstanding, a boycott, the social and economic conditions of the time, or a lack of talent, the repeated rejections must have sorely tested his creative imagination and his personality, which was held together by visionary thinking. The result was total alienation from himself, culminating in suicide.

The historical record is silent. The legends spiral out from his embitterment. On cold winter nights, the spirit of Lamont Young is said to appear on the tower terrace of Villa Ebe. Through the arched windows, he looks out in frustration over his beloved, despised city and wails in grief.

Young was born in Naples and lived and worked there all his life, yet he always felt British. That's also how other Neapolitans saw him. As the son of a Scottish father and a British Indian mother, he was labeled an outsider – reason enough to exclude him from local debates.

Yet Young made no compromises about his identity. Neapolitan pride went hand in hand with Anglo-Saxon bullheadedness. In his marriage contract with Ebe Cazzani, he demanded a mention of his British origins. His designs in pseudo-Victorian and Elizabethan styles express nostalgia for the homeland he never knew, adding a strange touch of exoticism to the southern architecture found throughout the city. Passing Castello Aselmeyer or Villa Ebe, you might entertain thoughts of a Lego set, a novel by a Brontë sister, a case of tuberculosis contracted within drafty walls, or a doomed love affair with a surprise happy ending. A vestige of a shelved era.

*

"Bracelet? You want a bracelet?"

The unrelenting English phrases divert my attention from my laptop screen. Under my nose is a cardboard sign with hundreds of colorful strings dangling from it.

"Come on, take a bracelet! It's beautiful!"

I can't help laughing, because the street vendor's work looks more like reels of wire than beautiful bracelets. He laughs along with me.

"Where are you from? Belgium? *Je connais la Belgique. Les Belges sont les plus gentils du monde!*"

The Belgians, the kindest people in the world? "I doubt it," I say.

His laugh is infectious. He points at my glass of Aperol. "Holiday?"

"Something like that."

"*Toute seule?*"

"Mmm, I'm looking for someone. His name is Lamont Young. He was an architect. A disappointed one, I guess. He shot himself in his own home. Villa Ebe? Castello Lamont? Castello Pizzofalcone? No?"

"Pizzofalcone, *oui, oui,* those people there *sont des clochards, des* refugees and banditti. Here, just take a bracelet. You can have it, for free, take some vacation, *voici, parce que j'aime les Belges.*"

While he kneels and loops the wire delicately around my ankle, I keep asking about Villa Ebe. But all he can really tell me is that it's now occupied by squatters.

"Please, *s'il vous plait,* a little money for a coffee, *l'arte d'arrangiarsi.*"

After our conversation he practices his art of survival at every table outside the bar where I am working. The British and the Germans are also the nicest people in the world, it transpires. He can name every player at Manchester United and praise the beauty of Cologne Cathedral in flawless German. I look on in admiration; he is a master of his art. When he's finished his round, he waves goodbye to me.

I wave back. "What's your name?"

"Dieudonné, of course!" he says with a laugh as he strolls into the distance.

I hunch over my screen again and refresh my inbox. Still no reply from Pasquale della Monaco. He is my last connection for now to Villa Ebe.

Pasquale della Monaco was born in Naples in 1948. He studied at the Porcelain Institute in Capodimonte and the Naples Academy of Fine Arts. Since 1970, he has, in his own words, "produced many beautiful paintings. I have received many prizes. I am much admired. A few of my personal successes have even been discussed on the television news."

Now seventy years old, della Monaco is active on Facebook. Most of the photos of him there were taken at galas, exhibitions and award ceremonies. On each of these occasions, he pairs his Italian suit with a different whimsical bow tie. For decades, he has been campaigning for the preservation and appreciation of Villa Ebe and the Rampe di Pizzofalcone. In cooperation with artists and other locals, he is trying to rescue the building from the negligent hands of the city authorities. He has organized events in Villa Ebe: chamber music performances, exhibitions, operas and monologues. He has held wild street parties outside its locked front door. He has staged a re-enactment of a Bersaglieri parade there: hundreds of young soldiers marching up the hill in the role of the legendary sharpshooters, wearing their signature white hats with black plumes. The English soprano Elizabeth Wellington moved her listeners to tears. The finest ceramics from Naples and Amalfi were put on display in the villa. Even the Italian fashion label Canzanella agreed to stage a show in Pizzofalcone, using the Rampe as a slanted catwalk.

Della Monaco is the apostle of Young's legacy, the source of his untold story, and he's not responding to my emails.

Despite the many minor victories showcased on his Facebook page, Villa Ebe remains a vacant, tumbledown ruin, in sad contrast to Lamont Young's hopes and dreams for the house, and perhaps an even sadder contrast to Pasquale della Monaco's.

Della Monaco, fearing that the Pizzofalcone site would become yet another car park, wanted to pay the ultimate tribute to Young's utopian genius by turning Villa Ebe into an architectural museum, with a studio for artists who "heard the call of Naples." He spent most of the 1990s lobbying for this plan. Thanks to his persistence and the popularity he'd earned with his cultural events, he won over the city authorities to his idea. Not only were his plans discussed, but through great, nepotistic effort he secured the promise of a green light.

In early 2000, about three days before the restoration work was slated for approval, a fire broke out at midnight in Villa Ebe. The archival footage from the news report stresses the ironic timing. It is a narrative, in-depth piece in three parts. In the first, we see della Monaco escorting a cameraman through the villa's interior as it was before the fire. Wearing an expression of pride and awe, he ushers the viewer up the grand spiral staircase. The broad, stately steps wind up the hillside to Young's study, where a bay window displays the elevated gardens. Another story up, the stairway leads to the tower room. The view is not especially good – it's a misty day – but della Monaco describes it so vividly that Vesuvius, the sea and the Vomero hill seem to emerge from the haze.

Then the tour is interrupted by a jarring cut to part two. A newsreader announces the "dramatic spectacle." The footage suggests how an eruption of Vesuvius might look: violent orange flames climb high into the night, followed by a few thick smoke clouds. Firefighters look on from a distance as the inferno blows the glass out of the tower windows, but they make no attempt to stop it – too much fuss to maneuver the engines all the way up there. Part three of the report shows the devastation: the rubble, the holes, the chandeliers covered with ash ... It's hard to tell which part of the interior was which. Della Monaco stands outside the ravaged building, responding to questions from a reporter. He puts on a brave face, deplores the vandalism and says it was probably just a prank, the work of delinquent youths. This is not the end of the story, he says. Despite the destruction, he believes enough remains intact that the villa can be restored. The reporter's follow-up question includes the word "illusion." Della Monaco corrects him.

"Hope," he says.

Five years after the fire, della Monaco completed a new application for funds for restoration and conversion into a museum, this one addressed to the European Union. The application was approved in 2005, but the project has yet to be carried out. The money was supposed to have been passed on to della Monaco's cultural organization back then by the mayor, but it vanished into a black hole of bureaucratic incompetence. By now everyone's used to seeing Villa Ebe this way, maimed by fire.

There is something sentimental about the figure of Lamont Young. In the only photo I can find of him, he is fiddling with the chain of his pocket watch, with his other hand shoved nonchalantly into his waistcoat pocket. He is thick around the middle and has a round head framed with medium-length hair, still quite full, combed into such a neat parting on one side that it resembles a wig. His eyes look far beyond the borders of the photo, as if he were daydreaming. He is dressed like an aristocrat, in what seems to be a deliberate attempt to look English. In contrast, Ebe Cazzani, steely-eyed and clad in black lace, is unmistakably southern, not really beautiful, but young. In this photo, she serves as half of a double portrait. The notion that Young named the house after her could be a legend. Ebe Cazzani is said to have gone on living there until her death in 1971. That would mean that she survived Young by forty-two years.

It's hard to make sense of that – was she so much younger than her husband, or did she live to such a venerable old age? – but when I look at their photos, I pretend it all adds up. I'm only too eager to believe that these two improbable people really belong together, that Young was a utopian in love as well and built that castle on the hill for his child bride.

That brand of eclectic romanticism is Villa Ebe's hallmark. The pseudo-Victorian tower topped with merlons harks back to some indeterminate past. At the same time, its osmotic adaptation to the hill anticipates the organic architecture of the following century. Original and old-fashioned, anachronistic and anatopic. An astronaut in the Middle Ages.

Can Young's tragic fate be explained by the simple fact that he was born too early? Can such a simple piece of bad luck validate a failed life?

*

The lower legs of some older women look vacuum-packed: their skin clings tight to their lean, wiry muscles. On the steep climb up the Rampe di Pizzofalcone, Giulia's calves seem in danger of snapping, but she marches on bravely, grumbling all the while about the run-down neighborhood. She wanted to see that Ebe place for herself – probably to make sure I didn't dream up the whole story. It's so easy to relegate the unknown to the realm of the imagination, far preferable to acknowledging the realm of ignorance. Giulia is the type of person who sees imagination as an assault on reality, even though her reality leaves plenty of room for magical, mystical Padre Pios and doesn't extend much further than the city limits of her beloved Naples.

It's already dusk. Monte Echia and the Rampe have no streetlights. The laundry has been taken in, the front doors shut.

When we reach the top, Giulia points: "That hovel? That's what you're planning to write a book about? Absolutely no one will read it! Besides, it's not normal for a young woman to be so obsessed with death. You shouldn't be making up books, you should see a psychiatrist."

Meanwhile, darkness has settled over the hill and is gathering inside me. Villa Ebe is still hiding part of its story. The ghost of Lamont Young does not appear in the tower. Inside the gate, the green front door refuses to yield. Afraid for a moment that Giulia may be right, I turn defensive: "Death isn't the point – the point is what drives people to that last resort. I want to understand why Lamont Young gave in to the temptation."

"Yes, it's sad that so many illustrious Neapolitans have been forgotten. Time erases them from memory," Giulia says. "It's not for others to remember them, and by the way, you haven't paid your tourist tax."

As I fish for the money, my disappointment seems to fill Giulia with some kind of remorse. She tells me Villa Ebe was definitely a prestigious building once. She thinks it was divided into two dwellings. The name Lamont Young still means nothing to her, she insists, but she believes the east side, the part of the villa enveloped in the hillside, was used by the Astaritas, a family of rich Neapolitan bankers, as their coastal residence. If memory serves, their properties were bombed in the Second World War. After that they muddled their way into poverty. Giulia turns up her nose a little as she tells me she's heard that "non–EU citizens" have now laid claim to the Astarita residence. Then she disappears into the dark skirts of the hill.

"It's a dream of mine not to have to sleep. There's still so much to do," Pasquale della Monaco writes to me weeks later out of nowhere.

He never responded to my repeated request to talk to him about Lamont Young. I suspect his English is too poor; likewise, my Italian is inadequate. The past is caught in the gap between two languages.

From November 2017 to May 2018, he sends me a series of newspaper articles about himself on Facebook Messenger, at intervals of a few days. Most of them are about his achievements, or prizes awarded to him for those achievements. Cavalier of Culture. Brilliant director. Founder of the Vulcano Metropolitana ensemble. Applauded by a crowd of eight hundred. Organizer of historical pageants. Driving force behind the tourist invasion of Napoli. Yes, Pasquale della Monaco is an accomplished man. At the same time, it's a little sad that in reply to my question about Lamont Young, his answer is himself.

On May 2, 2018, after months of silence on my end, della Monaco sends me a final link. It's a video of yet another interview, this one at the gate of Villa Elbe. It clearly dates from after the fire; the house already looks defeated, but it's spring, and the garden is budding into color. He is wearing a summery shirt and a weary expression. The interviewer asks when the architecture museum will finally be ready to open.

"*Il giardino di Villa Elbe prende vita di nuovo. E sono felice di realizzare,*" he says, and it sounds so resigned.

The garden of Villa Ebe is coming to life again. He's glad that at least he could do that much.

VIII

ROSSAUER BARRACKS (1864–1869), VIENNA

KARL PILHAL (1822–1878)

Dear Walter,

Back in Vienna. I've been here twice before. Once in September, a few years ago, for a reading. This past summer I returned to see the opera house, and the story of Eduard and Sicard wrote itself. Did I think I could pull off the same trick again?

This time it's snowing. February, and the streets are empty. I can walk the whole length of Kaiserstrasse and see only a few people. Most of the locals are away skiing, and the tourists won't show up until around April. An occasional horse-drawn carriage departs from St. Stephen's Cathedral, which is trembling in the cold in its lacy Gothic tracery. The temporary exhibition at the Albertina is devoted to a lesser-known artist. With the busy Christmas season behind us, the Rubens exhibition has traveled on to another city.

In this city on standby, what catches my attention is tae kwon do. Opposite the place where I'm staying in Kaiserstrasse, near the intersection with Neustiftgasse, is a tae kwon do center. The training hall has a picture window on the street side, as if showing off its wares. Yesterday, I watched the whole ten o'clock class through my window; the third from the right is by far the best defender. While out walking today, I passed no fewer than four other tae kwon do schools and one general martial arts center. I wouldn't say I'd especially been looking for them.

The other striking thing is the wedding-cake architecture. All the residential buildings are the same height, their roofs smoothed out with a spatula, buttery borders along the window frames. Spun-sugar decorations. Fondant moldings. Behind those façades, could there really be stairways, corridors, rooms and even light switches? The gaudy buildings somehow make the streets look even emptier – it's hard to believe the city is really inhabited. The white sheet of snow is too perfect to spoil; it's as if I'm an extra on a stage set, a figurine in a scale model made of wood and paint and cardboard, where a step through a door would lead me into emptiness. Once I reach the Ringstrasse and face the imperial architecture – the Hofburg, the Schatzkammer, the Nationalbibliothek – my sense of estrangement looms over me like those buildings. It's the same thing that sometimes happens to me when a place has become too familiar, like the one kilometer I've walked most often in my life: the road that leads straight from my childhood home to the Turnhout market. The market, the square, Begijnenstraat, the terraced houses, the junction, the optician, more terraced houses, our front door. Building front by building front, I know the way by heart, I know the way and the streets so well that they become strange, unreal. Admittedly, this estrangement usually takes hold of me as I come home from the café at night, drained by a day of work and an evening of drinking, but here in Vienna, it descends on me in broad daylight. Then I wish I could curl up against you and say, "I had that same feeling again on the way home: scale model." But you aren't here, and I'm the one who left.

Besides, it would be wrong to say that this city, this darling

Vienna, feels like a scale model – especially considering that the greatest accomplishment of Viennese architecture is the out-of-scale, the monumental. Incidentally, the critic Friedrich Achleitner claims that Vienna has never been the place for great architectural leaps. Instead, you have to see it as a storehouse of ideas, a place for reception, adaptation and contemplation. A place where systems that are alien to each other, or even mutually exclusive, exist side by side.

I believe Achleitner is right. His conclusion is confirmed by the city's many eclectic buildings in a romantic, historicist style, such as the building I actually mean to tell you about: the Rossauer Barracks along the Danube Canal, near Augarten Bridge, where the walls along the banks are covered with graffiti.

But what can I tell you about the Rossauer Barracks? It used to be called the Crown Prince Rudolf Barracks. Its red-brick walls and picturesque towers recall Tudor England, while its classical elements suggest a southern palazzo. With renovation in progress, what the barracks most resemble to my Flemish eyes is a new suburban mansion in a rustic style along the rural route between two cities. The building's blend of influences lends it all the vitality of a 3D foam puzzle.

Still, I had looked forward to the first sighting. It was a chilly hour's walk from Kaiserstrasse, and when, from the junction of Türkenstrasse and Schlickplatz, I finally saw the west side through the leafless plane trees, there was something alluring about it, like a bare shoulder thrust out among the garments of the city.

As I moved closer, I was not overcome by that secret sense of anticipation, that infatuated rush that drowns out the imagination, the way I have been every time before. I felt no trace of the excitement that ran through me when I spotted Borromini's voluptuous San Carlo or the crooked, phallic tower of Verchin (even now the memory makes me smile), or when I was cradled in the soothing symmetry of the Valletta library – you were there with me. I could have melted into it there and then.

The Rossauer Barracks is rather dull though still somewhat romantic. Red brickwork, recently sandblasted. Symmetrical. Rectangular. Huge. Two pompous towers on each of its four sides. Between the towers, the arched entrance gates are set off and decorated with dainty buttercream stripes, framed by cinnamon-stick pillars, and, oh yes, in the entrance are a barrier and a booth with a security officer to check incoming visitors. It's unmistakably in use as a government building. From all four sides, the barracks really does look exactly the same.

*

No pounding heart. It does nothing for me.

Without the pounding, I don't know if there's any point to all this: the snow, the isolation, the distance. The distance between you and me. Another dead architect.

In the evening, as I lie staring at the high ceiling in Kaiserstrasse, I think of my tragic builders. When I try to imagine them, they stand around my bed like the fourteen angels from the lullaby my grandmother used to sing. They haunt me, and at the same time they sing me so sweetly to sleep, a sleep that will not come.

*

It is not true, by the way, that military engineer Karl Pilhal simply forgot to install sanitation facilities. The top floors of the towers on the long sides did contain lavatories, each equipped with a single porcelain toilet bowl, four in all. There were also toilet bowls in the officers' quarters, worked discreetly into decorative chairs for the high-ranking gentlemen. All of these were *Plumpsklos*, dry toilets that did not flush, leading to a single central pipe down which gravity, it was hoped, would guide the excrement. Of course, the 2,400 soldiers quartered in the barracks did not have access to the private officers' toilets. They had to make do with those four bowls at the tops of the towers. Can you picture it?

Additional toilets had to be installed posthaste. This cost a fortune and caused considerable problems, and even with the new toilets, the no-flush system was still an unsanitary hell.

Soon after the barracks opened, in 1870, military engineer Karl Pilhal was discharged. He is said to have killed himself in shame when his mistake came to light. Suicide, because he'd forgotten the toilets.

And to think of all the other things that could have gone wrong. For example, the building site was in the alluvial zone of the Danube Canal. (I had to look that one up: the zone where the water deposits sediment; a rich, boggy surface, ill-suited to building.) The barracks were supposed to accommodate four hundred horses. Can you see them sinking into the Danube silt, the muscular forms of the drifting steeds trying to push against the current and back to safety? Or the drowned carcasses in the river afterwards?

But that never happened. Appropriate measures were taken. The foundations were firmly anchored and laid four meters deep; it took two full years of work. About twenty years ago, when the barracks was renovated by the national authorities, the excavations turned up the remains of skeletons. The foundations were discovered to have been made of soil from cemeteries demolished especially for that purpose.

The Rossauer is a barracks built on bones. The symbolism seems too neat, too heavy-handed.

*

It's been snowing all night. I saw it because the architects kept me awake, and all night I sat by the window. A pastry chef hidden somewhere in the sky gave the city a final dusting of icing sugar.

For days, the white of my paper has been unbroken. Failure can be a kind of emptiness. The chapter I wish I could write about military engineer Karl Pilhal suffers from emptiness. What can I say about him?

His life went according to the rules. He was born, baptized and trained as an engineer, after which he joined the army's committee for military technology. He remained in the military, gradually rose through the ranks, received the title of colonel as his reward for a life of service and was appointed director of the engineering corps.

A perfect human being is, above all, perfectly insufferable. He probably died dutifully, by the book, of some form of pneumonia that left him floundering long enough to receive the last rites. By now I'm more or less certain that's what must have happened. That suicide of his isn't even true.

Yet it's so easy to imagine – in a life and career otherwise so well managed – that the forgotten toilets in the Rossauer Barracks were the kind of mistake that could unmake him. Pilhal strikes me as the kind of person who tried to go through life with a minimum of fuss and mess. I almost wish he'd sullied his reputation. Yes, I'd like it to be true. His alleged suicide would at least lift him out of his colorless slot in history.

Pilhal was competent, yes. You might see him, if you must,

as a kind of representative of the nineteenth-century military engineer-architects who carried out functional and often repressive projects as part of the imperial program of urban expansion. The competence of his designs is matched by their lack of imagination. The Rossauer Barracks were already dated by the time they were opened in 1870. By then the romantic historicism that had briefly flourished in the previous decades no longer held much attraction, and the British Windsor elements simply looked old-fashioned. While the designers of barracks elsewhere took a more forward-looking approach, Pilhal's closed plan with towers harked back to the architecture of medieval fortresses. Pilhal was a builder in the service of the emperor, obedient and practical, with unshakeably traditional ideals. He designed for a Vienna that was already slipping into the past. The city's people were no longer interested in emblems of imperial might. Vienna was on the brink of modernization. The rising middle class was turning the city into its playground. As symbols of the old world, did Pilhal and his barracks draw the scorn of the bourgeoisie?

*

Whatever the case may be, my efforts to elevate failure in architecture into a gripping, dramatic tale of artistic destiny have foundered on the rocks of Karl Pilhal.

*

What am I really trying to prove?

This whole time, why have I been searching for underlying causes?

Am I doing the very thing I fear? By drawing a causal link between failure and suicide, I'm really implying that self-destruction can be justified, or at least explained. Is that what I'm trying to do, find explanations? The word "explanation" suddenly seems dangerous, and miles away from "understanding," or from that other word I sometimes say to you when you ask yet again why I have to write this particular book: "compassion."

Were you right? In the suicides of these architects, am I searching for false idols, forerunners, allies, to push me to a similar end when total failure hits me? Are you scared I'll let things go too far?

*

In the window across the street, the morning tae kwon do class has begun. Puddles of stone are forming through the snow. The white sheet has been broken open.

Love,
Charlotte

IX

FORT GEORGE
(1747–1769), ARDERSIER

WILLIAM SKINNER (1700–1780)

In Ardersier, a village on the Scottish bay of the Moray Firth, 18 kilometers from Inverness, the church is for sale. It could fetch a good price; after all, Helen Mirren once got married there. Besides, this is the home of Europe's largest dog cemetery. The post office closed a few years ago, but letters and packages can be sent and received at the local Spar. Just down the street are a McColl's corner shop, a hotel, a chemist, a barber shop and two pubs. More people pass through Ardersier than live there: families mostly, driving down Old Military Road, the coastal road that passes through the village before emptying into the car park of the local attraction: Fort George. From the outer wall of the historic fort and at the right season, you can spot dolphins cutting through the bay. There are no other cars there this morning, but the attendant maneuvers me into a parking spot as if every millimeter counts. He hands me a brochure with a few questions about my visit.

"Question 1: As you walk from the car park through to the ticket office, look around you. How would you feel if you were visiting the fort 250 years ago?"

It is eleven o'clock and the light is climbing towards noon. Here in the firth, the landscape seems to open up even farther. The wind roams free, yet it's pleasantly warm. I feel a sense of . . . open space?

Wrong. According to the model answer in the brochure, the pupil/visitor should respond, "I would probably feel very nervous and intimidated."

Even in this open landscape, the fort somehow manages to remain hidden. The path from the car park to the entrance gate passes between two rising walls, their tops covered by the well-maintained lawn. By the end of the path, I have vanished between the tall stone walls, or has the fort sunk down into the earth around me? High above the gates, the Scottish flag ripples in the wind. It looks fragile here, battered by the sea air. Yet the construction of Fort George – Dùn Deòrsa in Scots Gaelic – began in 1747, with the aim of intimidating the enemy. British military engineer William Skinner designed this defensive masterpiece to resist sieges.

A year earlier, in 1746, the original Fort George in Inverness had been blown up in the wake of the last Jacobite rising against the ruling House of Hanover. The Catholic Jacobite minority had been in rebellion against King George I, a Hanoverian and a Protestant, since 1715. The king was a distant cousin of the childless Queen Anne, the last monarch of the Stuart dynasty. The Jacobites contested his succession to the throne: he was a foreigner, and a damned German at that. Why should he be king when there were plenty of potential successors in Britain with closer ties of blood to the Stuarts? But those other candidates had all been passed over because they were Catholics. The 1701 Act of Settlement dictated that the crown could only go to an Anglican or other Protestant, even if the new monarch had to be plucked from the remotest branches of the family tree. All this to prevent a Catholic from claiming the British throne.

Many Catholics, especially in Scotland, were against the Act of Settlement from the start and were later opposed to the new German king. The Jacobites raised an army and defied the Act of Settlement in a series of violent battles and uprisings, but never won a decisive victory. Under the leadership of Charles Stuart, or Bonnie Prince Charlie, the Jacobite army waged its final battle in Culloden in 1746, and was defeated. That was to be the last Stuart campaign against the House of Hanover.

The Jacobites took their revenge by blowing up Fort George in Inverness so that the Hanoverians could never again use it as a base. A clever move, because the victor, King George II, did need a fortress to keep the peace in the Scottish Highlands. Almost immediately after hearing of the explosion, he ordered the construction of a new Fort George.

Military engineer William Skinner was appointed as the designer. He moved the fort to the Moray Firth, a strategically located inlet near Ardersier. From there Inverness could be protected from attack by sea, and the landscape offered further tactical advantages: not only did the inlet narrow at the chosen site, but there was a steep-sided promontory jutting out into the sea. That hard spit of stone, resistant to erosion, gave the fort its unassailable form.

Within the natural perimeter of the promontory, Skinner erected a fort in the shape of an elongated star, with two concentric defensive lines. The outer defenses take the form of a glacis, a grassy slope zigzagging around the heart of the fortress. Cut into the glacis are ditches with wooden palisades. These outer defenses are some distance from the white drawbridge leading into the fort. They slowed the enemy's advance and gave the fort's defenders more time to withdraw to safety. This type of fortification creates open spaces in which an attack can lose its momentum. It's an ingenious example of defensive architecture.

Because the fort juts out into the water, all the protection it needs on those three sides is provided by its mammoth ramparts. These days, there are also heavy machine guns on the corner bastions. The land side is defended by those same stone ramparts, many meters thick, and further inside by a draw-bridge over a deep ditch, which can be turned into a moat. The edge of that grassy ditch is marked by a yellow warning sign: "Caution: sudden drops."

Inside the ramparts, the fort covers the area of five football pitches. In the vast parade ground, two parallel worlds unfold: on the one hand the historical scenes reenacted by life-size papier-mâché mannequins, and on the other hand the modern soldiers going about their business. The 3rd Battalion, the Black Watch is still garrisoned here. Their uniforms make me keenly aware of the hot pants I'm wearing; I keep tugging at them, trying and failing to cover my backside completely. Other than that, I'm wearing pink Birkenstocks and a white T-shirt that shows the outline of my nipples. I'm starting to feel out of place here on this hot day, unintentionally provocative, as if I'm parading myself in front of these garrisoned men.

But they don't pay special attention to me. The discipline with which they go about their daily affairs keeps the world of tourists separate from the world of soldiers.

Unlike the Viennese Rossauer Barracks, built around a century later, Fort George reflected modern ideas about barracks design: the soldiers had more space and were not stacked on top of each other. Yet here too, living conditions were far from ideal. Fort George was known as "Fort Misery." One of the rearmost barracks, dot 12 on the plan in the brochure, is a his-torically authentic recreation of sleeping quarters for the lower ranks. The men slept eight to a small room, two to a bed, with a firepit in the center. On one of the beds, a papier-mâché woman is nursing her child. An information board tells me it was not unusual for a soldier's wife to live here with him, shar-ing a bunk with her husband and one of his comrades. Crossing my arms over my chest, I try to imagine her life with eight men and a baby in these cramped quarters. In so many ways, her body must not have been her own.

Opposite the barracks with the historical reconstruction is a field with the garrison chapel in the middle. This modest red-brick house of worship was designed by Robert Adam, the best-known scion of a family of Scottish architects. Robert's elder brother John was a contractor on the Fort George building site and dragooned his brother into contributing to the project so that some of his prestige would rub off on it. Robert's interior designs were all the rage at the time and led to the flowering of classicism in eighteenth-century British architecture. Inside the chapel, the light, graceful ribs of the vaulting form an almost mystical counterpoint to the misery of the barracks. There are no worshippers in the church, but there are books everywhere. Along the walls of the nave are tables with books of the dead, each one filled with the names of soldiers killed in action. On each chair is a hymn book with a red cover and a copy of the *New Life Holy Bible, New International Version with color features.* The brightly colored pages and plates make this edition of the Bible look more like a collection of New Age conspiracy theories than of sacred scriptures. Even so, it's an encouraging edition for the reader, with some friendly words from the publisher on the first page: "Those who have difficulty reading Scripture are advised to bypass the Old Testament and go directly to the New. Past experience has shown that the figure of Jesus Christ makes the New Testament an easier point of entry for Bible study. After the New Testament, readers can always return to the start of the book."

I leave the chapel and walk up the grassy slope to the rear rampart of the fortress, which offers a chronological overview of varieties of cannon. Unable to feign an interest, I walk up to the top of the rampart and sit on the parapet. From here, I have a view of the firth. Next to me, on one of the bastions, is a machine gun pointed out to sea. From a distance, the scene must look almost touching: a woman with a machine gun beside her like a faithful dog, the two of them gazing out over the water together.

"So this is where it all happened, my friend," I say to the gun. Below, outside the ramparts, is a small gravel beach. There's a pole sticking out of the gravel with a rusty chain attached to it. At the end of the chain I imagine the missing rowing boat.

On December 13, 1914, Lieutenant Owen W. Steele recorded the story in his diary. The tragic military engineer who had designed Fort George rowed out from that spot to admire his creation as the enemy would see it. The fort was intended to be invisible from the sea, surprising attackers who thought they could storm the Scottish mainland by way of the firth. In the narrow entrance to the firth, midway between Fort George and Chanonry Point, the engineer laid down his oars and, to his dismay, spotted a single chimney, which betrayed the presence of the concealed fort. Seeing this, the engineer drew his pistol and shot himself in the head. His death is a tale of shame inflated to deadly proportions and transformed into a masochistic performance: he took his own life in sight of his failure, in the certain knowledge that he deserved his self-imposed fate.

*

Of course, that never really happened. Ten years after designing Fort George, military engineer William Skinner was appointed Chief Royal Engineer of Great Britain. Having reached the highest possible rank, he continued his successful career until his death at the age of eighty-one. Skinner died at his drafting table on Christmas Day 1780, still hard at work.

He was a military engineer for sixty-one years and Chief

Royal Engineer for twenty-three. After numerous other successes, Skinner still considered his design for Fort George to be his greatest achievement. "My monument," he fondly called it. First he had planned it in painstaking detail, checking his work over and over again. Then he kept a careful eye on the building works, staying in close contact with the contractor John Adam; the two of them were in charge of the site and the thousands of soldiers working there.

Fort George is a success, a strategic fortress that responded to the needs of its day but was also far ahead of its time. The legend of the military architect in the rowing boat is not only incorrect, but also overwrought; even if he had rowed out to sea and been disappointed with what he saw there, couldn't he simply have returned to land and demolished that chimney, instead of blowing his brains out?

The story paints him as a thin-skinned perfectionist, who cast a minor mishap as a life-ending tragedy. Owen W. Steele is far from blameless; it was he who recorded the legend of the tragic architect in his diary in 1914, thus smuggling the false account into oral tradition. It's no more than a story, than folklore, of course, but it perpetuates the idea that architects who fail commit suicide and provides another tragic role model for the disappointed designers of tomorrow.

Yet this melodramatic tale contains a grain of truth. Skinner's hot temper and obsessive attention to detail are borne out by the historical record. And the boat may have come into the story through his son William Jr., captain of the 49th Regiment of the British army, who died in a sloop on August 27, 1761 during the occupation of the island of Dominica. He was struck by a bullet just off the coast. Stories sometimes lead each other astray.

*

The tragic architect of Fort George is a tourist trap, the tale of his suicide a lure to attract visitors to the area. A haunted castle is so much more exciting than your average stately home. You may know that there's no such thing as ghosts and that you probably won't run into one during your visit, but even so, the ghost story offers the imagination a way into the narrative of the building, where it may even write itself into the story. The haunted castle is a place where fear is embodied by architecture.

Has the legend of Fort George embedded an imagined narrative of tragedy into an architectural success? And what about the Rossauer Barracks, the Vienna State Opera, or the swimming pool in Turnhout? Regardless of the historical truth, they've all become sites of failure, every one of them. It's a valid way of looking at these structures, even if the failure is not immediately obvious. Whenever an architect – in reality or in rumor – takes the blame for a design flaw and imposes the death penalty, let there be enough entanglement between work and self for the building to preserve suicide in its structure, its skeleton, its history. Let the specter of Lamont Young roam Villa Ebe as the stories claim, let Borromini bellow his rage through the façade of San Carlino, let Eysselinck's raw grief become a sobbing audible in his blue Belgian limestone, let the human body and the body of the building share the wound.

In most cases so far, I've been confronted with buildings that show no physical sign of the alleged failure, and the tale of the builder's suicide usually turns out to be more or less a myth. The work asserts its independence from its maker's errors. The building refuses to take responsibility.

Maybe the relationship between creator and creation is something like a toxic love affair, in which the lover destroys himself for the sake of the beloved, or for an ideal of love. When the object of love decides to leave, as inevitably happens, the lover trots out trite phrases like, "You can't leave after everything I've done for you."

The conventional reply is, "I never asked you to do it."

In both cases, there is devastation and there is a guiltless accomplice, but that does not make the devastation any less complete.

*

When I started out as a writer – or I should say, when my writing began to find its way to readers and thus had at least some slight justification for existing – I knew one thing for certain: this is too much. Writing and leading a full life, I can't do both, something has to give. From the first awareness that I'd created something, and the surge of megalomania that ensued, I wanted to know if I could also destroy. A petty, despotic urge, but no inconvenience to anyone else, since as my object of destruction, I chose myself.

Writing is thought to require a turbulent lifestyle: a self-perpetuating cycle of excess, asceticism, ecstasy and exhaustion. I recruit accomplices in my self-destruction. I choose, for example, narcissistic lovers, read Céline and Cioran and sink naturally into a certain degree of cultural pessimism. I worry constantly about money, or about how impossible it is ever really to connect with another person, and then, when it happens, I fear the connection will break. All this adds up to a potent method of demolition, which screens me off from things like happiness, contentment, boredom and probably health in the long run. But the long and the short of it is, no one writes happy poems, it's just too hard. At least my inadequacy permits me to write; it contains, or so I imagine, the desire to make what is inadequate whole, or at least the possibility of doing so within the confined empty space of a white sheet of paper. By the way, the art of inadequacy isn't hard to master; in fact, it is our birthright.

Yet there are plenty of counter-examples, great thinkers and writers who took a different approach, leading simple, serene lives yet producing great, ecstatic works. Take Spinoza, the celibate lens-grinder and philosopher. He never experienced love or traveled far; for his experiences, he turned to the interior world of thought. He could write probingly about passions without ever having lived by them. In proposition 45 of part IV of his *Ethics*, Spinoza shows that my ideas about destruction as a necessity for creation are badly in need of reform:

> There's nothing against Happiness, except grim and gloomy superstition. Why should it be more proper to relieve our hunger and thirst than it is to rid ourselves of gloom? . . . No god or anyone else – unless he is envious of me! – takes pleasure in my weakness and my misfortune, or counts as virtuous our tears, sighs, fears and other such signs of a weak mind. On the contrary, the greater our Happiness, the more we move upwards in perfection.

Spinoza claims it is pointless to be gloomy; in fact, he considers it a sign of inner weakness. That's easy for him to say; but for most of us, "great happiness" and "perfection" are unattainable. That's not to imply that I have no interest in them; on the contrary, in all that I do, I aim for perfection. The unattainable sets me off; if I can't have it, I want it, with a reckless desire, heedless of consequences. Spinoza said it himself: We do not strive for what we think is good; we assume it is good because we strive for it.

That's how blind I want to be, how monomaniacally I want to write, in the delusion that the effort itself makes the question of good or evil immaterial.

empty place – not a house or tree or human form or any other
body in sight, only the grass and its undulations, and on one
slope a solitary gazebo, the only vertical element in a landscape
that is pulled apart by its own expansiveness yet proves to have
a border, where the grass slopes up into taller beach grass and
the low sand dunes begin, soon giving way to a thin strip of
white sand you can run your hand through almost without
moving, and even the sunshine is too simple, giving this place
the crystalline lightness of a scene in a dream, the sky opening
out into a blue expanse with small stepwise clouds, a grand
diffusion under which – in precisely this place, at Nairn
Beach – the Moray Firth opens into the North Sea, which
flows in turn into the Norwegian, the Baltic, the Atlantic and
onward. I am at the tip of a blue funnel.

The sky reminds me of the cover of a book from my childhood that I've never since been able to track down. The book's
C sticker meant it was too difficult for my age – that was the
very reason I had pulled it from the library shelf for teens. I've
forgotten the title but can still clearly picture the cover: a light
blue sky with naive clouds, which a boy is climbing. The cover
image was not a drawing but a photo, like an image of the sky
over Nairn today. The boy stepping up onto the clouds is the
brother, the main character, who dies after being hit by a car. It
stands to reason that you're the main character in your own
death, but he meets a truly tragic fate, snatched from his bicycle by a lorry. Much too young, only nine years old. Maybe
that's why his soul has to wander a liminal world in the clouds.
It's clear that the brother was killed instantly in the crash. But
for some reason, he remains present on earth but invisible. No
one can see or hear him. He, on the other hand, can see his
sisters, parents, classmates and friends grieving their loss after
the accident, attending the funeral, mourning and living on.
Fortunately, the book also goes into the advantages of his

ghostly condition: he can walk straight up the sides of sky-scrapers, walk through walls, fly ... Otherwise the story would be unbearably depressing.

The brother's soul is trapped on earth because the people he loved were so sad. I felt relieved when I read that, because it seemed to confirm my childish fantasy that after I died every-one would grieve for me forever. At first, of course, the brother is happy to see how much everyone loves him. On top of that, he thinks it's cool that he can walk on air. But after a while he starts to long for release from his lonesome, strangely lucid state. There is an overarching human desire to be seen, to have your existence confirmed in the eyes of another, and this boy is never seen at all. He does not exist, yet he is present – the **cruelest trap** between death and life. Not until the end of the book, when the people around him teach him to let go, is the brother's soul able to walk into the Great Sea, a kind of metaphorical ocean in the skies. There he dissolves into the heavenly ether.

Thanks to that book, I discovered as a child that I'd always misunderstood death. Yes, the body dies and goes to heaven, but after that, the soul must drown. Since then, I've learned it doesn't even have to happen in that order.

*

There is no one else visiting Nairn Beach, and I could just as easily not have been here myself. A forsaken presence in the landscape. Walter and I had planned this trip together – a holi-day after a busy, hectic year. We had a lot of distance to bridge. For both of us, the plan was like a frantic prayer in time of need. He let me pick the destination. The Highlands. We bought matching pairs of hiking boots, Deet to keep off the midges, and caps with headlamps. While counting down the days, we sent each other photos of rare bird species on the Isle of Skye: the snow goose, the Eurasian teal, the red-throated diver, the glossy ibis, the golden eagle. We watched a video in which an Atlantic puffin, looking like a cartoonish cross between a penguin, a toucan and a duck, befriended a passing tourist – we could *be* that passing tourist.

Walter put together a top ten of medieval ruins that we could visit. At number one: the ruins of Elgin Cathedral, the "Lantern of the North," from the year 1242. Although the skeleton is fragile, the ruins effortlessly evoke the original structure, reaching for the sky. Elgin, the most beautiful and most ambitious cathedral in all of Scotland, has been destroyed countless times over the ages by fire, cannonballs, sieges and thunderstorms, but rebuilt each time, larger than ever, with hard work and resilience – Walter stressed these words – the history of a bloodline, a church tower reaching higher than ever into the sky, well-preserved ornamental sculptures of grim demonic faces and fantastic creatures.

My job was to plunge into Scottish poetry and read poems about ruins to Walter, on location. We planned to go on pub crawls, to fill night after night with our ramblings about Roland Barthes as we did in our early days, to make love each morning with renewed affection, to have time for affection because we wouldn't have to work, to have time, too, for large and lavish meals. I told him I was looking forward to the long drives and to our playlists; he gave me permission to include an unlimited number of Billy Ocean songs. The Highland Games, the Cairngorms, the lakes, the folklore . . . we saw so many escape routes before us.

One evening shortly before our departure date, when I returned home late after a reading, planted a distracted kiss on his lips and then went straight to the kitchen table where I flipped open my laptop to make a few notes, he got angry. He started with the word "compulsive" and went on to shout a list of symptoms long enough for a diagnosis. Before I had time to shout back, before I could make him sick with adjectives, Walter must have caught a glimpse of the "suicide" folder open on my laptop, noticed the document "Scotland notes" and seen my crime for what it was: high treason. The trip that was meant to save us had become a Trojan horse, a chance for me to smuggle yet another tragic architect into our lives. Walter had the courage to give up on me there and then.

*

Built into the end of the stone pier in Nairn is a pane of glass, a window down into the water, just in case a stray bottlenose chooses to swim past that particular square meter. This is where the Phoenix Sea Adventures boat departs to explore the Moray Firth. I arrive early and spend quite a while peering down through the glass, but my determined stare fails to attract any dolphins. Joan and Connor arrive at the pier.

"Are you looking forward to seeing dolphins?" Joan asked.

"We see at least one every time!"

"I hope I will," I say. At the same time, I think of Walter and his absence. Dolphins are his favorite animals; he still has a dolphin duvet cover from when he was little, which we slept under once, with two dolphins on the pillowcases leaping out of the water, arcing towards each other.

The other passengers arrive, two families with children, and finally the skipper, an old sea dog with a heavy accent and a yellow life jacket. As we shuffle onto the vessel, he recites the introduction to the tour: "Welcome aboard! Enjoy the magnificent views and the gorgeous beaches. Out on the water, we'll see it all from a very different perspective. These waters are inhabited by a dizzying wealth of animal species: orcas, seals, porpoises and dolphins all pass this way. We'll also see a wide variety of birds."

The children run wild on deck, tipping the boat back and forth so it's hard to board, but Connor holds out a grandfatherly hand and pulls me across. It's a sturdy hand, large enough to steady all my shakiness. The skipper decrees who will sit in the pilot's chair and in what order, and we all check whether the people next to us have snapped on their life jackets properly. Only then does he start the engine. On course for deep water.

In the middle of the bay, it's easier than I thought to forget the coast. All around us, the sea is endless; it's easy to give myself over to the bobbing of the boat. The engine is off; our vessel sways a little. We're waiting for sea creatures from the deep to swim to the surface, each of us with our own reason for wanting to see a dolphin. The children hold their breath. Connor puts his arm around Joan; his love for her is so clear to see it's beautiful. One of the fathers fidgets on his bench; he's the kind who will ask for his money back if his kids haven't seen any animals by the end of the trip. The skipper is leaning on the wheel with one foot pulled up onto the pilot's chair. The atmosphere on the boat is tense with anticipation; something has us in its grip. At the same time, the bobbing makes me drowsy and my eyes keep closing. I try to fight my way to the surface, to stay awake, but keep making the same fitful descent into sleep. I nod off for a few minutes, until Joan's voice pulls me up from the depths:

"Charlotte, come and look!"

X

KELVINGROVE ART GALLERY & MUSEUM (1888–1901), GLASGOW

JOHN WILLIAM SIMPSON (1858–1933) AND EDMUND JOHN MILNER ALLEN (1859–1912)

Horticulture to a Victorian standard. Kelvingrove Park in Glasgow covers thirty-four hectares of well-groomed landscape around the river Kelvin, which ends its 33-kilometer journey just past the park, flowing into the broad river Clyde. Kelvingrove was created in 1852 as a green refuge from the slums around the factories in the center, an oasis in the rapidly industrialising city of Glasgow.

The banks of the Kelvin, thick with trees and shrubs, support a wide range of animals, plants and fungi. The park is home to the gray heron, the Barrow's goldeneye, the goosander and the great spotted woodpecker, as well as the otter and the brown rat. The ground cover includes wild garlic, wood stitchwort, pink purslane, Himalayan balsam, giant hogweed and Japanese knotweed. The park is kept in shape with intensive tree management, wildflower meadows and decorative borders of azaleas and rhododendrons. The best-known tree in Kelvingrove is a slender winter oak, the suffragette oak, planted in 1918 when women in Britain received the vote.

From various spots in the park, the greenery frames a view of the Kelvingrove Art Gallery and Museum, designed by two British architects, John William Simpson and Edmund John

Milner Allen. The building is topped with its own landscape of towers. In front of the central hall with its lantern roof, two towers thrust still higher, each with four turrets near the top and another four surrounding them one level below. I also count six smaller towers, and those are just the ones by the rear entrance. Still more towers grace the two wings, and the main entrance boasts a particular multitude of towers, decorated with shallow reliefs, columns, friezes, bas-relief figures and all sorts of other embellishments that give the building the sculptural quality of the Spanish baroque. It looks weirdly exotic amid the well-maintained landscape of the park, as if you'd stumbled across the monkey palace from *The Jungle Book*.

The rest of the building is plainer in style: solemn red sandstone forms a solid base for the pyrotechnics of the roof, with large symmetrical rows of windows adding rhythm to the whole.

When the museum opened in 1901, it was dubbed the Palace of Dreams. The pride of the collection was the stuffed Asian elephant Sir Roger, a peer of the animal realm and by extension the British Empire. Sir Roger still stands in the museum today and has become a kind of Kelvingrove mascot. In the lower hall of the west wing, the old elephant leads a troop of stuffed savanna creatures, all fleeing from a Spitfire LA 198 as it swoops down on them. The outermost tips of the wingspan stop just short of the walls; suspending it there must have been a delicate job. In any case, it's a peculiar sight: the warplane and the mounted animals united in a palatial Victorian interior.

I leave the west wing and walk back to the central hall, where I try to find Susan. We have agreed to meet under the organ above the rear entrance. I don't know what Susan looks like; our mutual friend Eleanor put me in touch with her. I try to wear the expression of a person looking for someone, so that whoever is looking for me will recognize me. I'm nervous about meeting Susan, mainly because she's an architect herself. I've reached the point where I can't pretend not to care. Architects now have a kind of glamour about them. When I'm around them, I go shy and quiet. I can't do a thing about it; a dumb fascination takes hold of me. At the same time, it frightens me to think that an architect is especially likely to cast doubt on my whole project and thus alienate me from my subject matter.

At first sight, Susan doesn't seem out to unmask me. She has a friendly face and thick red hair turning gray at the roots. She wears sandals under a simple purple linen dress.

"I want to show you a few select objects," she says. "There are eight thousand items on display, so we won't have time to look at everything. Besides, there's no logical connection between one gallery and the next. There are twenty-two sections, each with a different theme, so you always feel you've missed something."

I'm not opposed in principle to buildings that challenge their visitors, but in museums, I hate it when the floor plan seems to point me in the wrong direction. For example, I felt very uneasy in Museum Abteiberg in Mönchengladbach, where the celebrated postmodern architecture was not as hospitable as it might have been. From the outside, it all looked very promising; it's exciting to see how architect Hans Hollein integrated the building into its topographic setting, the sloped terrain of the Abteiberg. He also allowed it to converse with its architectural context: facing the museum is a Gothic cathedral, and next to that a car park from the 1960s.

But inside the museum, this integration seems to be called into question. The exhibition spaces are arranged not in a linear fashion, but in a matrix. A few are partly or entirely underground, connected to each other and the ground floor by an intricate network of ramps, corridors and stairways. Hollein's architecture invites visitors to put it to active use and make their own discoveries. Rather than a meek shuffle from one art work to the next, a walk through the museum is meant to be a dialectical experience.

In practice, despite these theoretical considerations, the museum made me antsy. As I entered each room, the last one I'd visited still occupied my mind. Right away, I would start to wonder whether and how I might be able to get back there. What route would I have to take? Would I need to retrace my steps? It made me so restless I couldn't focus on the art.

By comparison, the Kelvingrove's architecture is much more user-friendly. The central hall on the first floor, where the organ is, fans out on either side into west and east wings. These wings are symmetrical, each with a large courtyard surrounded by two levels of separate galleries. The challenge for the visitor is not to figure out how all the rooms are connected, but to absorb the overwhelming abundance of the collection: 6,000 square meters chock-full of objects, artworks and curiosities, a bombastic fusion of Rembrandt, dinosaur skeletons, Egyptian pottery, postmodern painting, a square millimeter of gold leaf from the Bronze Age, Art Nouveau furniture ... all this thrown together in delirious, gleeful disorder. If you don't start out well rested, your whole visit will collapse discouragingly on top of you, like a deceased hoarder's overloaded attic you've agreed to tidy up.

"The storage spaces under the building hold two hundred thousand more items," Susan tells me. "New ones are constantly being put on display for regular visitors. These little monkeys, for instance – look at those teeth! They weren't here last time."

We are in the main hall of the east wing, admiring three vicious-looking stuffed primates in a display case. "Diana monkeys," the sign tells me. The case to the left holds a mounted calf; her legs and neck hang slack, which suggests she never learned to walk. In the case to the right of the monkeys are two children's soccer jerseys, number 9 for Brazil and number 10 for Italy. The whole room is dotted with eclectic display cases like these, alternating with busts on plinths. I recognize Queen Victoria, whose likeness I saw earlier in Piazza Regina in Valletta. In this manifestation, she seems to be swallowing a disappointment with dignity; the look in her eyes is steely, but her nostrils betray real emotion. She is flanked by a Buddha carved from the same white marble and an Englishman with wavy hair and cherubic wings, who has the strangest look in his eyes, as if he's just cast a spell and is waiting for it to take effect.

The hall is bathed in light coming from large windows that sweep the whole length of the wing. It is filled with the installation *Masks and Masquerades*: a giant mobile suspended from the ceiling, consisting of one hundred white plaster heads. Their dangling faces show the whole spectrum of human expressions, from painful grimaces to blissful grins and every emotion in between.

Susan, growing impatient, pulls me away from the masks and leads me down an arcade to the left wing's side galleries.

"Look, a porpoise!" I point up at the huge creature hanging from the archway above us.

"This way," Susan directs me.

We enter a gallery called "Looking at Art." Here the excess of the previous space settles into a single focus: the paintings on the walls. Susan positions me in front of L. S. Lowry's *Seascape* and excuses herself to respond to a missed call.

It feels harsh of her to leave me alone with this particular painting. Right away I can feel its gloom bearing down on me. A few blue and green brushstrokes towards the bottom suggest water in motion, but for the most part, the painting is a grayish-white plane, shining bright. There is no escaping its painterly perspective; I am sucked inexorably towards the vanishing point. I try to keep my eye on the dark wood frame around the picture; if I can cling to that, then the light and the water won't swallow me. At the same time, the borders of the frame emphasize the unrelenting vastness of what lies within the canvas in front of me: the light, so improbably bright that I have to blink to keep myself from drowning, a gush of light that sweeps me into the sea, I must keep my head above water, where is the frame, this water, this light, it mustn't drown me, the reflection is unbearable, so bright it washes everything away, where is the edge, my God, I've lost sight of the edge, I'm out in the midst of that watery expanse, in the midst of that outpouring light.

"He took everything out."

Startled by Susan's voice, I gasp for breath.

"Literally, he emptied out the picture. Lowry started out by painting crowded, lively scenes from the industrial districts of Manchester, his 'Mill Scenes.' They look almost like Brueghels, with all the figures running this way and that, the hardworking masses. There's always smoke pouring out of a chimney somewhere, or an 'iron horse' churning out steam on a railway track. Those paintings were very successful: they sold well, and he was invited to join the Royal Academy.

"Sometime in the 1950s, Lowry grew tired of his subject matter. The same grim lives, over and over again. He abandoned those dark industrial scenes for paintings with a pure white background. Over the white, he placed figurative groups. In this period, his work showed almost no trace of architecture or landscape.

"In the 1960s, he began work on his 'Seascapes,' and even the figures disappeared. He took regular trips to Sunderland, always staying in the same hotel room with the same sea view.

There he painted dozens of sea views and a few deserted land-scapes, always restricting his palette to the same five colors: ivory black, vermilion, Prussian blue, yellow ocher and flake white."

"It looks so . . . desolate," I said.

"Here's how I think it works. At some point, you're too familiar with your subject matter to be able to do anything new with it. Either you stop — but most artists are too vain to do that — or else you use the emptiness in your art. Eleanor showed me some of your poems. I can imagine you won't write those kinds of run-on lines for the rest of your life. You're still very young."

As if worried she'll give the wrong impression, Susan makes the gesture of applying her principle to herself: "Or take me, I don't draw anymore. I'm now a senior manager at my architecture firm."

"Why did you stop drawing?"

"They offered me the new job. Besides, it was around the time of Oliver's death."

"Who's Oliver?"

"A friend, an old friend, we studied architecture together. Come to think of it, our class inspected the tiles here in the Kelvingrove, back in the 1990s. We were each equipped with a kind of poker for tapping on each individual tile: tick-tick, the sound told you if it was hollow. We all pitched in, but even then it took us three weeks to check every last one." She paused. "Are you a fan of Billy Connolly, Charlotte? There's a portrait of him here."

"Don't worry, I've never really been interested in comedians. I wanted to ask you about the museum's architects."

"Oh, right, the urban legend. What can I tell you? Simpson and Milner Allen were boring white Englishmen who had the same capacity for self-importance as so many other boring white Englishmen. They described the Kelvingrove as 'an astylar composition on severely classic lines, but with free Renaissance treatment in detail.' Blah, blah, blah. You can see for yourself that those towers come straight from the cathedral in Santiago de Compostela! Anyway, they never jumped off the top, if that's what you're after. What a sight that would be: Simpson on the left, Milner Allen on the right! Who will hit the ground first?"

"You're not a fan," I observe.

"How many women architects have you heard of? And I mean throughout history. Precious few, I dare say, when in fact the profession has attracted some very talented women. But no one's ever heard of them. They didn't make it into the history books, the tales of old men. Simpson and Milner Allen, on the other hand, are now famous for something they didn't even do. They never committed suicide. Milner Allen was already ill when the museum opened, and he died of the same condition in 1912. Simpson survived the reports of his death even longer. Meanwhile he designed the original Wembley Stadium and was even knighted."

Susan's tone is not strident but ironic and almost apologetic. I don't know who she's apologizing for – her profession?

"So in your opinion, what's the reason for the rumors of their suicide?" I ask.

In a low, drawling voice, probably meant to sound like an effete aristocrat, Susan says, "Oh, a few poor little rich men, in the very finite wisdom of their privileged positions, felt that the building was turned back to front. How they would have loved to ride their horse-drawn carriages through the park to the gallery. They were obsessed with the picturesque – the curse of Horace Walpole. Kelvin Park Road could have been a sweeping drive for their dramatic entrance, as they drank in the beauties of nature along the grand tour from their town houses to the magnificent front gate. But no, they had to approach from the street side! Worse, from Argyle Street, the filthy route to the slums! No architect could have intended such a travesty. As soon as they realized, they must have offed themselves!"

I feel like Susan is getting a little carried away, but to ease the tension between the two of us, I laugh aloud at her impression. She laughs with me.

There's no point in continuing to grill her about Simpson and Milner Allen. She has no sympathy for their fictional fate and no special admiration for their work. In her eyes, they are two tedious old coots who seized an unmerited spot in architectural history at the expense of yet another of the many unknown women.

We walk on to the corner gallery, an educational area where, lost in thought, I punch buttons on interactive panels. Susan is right; off the top of my head, I can't think of a single woman architect. An architect, more than a vet or a lawyer, seems automatically male; the phrase "male architect" sounds almost tautological. As if they have no gender, simply because they place themselves above such trifles. Women in the same profession, however, are just as automatically "women architects." Their minority status has to be made explicit, as if it defines the nature of their work. In any case, the tactic is effective: identifying women as a minority makes their work harmless, because whatever they do is seen in terms of their minority identity.

But what work? Thinking back to my architecture survey, prehistory to 1970, I cannot remember the work of a single woman ever being discussed. How are we supposed to learn more about women architects when they've been left out of our collective memory and the historical record?

In the section called "Mackintosh and the Glasgow Style," Susan perks up. Her ironic, resigned style of commentary

transforms into a kind of fighting spirit. Did I know, she wonders, that the Glasgow School of Art was revolutionary in the
field of gender equality? In the late nineteenth century, it
became one of the first art schools to admit women. Other
schools allowed women to take classes earlier, but they were
seen as mere hobbyists, whose real interest was in making not
art but polite conversation about art in the city's tearooms. In
contrast, the Glasgow School of Art offered them the same serious education as the men. Furthermore, the instructors there
approached and taught crafts, illustration and design – the so-
called feminine domains – as independent disciplines for the
first time.

*

Exhibition:The Glasgow Four. At the entrance to the gallery is a
large banner with four faces, one of which sends the blood
rushing to my cheeks. It's a portrait of architect Charles Rennie Mackintosh. His debonair mustache and the dark,
inescapable look in his eyes make me weak at the knees. For a
moment I fear I'm falling in love on the spot. Fortunately he's
been dead for the past eighty years. Next to Mackintosh is his
friend, the designer and teacher Herbert MacNair. Although
he wears a matching suit, with an eye-catching bow in his cra-
vat, Herbert lacks Charles's sharply outlined features, and he
has sloppy eyes. On the lower half of the banner are full-length
portraits of two women: the sisters Margaret and Frances Macdonald. Margaret stares into the lens, self-confident and a little
provocative, her attitude remarkably masculine. Her sister,
Frances, by contrast, is the embodiment of the ideal nineteenth-
century woman: a frail phantasm with a timid look. The
information panels tell me the four of them met at the Glasgow School of Art.

In 1884, Margaret registered at the art school for a number of evening classes. Her sister, Frances, nine years younger, began studying there in 1890, just after turning nineteen. Their father was an engineer and colliery manager. Thanks to their upper-middle-class background and their father's permissive nature, the Macdonald sisters, unlike many other women, received an excellent education and had the freedom to pursue their own interests. Mr. Macdonald supported his daughters' artistic ambitions, their interests in painting, design and architecture.

Fin de siècle. The world is discreetly preparing for a convulsion. After nearly a century of Victorian puritanism, more and more women are challenging their limited social role. Rumors of the femme fatale blow in from France and threaten to become self-fulfilling prophecies. Women's demands for autonomy throw established gender roles into disorder, but the yardstick of tradition is made of unbending wood. The powers that be, mostly male, leap to the defense, their yardsticks in hand. Rule-breakers are rapped on the knuckles, more firmly for some violations than others. For certain ideas, the time was simply not yet ripe. Public life would remain the exclusive province of men for a good while longer; admitting women to design school was one thing, but actually letting a woman design? Architecture regulated and upheld the established order. If women turned their creative powers from procreation to buildings, it would set too many changes in motion. Eventually, perhaps, a woman architect could *assist* in the design of kitchens, broom closets and reception rooms; the household was one domain where women had some authority. But most newspapers and magazines rejected the idea entirely, dismissing women with architectural ambitions as "irritable hermaphroditic creatures" whose obsession with sex might turn them into prostitutes and lesbians.

During their studies, Margaret and Frances became acquainted with Charles Rennie Mackintosh and his friend

Herbert MacNair. The four of them, drawn together by a shared aesthetic, embarked on a multidisciplinary friendship. Architecture, design, interiors, embroidery, metalwork, glassmaking, painting, masculinity, femininity, desire, abstraction, symbolism, verticality, geometry, eroticism, melancholy – all this converged in the meeting of their four minds. In their early, tight-knit years, until around 1900, they exhibited under their nickname, "The Glasgow Four." Their personal relationships and the artistic exchanges that grew out of them planted the seeds of the British Art Nouveau movement.

In 1896, Margaret and Frances left the school and set up a studio together in the heart of Glasgow. The sisters painted and designed posters, furniture and interiors. They shared a love of fairy tales, romantic epics, Celtic mythology, Dante Gabriel Rossetti and the Pre-Raphaelites. Out of these inspirations, they fashioned a shared style characterized by willowy, androgynous figures, whose long thin bodies display the vertical lines of geometric forms. Despite their epicene appearance, these ghostly beings have an erotic impact. Yet they differed enough from the conventional portrayal of female nudes that they raised no objections.

All the same, those distortions of the body were not rejections of sexuality, but explorations of a female sexuality that becomes possible when we see the body itself and put aside the standards imposed on it, put aside biological sex, put aside gender. Margaret hides an erotic charge in two of her favorite symbols of fertility: roses and ovoids. With a little imagination, you can see labial folds in her drapery and line-work.

Frances's figures are mysterious, free-floating and more feminine – isolated beings that show traces of ambivalence, inner conflict, still undefined, but forcing its way ever closer to the surface.

Around the turn of the twentieth century, the free-spirited

dynamics of their foursome, and the relationship between the two sisters in particular, were inhibited by an institutional intervention. Frances married Herbert; a year later, Margaret married Charles. These were both love matches, no doubt, but for women, especially independent female artists, marriage also offered a place in society. Yet this newfound security brought a dark side with it: stifling social constraints and expectations. For the rest of her life, Frances would go on struggling to reconcile her role as a married woman and mother with her desire to make art. Margaret, in contrast, found the liberty within her childless marriage to Charles to further develop her public persona. Driven apart by their diverging struggles, the sisters felt ever further removed from each other's work.

The estrangement between Frances and Margaret was not the direct result of their different roles within their marriages. The problem was that those contrasting roles led them in very different artistic directions. The Glasgow Four had a few more group exhibitions after 1900, but the magic ebbed away.

Margaret began working more closely with Charles, who was to become a famous name in the twentieth century, although less so in Britain than on the continent. The Mackintosh Hill House Chair is still manufactured today. His design for the new Glasgow School of Art building put him on the map as an architect. The early years of his marriage were a time of intense creative partnership. Margaret's visual idiom shines through in Charles's designs; he adopted her rose symbols and ovoids as central decorative elements.

Yet it is difficult to say exactly what role Margaret played in her husband's work. Like many female designers of her generation, she remained in her husband's shadow out in public life. Even if they were equal partners in their studio, the reception of their work minimized her contribution. Critics and historians have attributed most of their creations to Charles.

Frances too was eclipsed by her husband's ambitions. She and Herbert moved to Liverpool after he was offered a teaching position there at the School for Architecture and Applied Art. Their son, Sylvain, was born.

Frances, absorbed by the demands of motherhood, had less time for her art. After the school where Herbert had taught was closed, he was found to have made poor investments with the family fortune. They had nothing to fall back on. Their young household was threatened with bankruptcy. Herbert increasingly turned to drink; he gave up his profession and could not stand it when Frances went on painting.

In 1909, they returned to Glasgow, destitute and facing an uncertain future. Frances, with Margaret's encouragement and support, decided to leave Herbert. In this period, she was a prolific artist, mostly painting Symbolist watercolors: meditations on women's restricted social role and on her personal conflict between art and marriage.

Frances continued down a winding path, unable to reconcile her clashing identities of artist and wife. For the sake of her little boy, she went back to Herbert, a choice that sealed her fate.

Her last work is a black mirror made of beaten metal. At the bottom is a figurative element: a woman sleeping, or possibly dead. The figure represents Arachne, the prototype of the female artist from Greek mythology. There are various stories about how Arachne met her fate. The version from Ovid's *Metamorphoses* could be retold more or less like this:

Arachne is a young maiden renowned for her skill in weaving and spinning, the daughter of a dyer specializing in Tyrian purple, the most precious of colors. To make the dye, you have to crush sea snails, thirty thousand for a single pound. It is the color of sovereigns and emperors. His patient devotion to his work rubs off on his daughter Arachne, who from a young age spends countless hours at the loom. The beauty of her weavings is so otherworldly that her delighted admirers say she must have been touched by Athena. Arachne knows she should take this as a compliment, but since her weaving is so tangled up with her identity, she feels it "belongs to her" in some sense and finds it hard to give even a goddess the credit for her creations. Besides, she is proud of her work. Knowing false modesty often seems obnoxious rather than noble, she always makes the same response to her admirers, polite but firm: "Thank you, but Athena had nothing to do with it. I made this myself."

It doesn't take long for the news to reach the goddess. Who is this boastful girl, claiming her talent for herself? All mortals with any artistic skill should give thanks to Athena, goddess of art, whose kiss endowed them with the gift. Athena wants to see for herself whether Arachne's work at the loom really comes anywhere near her own. To be honest, the very idea infuriates her, but Athena realizes Arachne is young. Maybe her arrogance is no more than youthful overreach? She decides to pay the girl a visit, disguised as an old woman, and offer her the chance to repent.

"What a beautiful tapestry," the old woman says to Arachne. "Such superhuman beauty. As if Athena herself had woven it!"

"Thank you," Arachne replies. "It's very intricate and demanding work. I spend long, slow hours on it."

"You must make many sacrifices to Athena in exchange for the talent she has granted you."

"My sensibility comes from my father; my skills I taught myself," Arachne explains.

"Watch what you say, girl. Don't go acting as if you're a goddess. Beg for forgiveness, and perhaps your soul will be spared."

The sanctimonious sentiments of an old woman, Arachne thinks, and loses her patience: "Forgiveness for what? I'm telling you the truth. If Athena came down from Mount Olympus, she'd be the first to admit I'm right."

At that, the old woman throws off her cape and reveals herself as the goddess Athena. She challenges the girl to a weaving contest. The goddess, still trying to persuade Arachne to repent, weaves a lustrous tapestry with four exemplary scenes in which people who compare themselves to the gods are punished. The technique is outstanding, but the orthodox religious subject matter seems little more than self-congratulatory.

Arachne's weaving displays the same consummate technique but also courage and an original theme. Arachne decries the misdeeds of the gods in a series of scenes of Zeus raping and abusing women.

At the sight of it, Athena flies into a rage. Not only is Arachne insulting the gods, but her tapestry outdoes even Athena's creation. In demonic jealousy and wrath, Athena tears up the work of her mortal competitor. Then she strikes her three times, hard, on the head. Arachne struggles back to her feet but knows that she cannot escape. Even now, in her humiliation and mortal fear, she remains determined to decide her own fate. Accepting that her pride and skill have already condemned her to death, Arachne remains in charge of her life by hanging herself.

Athena, seeing Arachne string herself up in her tapestry, interprets this desperate act as the ultimate form of hubris. Does the girl think even life and death are hers to decide? So the goddess transforms Arachne into a spider, to weave and hang forever in her web.

Frances Macdonald committed suicide in 1921. Soon afterwards, her art became a commercial success, partly because of her sister's efforts and the tragedy of Frances's deliberate death. Her husband, Herbert – frustrated, jealous and feeling like a failure – destroyed most of her work. Maybe he saw this as vengeance for a difficult marriage, a difficult wife. *Damnatio memoriae.* His violence denied her art, and therefore the memory of her life, a place in history, where there had never been any place for a woman to begin with. In life and death, Frances was deprived of her voice.

Margaret Macdonald achieved a degree of autonomy as an artist and remained somewhat active as a public figure. She had the good fortune that she and her husband were equals in their marriage and inspired one another, which made it possible for her to go on exhibiting alongside him.

From 1914, Charles Rennie Mackintosh struggled with declining mental health. Depression, alcoholism and a series of financial and artistic setbacks left him needing a great deal of support from Margaret. In the years that followed, there were some happy periods, with watercolor landscapes and pencil sketches, but she never again found time for her own work.

When Charles developed tongue cancer and lost his ability to speak, he also stopped signing his sketches and drawings. A number of drawings from this period may have been made by Margaret.

From his sickbed, Charles helped medical students improve their anatomical drawing. Margaret claimed that at his death in 1928 he'd had his pencil in hand.

The wives of male artists are often central in creating the myths about them. Margaret died five years later. Their work from the height of their joint career, 1890–1910, is mostly attributed to Charles Rennie Mackintosh. In recent years, a few dissenters have tried to rescue the "Glasgow Girls" from oblivion, but most critics claim that Mackintosh's foolish infatuation with Margaret led him to exaggerate her role in his work.

*

When Susan and I reach the end of the exhibition, we return to the main hall of the east wing. Through the large windows, the sunlight pours down on us.

Susan points to the other side. "There's another gallery with work by the Glasgow Boys. Have a look on your own if you like. I hope one day they'll do the same for the Glasgow Girls. I want to show you our Salvador Dalí now, and then I have to go."

Susan climbs the stairs ahead of me to the upper galleries. The colonnades are made of blond sandstone that seems to glow with the honey color of stored sunlight.

"The stone was recently cleaned – they coated it with latex and then peeled off the grime. You should have seen the museum before the renovations. The walls were black with soot. There were false walls and waist-high partitions everywhere; the interior was divided into lots of dark little corners. The roof leaked so badly that every night the caretaker had to put out buckets to catch the water," Susan tells me.

It's hard to imagine this gallery without the sunlight flooding in from above, the honey-colored walls, or the tongue-in-cheek humor of the eccentric collection. It is a weightless place. Soot, damp and stale air seem like mere legends from a forgotten world. I think of my own heaviness, how intense it can be sometimes, but this building's power now lifts it out of me with ease. And in that swift moment of lightness, I recall other, similar moments when I thought I was experiencing what self-help books and greeting cards call happiness, but is in fact a kind of mercy: permission from yourself for everything to be all right in spite of everything, a state in which even the heaviness that came before was part of something larger, has meaning by negation, is a dark side indispensable to reaching lightness, a shadow already hanging over me again – since the lightness, as I've learned from experience, never lasts but segues into a new heaviness.

So, absorbed in that moment, I allow the full weight of the building, the stone, the roof, the columns, the arches, the marble, the stairways, the metalwork, the glass, the mortar, the earth to drag me into its depths. I think of Frances Macdonald. If the depths last long enough, if the depths can overwhelm you in the midst of the purest balance and go on and on, maybe that's the suicide, it occurs to me now, and not the final act.

Susan breaks the silence. She's paused on the stairs, lost in memories of her own. "Oliver, my friend from university, was involved in restoring the museum in 2003. He used to tell the funniest stories. Once he helped to disassemble the sarcophagus of Pa-ba-sa in the west wing – Pa-ba-sa was some high-ranking official under Pharaoh Psamtik I in ancient Egypt. As they were removing it from its base, the lid slid open. In the sarcophagus, they found a pornographic magazine from the 1950s. Oliver loved that sort of thing."

I laugh. "Thanatos and Eros, the mummy and the porn mag!"

"Still, it's a dangerous form of attraction. You shouldn't eroticize death too much, Charlotte. Towards the end, Oliver started to see death as a kind of perfection, maybe because so many other things in his life went awry or became undependable, I don't know. In the end, you never know why people do it."

"Did Oliver do it?" I ask her.

"He'd got himself into a jam. Bought an Art Nouveau building that cost the earth and couldn't keep up with the payments. He wanted to restore it with all the original details, to take the whole thing back in time. A typical delusional architect, thinking you can resurrect the past and time won't crack it to pieces. There were all kinds of problems. He made errors of judgment. The costs were crippling. Oliver saw no other way out . . . I can still hear him the first time he showed me the building: 'This is the house I want to die in, Susan!' He saw the building for what it had been, for what it once again could be, and was blind to what it had actually become, a hideous pile of work. It's a trap, I can tell you that. You're an architect, so you fix up your house exactly the way you want it, and then you expect your life to conform to the same ideal shape. Goes without saying that's never how it works. He jumped off the landing. This was a few years ago."

*

The Dalí is on display in a space designed especially for it, like a little chapel. Black walls and bathroom tiles. *El Cristo de San Juan de la Cruz* is the title of the painting from 1951.

The image came to him in a cosmic dream, Salvador Dalí claimed. The perspective is idiosyncratic. The cross to which Christ is nailed is viewed from above, from beyond the skies as it were, as if the painter has taken the place of God. Despite that perspective, the picture does not have a vertical effect; three quarters of the canvas is a dark black void that seems to project forward into the gallery. Through this void, the cross seems to stretch almost horizontally, hovering menacingly over the scene below, a bay with a little boat.

The painting has a stormy history. In Dalí's surrealist oeuvre, it is almost a step backwards, a sudden attempt to imitate the work of the old masters. But by then the twentieth century had come too far to be satisfied with that. The public wanted his melting clocks and mechanical elephants, disruption rather than the old paradigms.

When the painting was exhibited in London in the 1950s, the British press eviscerated it. But the city of Glasgow bought it anyway, for about eight thousand pounds, a considerable sum in those days, but small fry when you think that Spain recently offered eighty million euros to buy the painting back. The curator would not dream of ever selling the Dalí; it's the Kelvingrove's treasure. It is however often sent out on loan to other museums, to burnish Glasgow's international reputation. After these missions of cultural diplomacy, the painting returns to its little chapel in the Kelvingrove. It is always a happy homecoming.

"Once we almost lost the painting forever. Here in the museum, a fanatic once chucked a stone at it. After that, he grabbed it and tore it. A real nutjob. He believed the painting was blasphemous because of the perspective, as if the painter had thought he was God. He also said Dalí trivialized Christ's sacrifice for humanity by leaving out the blood, the crown of thorns, and the nails through the wrists and ankles. That weirdo did considerable damage. They sent him off to an asylum. Fortunately, the canvas could be repaired."

Susan crosses herself. "Sorry, force of habit," she says.

We say our goodbyes in the central hall under the golden coffered ceiling.

"Best of luck with your book. Take care of yourself," Susan says as she passes under the organ and hurries out of the rear exit.

I stroll over to the west wing. Sir Roger and the savanna creatures are still fleeing the Spitfire. At the entrance to the "Creatures of the Past" gallery is a life-size Elvis doll. Inside the gallery is an eight-meter-long canoe from Mesopotamia. A square millimeter of gold leaf from the Bronze Age. A ceratosaurus skeleton. A mummy on loan from the British Museum.

I consult the floor plan and discover the order within this chaos. The west wing, where I am now, is called "Life." On this side of the central hall is everything related to human beings and their habitats: human history, archaeology, anthropology and paleontology. The east wing I visited with Susan is called "Expression" and holds all forms of expressive art, such as painting, sculpture and design.

When I think of the Macdonald sisters, this dichotomy between "Life" and "Expression" has a newly bitter aftertaste.

I loop around the landing of the west wing's upper gallery, wander aimlessly over to the upper level of the central hall and take a right past the organ, along the rearmost staircase to the ground floor. Here I find the ceremonial foundation stone of the Kelvingrove Art Gallery. White marble with inlaid gold letters:

> THIS STONE WAS LAID ON THE
> TENTH SEPTEMBER 1897 BY HIS
> ROYAL HIGHNESS THE DVKE OF
> YORK K G
>
> JOHN W SIMPSON
>
> E J MILNER ALLEN
>
> JOINT ARCHITECTS

Their names suddenly look strange to me; I just can't get them in the right order. John Milner Allen, W. Edmund, Milner Simpson, Allen John Edmund, John John W., Simpson Johnson. As if I'm reading a Tolstoy novel and keep getting the characters and their three Russian names mixed up.

I'm tired. I turn round, ready to head back out into the park through the rear exit. One last work holds me back. Straight across from the foundation stone, there's a painting on the wall: *North Corridor* by David Pugh Evans. A man in a beige trench coat stands in profile in front of a large window. He cannot see through the window because outside it, strange to say, is a closed curtain. The material of the curtain is thin. Through the fabric, through the window, light seeps in. The man is frozen in his own gaze, which reaches neither through the window nor through the light. Perhaps it's now all I can see, but in some uncanny way, I feel certain the man in the painting is suicidal.

The beige tones of the room and the bloodred wall-to-wall carpeting confirm that. Everything in the picture is drenched in melancholy.

David Pugh Evans is an anti-Hockney. His figures share the same realistic treatment, and his backgrounds often have a similar architecture of monochrome planes, but Evans's palette is a good deal more sinister. The flirty openness of Hockney's scenes of leisure is nowhere to be found. His work turns inward. There is no background, only the enigmatic empty room.

In a reflex, I try to decipher the story behind the image; what on earth is the man in the beige trench coat looking at? Whatever it is, it appears to be holding him captive.

The different directions of the gazes – viewer–man, man–window, light–window – give the painting a many-layered quality that challenges me to solve the riddle of the image.

The longer I look, the more it dawns on me that there is no solution, no narrative. There is only this frozen image on canvas and the act of looking. A confrontation with the suffocating and partial limits of what we can see. The image is cut off from time and context and motion. It's a second-hand relationship to the world.

XI

PINE VALLEY GOLF COURSE (1910–1918), PINE VALLEY

GEORGE ARTHUR CRUMP (1871–1918)

"SHINE ON WHITE NEW PINEAPPLE," screams a Sunkist billboard along Interstate 76 out of Philadelphia. Canned white pineapple soft drink sounds unappealing, like some elixir for men concerned about their sperm count, but I do take careful note of the slogan. After all, in F. Scott Fitzgerald's novel *The Great Gatsby*, the billboard is a central motif.

In *The Great Gatsby*, the eyes of "Doctor T. J. Eckleburg – Oculist" stare out from a faded billboard en route to the home of the millionaire Jay Gatsby in West Egg. Two gigantic blue irises peer ominously through yellow spectacles. The eyes are not part of a face; the spectacles do not rest on a nose. Against the billboard's blank background, the eyes stare out of their floating frame at the passing cars. In the book, Fitzgerald uses the billboard in various ways; it shows up as a warning when trouble is coming and serves as a watchful divine presence, bearing witness to everything and providing the moral compass the characters lack. And besides these religious concerns, the eyes are also simply an advertisement for a local oculist.

In view of the prophetic power of that billboard, it would be unwise of me to dismiss the potential relevance of the Sunkist billboard to my own quest. I have come too far to endanger my story now, with my last few hundred euros in my pocket. This is where it has to come together.

"Shine on white new pineapple," I murmur to myself behind the wheel, a cryptic message I will carry with me on the way to Pine Valley.

At the borough of Bellmawr, the interstate turns into a state highway, New Jersey Route 42. It's the week after Christmas, and the outdoor decorations are blinking in broad daylight. Front yards, porches and roofs are littered with candy canes, LED snowflakes and all sorts of light displays: Santa Claus on his sleigh, Santa on a Harley-Davidson, a solar-powered nativity, laser-light pine trees, a galloping unicorn, Mickey Mouse in a Santa hat, a reindeer family carved out of shrubs, Nutcrackers, inflatable polar bears and tons and tons of fake snow. It goes on and on until Blackwood Clementon Road, a traffic artery leading past a shopping mall: another long series of blinking lights, this time advertising chain restaurants and megastores.

*

At the Clementon Park & Splash World turnoff, the screechy suburbs come to an abrupt end. This is the start of a wooded enclave along Clementon Lake. From the road, you can see part of the water park: a Ferris wheel, a wooden roller coaster. A labyrinth of pastel waterslides – or maybe the colors were vivid once, bright red, dark green, deep purple, now bleached by the sun. My hand reaches absently for my shin as I think of my brother again, and of the flap of skin he lost as he sped down that plastic waterslide in Ostend. This time I don't think it happened to me. Instead I think I don't know how he's doing, that really the last time I knew was when we were children. The park seems to have been closed for a while.

Past the lake, the woods grow dense and close on either side. I am nearing the village of Pine Valley on the western edge of the New Jersey Pinelands National Reserve, better known as the Pine Barrens. This thickly forested coastal area covers seven New Jersey counties, from Cape May in the south to Seaside Heights in the north. The Pine Barrens are a strange and mysterious stretch of backcountry, to which this road is the prelude. Here and there a house is visible among the conifers as they glide by, but the farther I follow the road into the woods, the closer and more interlocked the evergreens are. Within their overgrowth, they conceal depths as ancient as a primeval forest.

It was in the Tertiary period, some sixty-five million years ago, that the Pine Barrens began to form. For millions of years before that, the Atlantic coastline had been shifting back and forth through a series of ice ages. Meltwater covered the coastal plains completely, and the ocean deposited minerals underground. Centuries later, when the water receded, it left deep layers of sand, silt and clay. This cycle repeated in different geological epochs. Today, those materials are still the main constituents of the Pine Barrens soil.

In the second half of the Tertiary, in the Miocene epoch, a new layer of sediment was added: Cohansey sand, so named by the geologists Knapp and Kummel in 1904 because they took their samples by Cohansey Creek. Cohansey sand consists chiefly of yellow shards of ironstone and quartz, combined with trace amounts of chert, white sand, silt and clay. These diverse particles stick together, forming large grains.

Sugar sand, the people of the Pine Barrens call it. This particular type of coarse sand limits what can grow there. The first European newcomers to move inland from the coast of New Jersey could do nothing with the soil. Not a crop could they find that would take to it. They decided the area was unsuitable for agriculture and moved on, leaving behind the name Pine Barrens as their verdict on the barren earth of the pine forests.

But that name is based on a misunderstanding. The soil of

the Pine Barrens is not arid. On the contrary, the area is veined with rivers, wetlands and aquifers, transporting water through many ground layers. It is the Cohansey sand, that granular sugar, that makes it so hard for farmers to work the land. The coarse texture makes the soil extremely porous; everything trickles through it as if through a sieve: water, snow, the remains of dead animals, rotten leaves, compost, all absorbed into the subsurface. The soil sucks it all into the depths without retaining any nutrients or organic material. Minerals are likewise swallowed whole, so they have no chance to neutralize the acids. The result is soil that is too acidic for most plants and crops.

*

At the end of the road is a sandy parking lot beside a formidable two-and-a-half-meter-high electric fence. On the fence is a sign: "Borough of Pine Valley." The fence appears to completely surround the site.

Pine Valley originally fell under the borough of Clementon, but since 1929 it has been an independent borough and evidently a gated community. Behind the fence is a drive leading up to two small houses. Outside the one on the left, the American flag is flying; the door is marked "Reception." In the house on the right, a light comes on. A man comes outside and heads towards me.

"We're closed!" he says.

"The borough is closed?" I ask.

"This is private property. You are unlawfully trespassing. Please step back from the fence, ma'am. I have every right to call the police."

I take a step back. That's enough to calm him down, at least for the moment.

"I'm looking for the Pine Valley Golf Club," I say.

"This is the Pine Valley Golf Club, the number one golf course in the world."

"I thought this was the borough of Pine Valley, but the road stops here. So how do I get to the golf course, exactly?"

"Look, ma'am, the Pine Valley Golf Club and the borough of Pine Valley are different places on paper, but in reality it's a different story."

"So this is the golf course? Then I've found it after all."

"What I'm trying to tell you is that Pine Valley is organized as a borough, but it's basically private property. I never heard of anyone questioning our way of doing things."

"What do you mean, the borough is private property?"

While asking this question, I must have stepped forward again without realizing, because the man repeats that I'm unlawfully trespassing: "This is your second warning, ma'am."

"So you're saying I can't go inside – and not just the golf club, but also Pine Valley, because they're the same place?"

"Well, you certainly can't enter the golf club. No women allowed on the property."

"Excuse me?"

"You heard me. It's for their own good. The level of challenge is, uh, how shall I put it, too disturbing for women. And, well, they hold up the game. Most women figure that out on their own, actually, and they're fine with it. Women can play when invited by a member, but only on Sundays after three p.m."

"And the member must be a man, I suppose? You can't bar women from the entire borough, can you? That's unconstitutional."

"As I said, ma'am, this *is* the borough, a fully equipped borough with all required services. That building there on the right houses the mayor's office, the police, the fire department, the council, the school board and the tax assessor's office."

"Right. And how many clowns fit into a circus car?" Now I've let my frustration run away with me.

"What a weird thing to say. Are you from Europe? We open the doors to the public in September for the final day of the Crump Cup. You can sign up on our website. It's the birthday of Pine Valley's architect and founder, George Arthur Crump. I should add that no cell phones or cameras are permitted during the tour, if it's photos you're after."

"You don't understand. I can't come back in September. Is there anyone here I can talk to about this?"

"Well, gosh, ma'am, there's a population of twenty-three on paper, including the mayor, the chief of police, the fire chief and the tax assessor, but all twenty-three are basically golf players or club employees. Since the club's closed right now, there's no one here to talk to, no."

"In other words, Pine Valley doesn't really exist? You made up a borough so you can do whatever you like inside this fence?"

"Now you're going too far, ma'am. I'll have to ask you to step away from the fence."

"I bet every single one of you is a Republican."

"I'm calling the police."

The man sprints inside. He's serious. In the lit-up window I see him lift the receiver from its hook. I raise my hands into the air in surrender. He nods, hangs up the phone and waves an insistent goodbye.

*

Pine Valley is reputed to be the world's most exclusive golf club, so exclusive that even Hollywood stars and well-known athletes can't pay their way in. Obviously, I hadn't expected they'd let me waltz straight onto the fairway.

Now that I've seen the electric fence, I understand why so few stories about the Pine Valley Golf Club have reached the outside world. An indiscreet caddy once bragged that he'd had the honor of lugging Sylvester Stallone's clubs. One of the gardeners has a framed print in his house of a selfie he took with Sean Connery; George W. Bush didn't want his picture taken. In general, there seems to be an unwritten agreement that what happens in the club, stays in the club. All questions elicit the same response: "We can't tell you that, because it would intrude on other people's privacy. But the club is an unbelievably quiet, peaceful place."

Topsy Siderowf, an associate editor at the renowned magazine *Golf Digest*, has played there. In an interview in 1996, she told the *New York Times*, "It's a beautiful place in impeccable condition and everybody seems to be in a good mood. It was a privilege to play there. But I don't think you should write about it. I just don't think it belongs in a newspaper."

I take one last look back at the man in the window. He's turned on the TV and already seems to have forgotten me. I follow the fence into the woods.

*

The plants that manage to grow in the inhospitable soil of the Pine Barrens form unique communities. Three flowers that have become extinct elsewhere in the world survive there: a gentian with petals like blue flames, the swamp pink and the bog asphodel.

Thirty varieties of wild orchids shoot up, untamable, from the open swamps and wet meadows, including the rose pogonia with its snakelike mouth, the upper lip raised in a sensual curl.

In the sandy woods lie the beds of the rare pink lady's slipper. Its two lower leaves form a flower pouch that is practically pornographic, opening into a slit that shows every tint from magenta to white. The same sandy ground gives rise to a variety of carnivorous plants: bladderworts, which snap up insects, sundews, which stretch out their sticky tentacles, and gluttonous pitcher plants, with cavities deep enough to trap a whole mouse.

Most of the shrub layer consists of blueberry bushes, a masochistic species that thrives on the harsh soil. The idea that the region is too acidic for agriculture is belied by the millions of dollars' worth of Pine Barrens blueberries consumed annually. Rich growths of bracken fern, mountain laurel, swamp azalea and broom crowberry form other insurgent elements on the barren ground.

Despite the stubborn persistence of some rare plants and flowers, others struggle for decades and then lose out to the acidic soil. Wild lupine, for example, was one of the toughest native flowers in the Pine Barrens in the early twentieth century; today, it is a threatened species.

Still others try to crowd each other out. The oak and the pine are embroiled in an ongoing clash of the titans. The *Pinus rigida*, or pitch pine, is the most common type of tree in the Pine Barrens, a tough, gnarled conifer that grows up to 25 meters high. Its roots find nutrients even in unpromising soils, branching out underground and delving through the sandy layer to the water below. The pitch pine has tough needles in bundles of three, which grow to be 12 centimeters long.

In objective terms, the pitch pine's archrival, the oak, has more natural advantages. Oaks grow faster, reproduce more easily and have large flat leaves better suited to photosynthesis than pine needles. They steal the sun, as it were, growing taller than the pines and suffocating them with their overhanging foliage.

These two competitors also share a greater enemy: the frequent forest fires.

Although the oak grows fast, it recovers slowly from

burns — if at all. The pine is more flame-resistant; in fact, it needs fire to grow. The blazing heat is what opens its cones. To the pine tree, a forest fire is a welcome catastrophe, like the biblical Flood, cleansing the earth and wiping away everything — including its rival's acorns and fallen leaves. In the new open spaces, the seedlings from its pine cones have a better chance of establishing themselves.

The pine also has a secret weapon, an almost magical property: under its bark, it has dormant buds which, when awoken by fire, begin to form new branches. After the fire has burnt itself out, you can tell the pitch pine from the oak among the charred skeletons by the green shoots sprouting through the blackened surface. After the fire, the advantage belongs to the pine. Blow by blow, the cycle of death and growth repeats itself. The pitch pine must be destroyed to live again.

Some biologists hypothesize that the pitch pine's needles are evolving to catch fire more easily, so that they make better kindling and fuel for the flames. They are developing properties that aid in their destruction, a kind of suicide mechanism — but not really, or not absolutely, since unlike other living things, they can regenerate.

Meanwhile, in the wetter areas of the Pine Barrens, the range of tree species is starkly different. Here, the dry world of sand and fire damage seems very far away. Tall Atlantic white cedars grow. Sedges and rushes spring up among patches of peat moss. The surface of the river is dotted with many species of water lilies. They meet with hardly any resistance.

*

Two kilometers down the path, the small town of Berlin breaks up the forest around Pine Valley. It is the last stop in the inhabited world. Beyond Berlin, the Pine Barrens stretch out in the fullness of their wide expanses. It's 75 kilometers as the crow flies through the forests from here to the Atlantic coast.

The fence around the golf course does not run parallel to the forest path. Enigmatic bulges in the landscape and a barrier of tightly packed pine trees have hidden the fence from me along the way. The golf course must make an inward turn somewhere, but the path continues straight. Yet I can't shake the feeling that it's me who turned away, that I should have kept going, straight ahead, if I wanted to stay alongside the fence.

How did I end up in this street? Probably just woozy with hunger. The path was definitely straight. When did I eat last? I take a left onto Cross Keys Road and pass the fire station, reaching a gas station with a roadside diner. Let's Wingette!, the place is called. All they serve is fried chicken wings and fried fish; not my favorite lunch, but the restaurant is open and there's no alternative in sight.

"Chicken, fish, or shrimp?" the waitress asks even before I'm seated.

"Coffee," I reply.

"I'll have to ask you to order food with that. If you don't mind me saying so, you could use it. You look pretty pale. Six, eight, or eighteen pieces?"

"I'm just tired, I think."

The waitress interprets this as an order: a mixed plate with potato salad. She pours the coffee.

"You passing through?"

"I wanted to visit the golf club."

"You tried to climb over the fence, you mean? The entrance is in the other direction."

"I'd like to see the grounds, the landscape, not so much the club."

"Well, I hate to tell you, but you're not gonna get to see it.

There's a little airport a couple of blocks away. Presidents and bank directors land there in their private helicopters. And on top of that, you're a woman."

"Yeah, I already heard we're barred."

The waitress gives me an eye roll of solidarity and plunks the plate of mixed fried pieces down in front of me: "That'll be $16.95. My dad had a soft spot for that golf course. All his life, he dreamed that one day he'd be rich enough for a membership when he retired. He owned a car repair shop right near here. Used to have big shots coming in now and then for repairs to their Buicks. They prefer to drive low-key models, so they don't attract attention."

"Did he ever play there?"

"Nah, things never work out like that in real life, of course. But he claims a friend of his, who's a gardener there, let him walk around the grounds once – could have cost the guy his job. My dad was never a big talker or anything, but when he told the story of that one time in Pine Valley, he turned into a regular poet. He made me sit through it dozens of times."

"So what did he say?"

"Oh, stuff like, 'First there was a sense of calm, of profound harmony with the challenge of the game. As if the course had always been there, as if it had always been ordained to be there, from the beginning of time and quite possibly to the end.'"

"What did he mean by that?" I asked.

"Oh, he was just getting carried away. This was in his last years, when he was *really* old. That's when folks tend to say stuff like that."

*

The grounds of the Pine Valley Golf Club have a mythic reputation. It's said to be easier to walk barefoot to the North Pole than to play golf in Pine Valley. The course has been described as enigmatic and downright treacherous. Its design blurs the boundaries between the natural and the artificial landscape in an ingenious way. You might easily forget you're in the Pine Barrens, but if you wander off the fairway in search of a lost golf ball, you soon run into the sandy, undifferentiated expanses surrounding them. Like some godforsaken lunar landscape, that barren sand and those pitch pines creep into your throat. Just a moment ago, the lush green of the turf was all around you; now it seems like no more than a mirage.

Most descriptions of Pine Valley come from people who brag about having played there. The ones who have actually seen it don't say a word. Inside the fence is a secret that covers about two and a half square kilometers of land.

From Pine Valley's public records – it's an official borough, after all – we can deduce that those two and a half square kilometers must contain not only the reception building and the so-called town hall at the entrance, but also twenty-two luxury homes. The houses are all owned by elite club members, but the land on which they were built belongs to the borough of Pine Valley. The owners pay property taxes to the borough, but since the borough is identical to the golf club, those dollars go on circulating in the same closed system.

George Arthur Crump came up with the idea of Pine Valley Golf Course in 1910. An avid golfer, he dreamed of professionalizing the sport in the region. His eighteen-hole design for the course drew on the natural landscape to create an Eden for all experienced and aspiring players in and around Philadelphia. I wonder what he would think of the club's electric fence and self-perpetuating capital flows if he could visit his "valley of dreams" today.

*

In her book *Pine Valley Golf Club: 100 Years of Mystery at the World's No. 1 Golf Course in Pine Valley, New Jersey,* J. E. Souders explores Pine Valley's shadowy history. Souders begins her story in the late nineteenth century, with Virginia Sumner, a slender socialite with pale blue eyes. In 1881, having just turned sixteen, she married the up-and-coming ad man Howard Ireland, a powerhouse of spunk and promise. In short order, he built a successful advertising firm in Philadelphia. In 1885, Virginia began buying up parcels of land that overlooked the Delaware River near Clementon, New Jersey. She indulged in this new hobby in her own name; the deeds identify the purchaser as "Mrs. Virginia Sumner Ireland."

Five years later, she owned a continuous area measuring four square kilometers, which she dubbed Pine Valley. It included Timber Lake, where Howard and Virginia had a sprawling mansion built. The house has a granite façade and more than twenty-five rooms. Their first years there were happy ones: Virginia made the most of their lavish lifestyle. She bred racehorses on the property and galloped around the Pine Barrens, free to roam the wilderness. In her first automobile, she sped down the country roads, rattling past the pines. She opened an airport on her estate and learned to fly an airplane. She traveled widely, living life at full throttle. When she was at home, she succumbed to extravagant urges, striving after the decadent spirit of fin de siècle European culture. In the house by the lake, she held wild parties, concerts, art exhibitions and banquets. Virginia Sumner Ireland inhabited the same world as Fitzgerald's Gatsby.

By 1912, those happy years were probably a distant memory. That was when Virginia Sumner sold 700 square meters of land to a hotel owner from Philadelphia, George Arthur Crump. This time, the name on the deed was "Widow V. Sumner Ireland." But her husband, Howard, did not die for another ten years. Furthermore, the divorce papers from 1896 have been preserved. Since then, the countryside has swallowed up their secrets.

*

When George Arthur Crump bought the land from Virginia Sumner he was forty-one. His wife, Belle, had died a few years earlier and was irreplaceable. The Crumps had no children, so George was left without any responsibilities and had nothing to lose. To buy the land, he had to sell his shares in the Colonnade Hotel, a six-story corner building in Chestnut Street in Philadelphia. The Colonnade was a smoothly functioning family business, but Crump had played no real role in its operations for years. He had delegated his duties to others and taken a room there, not so much for business as for leisure.

His father, George W. Crump, enjoyed outdoor activities and often took his four children out to hunt, fish and play sports. George Arthur's sister Helen became a tennis star with a nationwide reputation, while George Arthur himself made a good showing in regional squash tournaments.

In the 1890s, George Arthur took up golf. From then on, he was at the tee more often than he was at his desk. The game had awoken something in him, something unreasonable; he always wanted to play, and when he was playing, he wanted to play better. He brought an inquiring mind to every stroke, always thinking about how the next one could be more effective. He came down hard on himself over every chip, slice and mulligan, until his nerves couldn't take it and his hands became too shaky to hold on to the club.

Although Crump loved competition, more than that, he was good-natured and sportsmanlike, never wanting his own enjoyment to come at anyone else's expense. When golfing, he never had to worry about that; he was really competing not with the other players, but with himself. His obsession with a flawless swing didn't bother anyone else. With monomaniacal focus, Crump devoted himself to improving his game. Only a few years after he'd started playing, he had made a name for himself as one of Philadelphia's best golfers. Crump received many compliments on his style and execution, even from seasoned professionals. Now and then, he won a tournament. But along with this recognition came the sobering realization that he had started too late to become a great player. He never said it out loud, but he was haunted by a sense of lagging behind. To drown out this gnawing feeling, he redoubled his efforts.

Although he was never a professional golfer, his fanatical devotion turned the game into a full-time occupation. When the course at the Philadelphia Country Club was waterlogged and the nine holes in Merchantville became tedious, he would venture out to more distant clubs. In one eighteen-month period, Crump went on fifty golf trips. His circle of friends grew ever wider. Golf offers ideal conditions for sociability: like-minded people in an easygoing atmosphere, whacking a ball together against a scenic backdrop. What more could a man desire? Time after time, Crump's days on the links were full of camaraderie and good cheer. Numerous surviving letters speak of his many friendships and reveal something of Crump's personality. His friends describe him as quiet and reserved, modest but generous, always empathetic and frequently capable of true selflessness. A few praise his humor but wish it were not so often at his own expense.

When his wife, Belle, died unexpectedly in 1906 – struck without warning by a heart attack on a ferry from Manhattan to Jersey City, dead before the boat reached shore – Crump gave up golf for a few years, apart from one trip to Atlantic City every winter. This annual outing had given rise to a tight-knit brotherhood of players known as the Philadelphia Ballsome. In the years that followed his wife's death, Crump found real solace in those friendships.

Maybe he believed he ought to do something in return for their support. His friends sometimes complained about the second-rate golf courses around Philadelphia. How were golfers from Philly ever going to win championships when they didn't even have a decent place to practice? Crump listened to these exchanges in pensive silence, with enough detachment to see what was needed: a professional course. And he had very firm opinions about how it should look.

When he weighed his options, the outcome was clear. Belle had died four years earlier, much too early and much too unexpectedly. His father too had died young, soon after his fifty-second birthday, before he could take the time to enjoy the fruits of his labor. Crump himself had reached a turning point in his life: he was past forty, with a lot of living behind him, and the years ahead demanded nothing of him. His life consisted largely of golf and the people he played golf with. If he sold part of the hotel, he would be wealthy enough to remain independent and do whatever he wished. The truth was he had nothing to lose. Not too far from Philadelphia, he knew of a place where he'd gone hunting now and then, near the estate of the high-living Virginia Sumner: a sandy wasteland, overgrown with a mosaic of pines, oaks and bushes divided by streams and ponds.

The waitress refills my coffee cup and takes away my plate of chicken bones and shrimp tails.

"Why do you care so much about seeing that golf course? Are you the nosy type?"

"Not by nature. I want to see it so I can describe it properly. I'm planning to write a book." I try to say this airily and not sound too driven. When she doesn't follow up with any other questions, I feel a little hurt. I'd like to have told her about the architects. When I talk about them, I feel less guilty about hardly having put anything down on paper, and less afraid that what I *have* written isn't good enough.

"What's your regular job?" the waitress asks.

"This is my regular job."

"You make a living writing books?"

"Not really. Well, sometimes I have money, sometimes I don't."

"Why don't you get a job if you need money? There's nothing wrong with working hard for your paycheck."

"I don't have time to write and hold down a job. I think if I had a job, I wouldn't find the opportunity to write, and I'd probably stop. It's all or nothing."

"If you stopped, you could do something else, right?" And she shrugs, as if the choice is obvious. She clearly has more talent for living than I do. Then she strolls back into the kitchen with my plate, oblivious to the existential turmoil in which she's left me.

There are days when I dream of earning wages. In this dream, a sum is deposited in my bank account on the first day of every month. It's always the same old reliable amount, and I know exactly how hard I have to work to earn it. I deduct my rent, utility bills, insurance payments and living expenses, and I'm left with a reassuring buffer. Money is security. In the supermarket, I don't have to add up the prices as I go and hope the cashier will arrive at the same total. At the café, I buy a round for my friends. Two rounds. Birthday presents aren't sources of anxiety. I buy a merino wool sweater, just because I like the way it looks on me. I can save a little every month, and I make sensible financial decisions, like buying property. I'm not always reserving mental space for my latest project, so in conversations I seem less absent, and I'm more fun to spend time with. My sleep pattern is not disrupted by second thoughts, self-corrections, brilliant ideas, or the fear of failure. I feel less down, because I don't cultivate strong emotions for the sake of my writing – a truly second-rate habit in any case, which can lead to nothing good, so in my dream I choose to earn those monthly wages in some line of work that doesn't depend on cannibalizing my life and experiences. Alongside my work, I can be a whole person, an appealing thought; my work does not shape my whole being, I exist without manifesting my existence through writing, I do not share myself with writing that is ever present and never finished, that exhausts me and makes sleep a struggle at best – body wants to rest, mind shakes it awake, get up, flesh, make haste, the words are on their way.

When I awake from that dependable dream of security, I am always relieved. From an objective point of view, it makes no sense, I know, but I can't make concessions. Quitting my writing would be the worst possible failure, a crushing disappointment, a fatal shift in perspective.

*

I leave Let's Wingette! and walk back down Cross Key Road to the woods, back the way I came, towards the entrance to Pine Valley. The pines make room for my retreat and then link arms again behind me. How long can you keep fighting failure? At what stage does dogged resistance descend into farce?

*

In the end, the Pine Valley Golf Course was known as "Crump's Folly." Crump was not an architect by training. He had been introduced to the profession by his uncle John, who had built the Colonnade Hotel, and he'd picked up a little knowledge, but to build the golf course of his dreams, he needed to learn more.

After selling the hotel, Crump went on a study trip to Europe in 1910. For three months, he studied golf courses in France, Switzerland, Austria and Italy and took a special interest in landscape architecture in England and Scotland. On his return, he called a meeting of the Philadelphia Ballsome to lay out his plans. An all-season facility. A masterpiece of golf architecture. A high-stakes wager, considering the wilderness where he planned to build the course. If he succeeded, it would be a paradise, a valley of dreams.

Like Virginia Sumner, his friends were easily persuadable of his genius. When Crump described his plan to build the world's most challenging golf course in Pine Valley, her icy eyes glittered, and she sold him the land.

In the place where the clubhouse stands today, he pitched a simple tent. For the first two weeks, he lived there under the open sky like a hermit. He studied the land and the soil, made calculations, divided the surface into eighteen holes. Now and then his friends came out to see him, but most of the time he wandered alone among the conifers. He got to know the landscape – its enchantments and its snares – and he investigated its quirks.

He very soon realized how stubborn the soil could be. Large areas of trees and undergrowth had to be uprooted to make room for the holes. Crump used sticks of dynamite, but the explosions barely ruffled the deep-rooted pitch pines, and the sandy ground easily muffled the shocks.

He switched to pulling up the roots with steam-powered winches. An army of men, horses and machines went to work on the site, with the goal of removing some 22,000 tree stumps. Part of the site was marshland that had to be drained. In other places, the land had to be raised into artificial mounds for bunkers and other hazards. It must have seemed insane at a time when golf courses were built without moving the earth.

By March 1913, these earthworks were largely completed. The course was starting to take shape; the first seven holes were under construction. With spring on the way, it was time to sow the first grass seeds. Crump had learned from his research how unyielding the sugar sand of Pine Valley could be; that acidic earth repelled even weeds, let alone the smooth green lawns he required for his picturesque fairways. After experimenting with several varieties of grass in various test soils, he selected rich peat from the Netherlands, which he imported by the shipload. In Pine Valley, he mixed the imported peat with sludge scooped from the bottoms of the ponds. He spread the mixture over the sand to form a fresh layer of soil in all the areas where he planned to build greens and fairways. He seeded this peat with red fescue grass and closely supervised the fertilizing. Every grass seed passed through his hands. Every bit of greenery served the overall design. He wanted the course to look as if it had sprouted naturally from the barren soil, in defiance of all nature's laws, as if it had always been there, ordained to remain there until the end of time.

*

Crump's philosophy of golf course design demands a mental toughness from the players. To master the course, the player needs not so much talent as deep inner resolve. The design cunningly makes this point by exacting a high price for each mediocre stroke; a momentary lapse will land your ball in a deep bunker, a sandbank, or a water hazard. To escape these sudden-death obstacles, you must take risks and, above all, keep a cool head. Crump saw golf players as men whose greatest virtue was self-control. His favorite story was about an unflappable player from Philadelphia who, while executing the perfect stroke, had the bad luck to find himself right underneath a hot-air balloon with leaky sandbags. The sand dropped out of the sky straight onto his bent neck. God knows how, but he completed his stroke. Only after he'd seen where the ball had landed did he look up to find out what was falling on him and where in the blue blazes it was coming from.

In May 1913, Crump persuaded the well-known British landscape architect H. S. Colt to come overseas for a visit to Pine Valley. Colt was a living legend in those days, a pioneer who had turned golf course design into landscape art, and into a science. Crump was not too proud to ask for advice; he believed Colt's professional experience could not fail to elevate his design to a higher level. Nor was Crump thinking of his reputation; he was happy for Colt to rake in all the credit he deserved. Besides, there was a little problem with the grass.

The experiment with the Dutch peat and the red fescue had not worked out quite as Crump had hoped. Colt had ties to Carter's Seed Company, a first-rate British grass dealer that had established a foothold in the American market. With Colt on board, Crump could easily cut a deal with Carter's for his seed.

When Colt laid eyes on Pine Valley, he could hardly believe it: such perfect conditions, so close to the drab landscape around Philadelphia. The site was a leftover pocket of Eden, blessed by God, sublime in its union of contraries: its unruly beauty, its brook-riddled barrenness. Colt had nothing but praise for Crump's attention to detail; it really looked not as if a golf course was being built among the conifers, but as if the course had always existed and the trees had been planted around it. And that was not all. Colt believed Pine Valley might just have the potential to become the most challenging golf course in the world.

Colt made a few suggestions for routing the holes, which Crump took to heart and adopted in his design. Their only disagreement was philosophical. Colt agreed that the course should be "severe" for "the first-class player," but felt it should also show sympathy for "the weak." This is the one point on which Crump refused to compromise; Pine Valley was to be a brutal test of nerve and endurance, not a walk in the park.

To make this absolutely clear, he is said to have hung a sign above the entrance gate with Dante's infernal warning: "Abandon hope all ye who enter here."

Crump put Colt's advice into practice with zeal. This delayed the work somewhat, and the first holes were not reseeded until September. A new contractor installed an advanced irrigation system, in the hope that this one would be up to the job of keeping the grass green.

*

Meanwhile, Crump had a bungalow built for his own use near the fifth hole. He stayed in that humble cottage through both summer and winter. Every evening, he sat next to the small coal stove, going over his diagrams and calculations by the light of an oil lamp. His friends could hardly wait for the golf course to open. In the meantime, they paid fewer and fewer visits.

In the spring of 1914, a representative of Carter's Seeds inspected the turf. Crump had already spent $45,000 on the lawns; he was told another $25,000 would be needed. Otherwise, the whole round of seeding would go to waste.

These emergency measures by Carter's Seeds set the whole plan back again. Still, the sponsors and the players were unconcerned. The news that the opening would be delayed was accompanied by the first eyewitness reports. Crump had invited a few close friends to preview some of his holes. The lucky few who were the first to play in Pine Valley all agreed: "The world's greatest golf course – if grass will grow."

A year later, close to the planned opening date in March 1915, the work on the final holes ran into further delays. When a patch of woodland was cleared, the ideal terrain was revealed for the thirteenth hole. Crump decided to alter the course to take full advantage of this natural treasure. As the project neared completion, his perfectionism was coming to the surface. More and more often, he saw only what could be better instead of what was right in front of him.

In October 1915, Crump met with a huge setback. Despite his investments in the Carter's Seeds method, the grass died for the third time. The green looked like a teenage boy's stubble, a sparse coating with bare patches everywhere. The problem was simple: the ground was too acidic. The entire lawn was in need of replacement. Thanks to the heroic effort Crump had put into import and irrigation, he had succeeded in planting grass, but he could not make it flourish on the sandy ground. Each time, the early signs were promising – the seed germinated and formed a cover, though a thin one. But the first heavy rainfall would wash away much of the grass, because of the sugar sand below.

Again and again, Crump refertilized and reseeded. The costs were astronomical; he spent $200,000 on compost and manure. The money he'd made by selling his shares in the Colonnade was almost gone, but if that meant the grass would someday grow, it was worth it to him. There had to be a way. After all, the initial results were always so encouraging!

But there was a fundamental problem. Constant fertilization was providing the grass with all the nutrients it needed close to the surface. That made the roots lazy, so they never burrowed down through the sand to deeper sources of water and nourishment.

When the hot summer of 1915 arrived, the grass didn't have a chance. The whole field turned brown. In the autumn, nothing of the lawn could be saved.

Crump, in his desperation, threw still more money at the problem. The grass guru Robert Bender inspected the turf and advised that all the dead grass be removed once again. There was nothing for it, he said, but to replant the whole course. For the entire winter, Pine Valley was slathered with tons and tons of manure. When the wind blew in the wrong direction, they could smell it in Clementon.

In February 1916, it looked as though, against all odds, the grass had taken root. It was germinating, greener than ever before.

The ground is learning, thought Crump, triumphant.

*

From the spring of 1916 onwards, there were no more newspaper articles about the progress or otherwise of the work on the final holes, and not a word about the expected opening date. That's not so strange, since America's entry into the First World War provided plenty of material for newspaper columns.

When the silence surrounding Pine Valley stretched on into 1917, it was widely suspected that the grass was still causing trouble, and that the time had come for Crump to face the facts.

On January 24, 1918, the silence was broken by a shot. That morning, Crump was found dead in his house. The coroner reported a "Gunshot wound, Head."

The *Philadelphia Inquirer* announced that Crump had died of toothache. According to the newspaper, a large abscess in his mouth had put pressure on his brain, and that condition had led to his death. The reporter observed that a man with a powerful death wish is very likely to choose a method that is fatal and, above all, cannot be discovered in advance.

*

I must have walked for hours by the time I arrive at the parking lot and the gate. My legs are heavy and I have a gritty thirst in my throat. I'd swear that path was much shorter in the other direction, two kilometers at most. As far as I know, I didn't wander off it. The path is straight. The pitch pines are playing dumb, but I'm almost certain they have a hand in this, they tangle up time in their needles. Just look at them huddled together in threes, as if whispering secrets.

Now that the gate has re-emerged from the woods, the entrance is also in sight. I feel like grabbing the bars and rattling the gate, ramming the car into it, or maybe just climbing over it in plain sight. If I run fast enough when I land, who knows how far into the grounds I'll get. And if the misogynist gatekeeper catches me, who cares? I'm so close. I can't let this gate stop me.

As I gather my courage and survey my options for storming it, I am struck by the undeniable truth that this gate is so much more than a physical boundary separating me from what I hope lies beyond it. Even if I make it past the gate, there is still the utter powerlessness to capture human existence in a fundamental way; in that sense, you might just as well say that the fence is inside me, imprisoning me in my ambition to find the one complete story that will bring everything to life. I am doomed from the start. I am failing at every turn. What do any of these architects have to gain, at this late stage, from a "narrative context"? The very thing that the act of suicide forever amputates. What do I hope to find inside that gate that might redeem George Crump? He died just like the rest of them, hopeless and alone with his failure and his self-judgment, with his inability to achieve something magnificent, after all those years that his work, his creation, had lied to him so persuasively, saying he could do it, telling him he wasn't a fool to want to make something that touches on everything.

XII

CRANDALL'S KNICKERBOCKER THEATRE (1917–1922), WASHINGTON, DC

REGINALD WYCLIFFE GEARE (1889–1927)

Two evenings a week, Dr. Joseph Elward makes house calls. He is out tonight in spite of the storm. One of his regular patients, the young widow Mrs. Wilson at 1704 V Street NW, has a bad case of bronchitis that cannot go untreated. Under normal conditions, the walk from his suite at the Northumberland Apartments takes five minutes at most, but tonight he sinks into the heavy snow with every step and arrives fifteen minutes late. According to the latest measurements, the city is covered in around two feet of snow. The whole street has been whitewashed. It hasn't stopped since yesterday afternoon; more flakes keep falling, sharp stars of frost, hundreds of microscopic razor blades – the snow feels like it's scratching out his eyes.

"My God, doctor, your pants are soaking wet!" Mrs. Wilson cries, standing in the doorway. He squeezes past her into the building. She makes to beat the snow off his pants, but he steps away in time. "You are strictly forbidden to stand in the draft, Mrs. Wilson. Go back upstairs now, please, and I shall follow."

In her two-room apartment the coal-fired furnace is belching out heat; the atmosphere is stifling. Without awaiting his instructions, Mrs. Wilson unbuttons her woolen pinafore dress and the blouse underneath, revealing her bustier. Under the wet fabric of his trousers, he feels his skin stretching, so cold it burns.

He produces his stethoscope from his medical bag and listens to her lungs. When she inhales, he hears a rattle in her chest like rosary beads and a wheeze rising out above it. Things are clearly getting worse. "Are you coughing up blood, Mrs. Wilson?"

Before she has time to admit it, he hears the boom. The noise is overwhelming and difficult to place at first, as if it had several parts; in any case, the sound is so violent and inexplicable that he cannot take in its full impact. The mighty quake of the first boom is soon followed by a series of smaller tremors, which trail out in turn into sharper sounds, yet still heavy, like clumsy shards, stone rattling into rubble.

Dr. Elward grabs his medical bag from the floor. Instinctively, he starts running towards the noise, down Mrs. Wilson's stairs, out of the front door, to the left, all the way down the street, then another left, and now through the tumult he can hear the screaming, still far away – not cries for help, but the kind of screams Dr. Elward remembers from Europe, from the field hospitals of the Great War, the screams beyond helping, the yearning and pleading for death. There is so much noise, such a great deal of resistance for him to plough through, that he's hardly aware of pushing through the thick snow; the screaming comes at him like a solid wall of sound.

At the junction of Kalorama Road and 18th Street, he runs into the first crowd of onlookers. Before Dr. Elward has time to ask what happened, he spots a boy, half-conscious, losing his footing on the slippery surface and collapsing. His right arm is missing.

"I'm a doctor! I'm a doctor!" Elward shouts as he runs to the boy in the middle of the road. He is shouting so loud; passing tires have packed down the snow and half-melted it; in the slush, the blood is spreading fast. Dr. Elward slips, his stethoscope swinging around his neck like a noose snipped open.

Mrs. Wilson in her bustier in the stifling hot room flits invol-
untarily through his mind.

"Hold still, son. I'm a doctor. I'll bandage the wound."
Elward tears a strip from the lining of his coat and wraps it
around the demolished shoulder blade.

"My God, doc, you're cutting my arm off, please, don't cut
my arm off," the boy moans; his eyeballs roll back in their sock-
ets, but he remains conscious. He must have left his right arm
in the place he was running away from, but the whole street is
dark and heaped with snow, and Dr. Elward has learned to turn
off his imagination in situations like this, so he does not picture
the place where the boy's arm may lie or what must have happened there. It's a little after nine, and he has to stanch the
bleeding in the spot he can work with, the spot where the
right arm is missing; that's all Dr. Elward needs to know.

In the moments that follow, the 18th Street junction fills
with vehicles. Help has arrived. Firemen and police officers
march down Columbia Road, instructing the bystanders to
follow them to the Knickerbocker Theatre. A priest identifies
himself and leads the way. Still that ceaseless screaming, now
coalescing into words.

"My wife's in there."

"What happened here, officer?"

"Sweet Jesus, thousands of people must have been crushed!"

Dr. Elward leaves the boy behind with an ambulance man
and rushes after the astonished bystanders and emergency
workers, into the dark street, through the drifts of snow and the
shower of razors on that calamitous night of January 28, 1922.

*

In the late afternoon of Friday January 27, 1922, a meteoro-
logical fluke six miles off the ground leads to the start of the

snowfall in Washington, DC. It's a kind of atmospheric traffic jam. Polar winds from a high-pressure area over Greenland are caught in the jet stream that leads to the northeastern states. A current of frosty air is drawn down from the Arctic through a depression and reaches the East Coast. Snow falls from Rhode Island to Cape Hatteras, and skates and sleds are hauled out of storage. The DC weathermen warn that this enthusiasm is premature; they don't expect the snow to stay on the ground.

But it snows all night. By the morning of January 28, Washington is submerged in eighteen inches of snow, and it keeps falling. The whole city is paralyzed. Between Virginia and DC, nine trains have to be evacuated. Trams grind to a halt on their rails. Drivers abandon their cars in the middle of the road. The only way of getting around is on foot, and even that is not without its risks; in the middle of the snow-covered field in front of the Smithsonian Castle, a man sinks to his waist and sincerely believes he may go under. It takes two firemen to calm him down; each gripping one arm, they steer him out of the snowy sea. One hundred and fifty extra street sweepers are assigned to each district. Dozens of snowplows take to the streets, until they too are stranded. Most shops take a snow day; a few small stores soldier on, like Mr. Bernard Nordlinger at the men's apparel store on M Street, who hires four of his nephews to keep the sidewalk clear; the boys shovel without stopping, a Sisyphean task as the snow keeps falling with renewed intensity. According to the meteorologists, it is piling up at a rate of one inch per hour.

Four p.m. The snow reaches a depth of two feet, and the mood shifts. What was a hassle at first now has the glamour of a record, of novelty: it has snowed for twenty-four hours straight. The abandoned vehicles, the stranded travelers and the helpless slipping give way to epic snowball fights. One dauntless woman begins to dig out her car. A shy fellow in his twenties tosses the object of his silent adoration over his shoulder, lifts her high above the snow, and carries her across the street. Photographers seize the opportunity, taking historic winter scenes of the White House, the Capitol and the Treasury Building, destined to become archival images in our day.

A scattered few city-dwellers close their curtains and count the cans of food in the pantry. A few others whisper of an apocalypse. One woman nods off for a few minutes and dreams that the snow has risen to her ninth-floor window. Flinching awake, she thinks, *I dreamed of death.* Every half hour the radio provides updates on the weather situation and tips for keeping safe. The frail and the elderly heed the advice to remain indoors. The Potomac lies motionless under a thick layer of ice.

Just like that, in a single night, the world is buried. Snow lies over DC like an unmoving shroud. Things lose their definition. Under it could be a skyscraper, or the towering trunk of some gigantic tree, but in fact it hardly matters anymore what lies beneath the snow. White itself has taken a form. This white new world has new laws and different meanings. Maybe this used to be Mr. Robertson's town car; now it has changed into a fort for several neighborhood children. Taking a step no longer simply means putting one foot in front of the other, but sinking it into the depths of the piled snow. Time becomes flat, and cheap, since the economy is more or less at a standstill. People resign themselves to the constant feel of a sodden overcoat.

At 8:00 p.m. on January 28, twenty-eight inches of snow are measured, and the flakes are still coming down. The overwhelming volume and uninterrupted fall make the snow seem somehow deathless; from now on, the world will always look like this, redrawn, wiped blank.

Amid this confusion, the inhabitants of Washington do their best to recreate their old lives under the new ministry of frost. On Saturday evening, a few cabbies – full of chutzpah, all confident they're the city's best drivers – decide it's time to venture out again into the snow-packed streets. It's a good night for business; more than a few pioneering spirits are already braving that snowbound, spellbound world in search of nightlife – after all, it's a Saturday.

Some cinemas decide to go ahead with their scheduled showings. At the Knickerbocker, it's comedy night, the most popular night of the week. Despite the storm, 300 of the 1,700 seats are sold. The film is *Get-Rich-Quick Wallingford*, a light-hearted caper. Sam Hardy – who will later perform in the first King Kong movie in 1933 – and Norman Kerry play two convicted con men, Wallingford and Chester. Disguised as businessmen looking for investors, they raise money from the residents of a small village to set up a carpet tack factory. The villagers soon smell a rat, but Wallingford is a professional and calms them down with reassuring lies – until someone appears out of nowhere and tries to buy the factory . . .

A wave of anticipation and laughter rolls through the theater, just before Wallingford sits on a tack, yelps, and grabs his rear end. It's a little after nine. Outside, gusts of snow are ripping the darkness to shreds; through the whirl of white the neon letters burn.

CRANDALL'S KNICKERBOCKER THEATRE

The blizzard has now been going on for twenty-nine hours without pause. In that time, a two-foot layer of snow has accumulated on the roof, weighing 14 pounds per square foot. The snowflakes on the roof have a cumulative weight of close to 8 tons. A single snowflake's crystalline structure is too fragile, in most cases, to reach the ground intact, but the accumulated mass is enough to collapse the steel truss roof, some sections of which weigh around 2,000 kilograms, and others more than 10,000 kilograms. The mass of steel and stone and snow comes crashing down in one piece, the entire area, as if someone had cut out the roof along the edges. The balcony breaks the fall for a mere instant before the collapsing weight drags it down too.

"A hearty peal of laughter" and then "a roar, mighty as the crack of doom," one survivor later recalled for the newspaper. He said he wished the merciless roar had left a little scope for human resistance, however feeble. But it meant nothing to the stone and steel that bones were wrenched out of their flesh. The patrons did not have the ghost of a chance.

*

The painting *Cupid Complaining to Venus*, made by Lucas Cranach the Elder in 1526–7, contains an alarming anamorphosis. Casting a quick eye over it, we note that Cupid's nude, squat, childish form wears the face of Donald Trump. Beside him is Venus, dressed in nothing but an ostentatious hat, with the branches of a richly laden fruit tree winding over her palm and between her feet. The two figures stand in the foreground of the painting, in a rural setting at the edge of a dark forest. The tree, which bears peach-like fruit, forms a dividing line in the landscape, which opens out into a distant background of water and a rock formation. Half-dark, half-light.

The scene Cranach painted comes from Theocritus's *Idylls*, in which the little god Cupid is tormented by bees. Whimpering, he runs to his mother, Venus: "They're stinging me! It hurts so much!"

To Venus, the incident does not come as a complete surprise. After all, Cupid is still holding the honeycomb, his mouth still sticky with freshly stolen honey. Yet instead of just telling him it's his own fault, she uses this formative moment to explain to Cupid that love always has two sides: "Sometimes it's sweet, sometimes devastating."

"But how can something as tiny as a bee's sting cause me so much pain?" Cupid asks – a naive, perhaps hypocritical question.

"You're just a tiny little thing yourself, but your arrows cause much greater pain," Venus reassures him. Violence can always be outdone by greater violence. Power goes to the highest bidder. Just what the little tyrant wanted to hear.

I saw the painting in the summer of 2016 at the National Gallery in London. The distortion of Cupid's face into Trump's was an optical illusion, a moment's distraction, a chance confusion of images.

I cannot rule out the possibility that Cupid was not my favorite mythological character at the time – I was going through an episode of heartache – and that I may therefore unconsciously, or even deliberately, have demonized him.

Yet at the time it felt like a sign. After Trump's election a few months later, as I spent days in a state of useless outrage, I thought back to the painting and the little Cupid, in a frantic search for the meaning behind the distortion.

*

It is January 2019; I'm in Washington, DC, and the United States government has shut down. Two years after Trump's inauguration, outrage can no longer keep pace with political events. The government has been shut down for a few weeks now. President Trump has loosed his arrows, putting a stop to the business of governance to push his plans for a grotesque, dystopian wall, and the Democrats won't have it. He's determined to go on whimpering despotically about the injustice of it all on every news broadcast until he gets his way. On the TV screen, his mouth dripping with stolen honey, he does not hesitate to blame the bees: *For five billion dollars, the wall will stop illegal aliens from crossing our southern border and at the same time keep our economy great and protect our country from the terrible drug flow. Jobs numbers will be better than ever for Americans, especially my people and the people that support me. The wall will pay for itself many times over, because Mexicans want to steal American jobs and suck drugs and death right into the United States. If we'd had the wall earlier, El Chapo and the whole Sinaloa cartel would never have come through our border.* Or words to that effect . . .

Taxi drivers prowl DC's empty streets like predators. Because of the shutdown, there are few if any businessmen, members of Congress, or journalists in need of rides. Any pedestrian is a potential target. If you stand still, or stray too close to the edge of the sidewalk, you might be whisked into a taxi and forced to come up with a destination, preferably one on the far side of town that will really run up the meter.

I am at the corner of 3rd Street and Pennsylvania Avenue, in the lion's den, unmistakably a tourist, with the Capitol to my right and the National Mall stretching more than a mile to my left. There is literally no one else out in the streets. The city's broad avenues are deserted, only a few joggers have ventured out on the National Mall, the Smithsonian Museums have shut their doors, and the Capitol Visitor Center is closed.

I wonder if I will ever in my life be so alone – so overwhelmingly, Spielberg-apocalypse-movie alone – with . . . the Eiffel Tower, say? Monumental buildings on this scale are not designed to be experienced by individuals. They require a crowd: passersby, visitors, patrons, travelers, enthusiasts – one way or another, they demand the collective gaze, which confirms that they are part of a shared space. The fact of my aloneness with these buildings overwhelms me.

The taxis are coming on strong, but I have a date with Georgia and her gray Escort. Like so many government employees going into their third week without income, Georgia is trying her luck as an Uber driver. No sooner am I in the car than she starts to explain that this is the American way: self-reliance, surviving and thriving without handouts from anyone. You just pick yourself up, dust yourself off, and get back on your own two feet. Her catering company, which works for Congress, hasn't had any work in three and a half weeks, so she's turned to Uber. The bills won't pay themselves, and she has three growing boys to feed. In the rearview mirror, I can see her game face. She drops me off in the Adams Morgan neighborhood, where 18th Street and Columbia Road meet at the tip of an isosceles triangle. This was the location of Harry Crandall's Knickerbocker Theatre, named after the contractor and businessman Harry Crandall and designed by the young architect Reginald Wycliffe Geare. Now it's the site of a branch of SunTrust Bank, a reserved brown brick building shaped like a typewriter. Georgia asks me not to forget to give her a five-star review.

*

Reginald Geare is twenty-eight in 1917, when he completes the Knickerbocker Theatre. This palatial cinema, made out of Indiana limestone, forms a turning point in his early career. No expense, no effort has been spared. Harry Crandall bought the land for $60,000. The construction costs, as calculated by Geare, are $150,000, a fortune in those days and a fabulous risk. But they expect the building to pay for itself many times over.

In 1910, after a few failed investments in casinos, Harry Crandall turned his sights to the film industry. He had a feeling that was where it would all happen, and he knew he had to take that feeling seriously. After all, didn't he see them everywhere he looked: the bank directors, the stockbrokers, the Congressmen, the wealthy heirs, all with the same fat wallets and the same utter lack of imagination when it came to spending their money, all caught in the same rat race, all chained to their bourgeois comforts, minions of greed, all seeking distraction from the terrible awareness of their own predicament, from the play of shadows in their stifling caves, all yearning for fictional worlds, vaudeville, picture shows, doe-eyed young actresses, concerts, red carpets, the whole shebang?

Yes, Henry Crandall saw them. He saw that the rich, just like their lower-class compatriots, wanted to be dazzled by glamour, commerce and escapism. He saw that they were not in fact searching for intellectual stimulation; what they were really looking for was a good time. He saw the First World War shifting the center of the film industry from Europe to America. He saw the success of the Hollywood formula and its mass reproducibility. He saw the border disintegrating between low and high culture. Harry Crandall saw it all. The only job left for him was to give all those new dreams the sanctuary that they deserved.

Not by chance, his first cinema, built in 1916, was at 437–439 9th Street, in the heart of Washington's business district. His foresight did not let him down. The five o'clock showing sold out every time, and most of the seats were occupied by men in three-piece suits, slumped back in the plush seats, their waistcoats unbuttoned. Crandall's success propelled him to the status of movie mogul. It would have been bad business not to consider expanding immediately. It was time to open a major cinema downtown – ah, what the hell, a major cinema in *every* part of town. It took Crandall only a few months to make enough profit to pay for this expansion. He bought the Savoy

Theatre on 14th Street, a building in the stately traditional Colonial Revival style. Eight weeks and a few thousand dollars later, he'd transformed that brick box into a Beaux Arts palace with a balcony, which doubled the number of seats. He also made the lobby substantially larger. Its spacious interior, adorned with green marble columns, offered a grand entrance into the building. He transformed the theater itself into a gold, pink and ivory boudoir. Grandeur for the masses. Low culture in an opulent palace with operatic appeal. Luxury enough for the captains of industry, and a backdrop for the dreams of less prosperous visitors.

Crandall turned this formula into a strategy to dominate the market. The crucial idea came from the young architect Reginald Wycliffe Geare, who had renovated the Apollo Civic Theatre in Martinsburg for him. A recent graduate of George Washington University, Geare had just completed further training in draftsmanship. Seeing the gloomy façade of the Apollo Civic, he pictured a lavish interior in light blue velvet with golden decorations for contrast, like a jewelry case in a charming contessa's bedchamber. Crandall saw brick transmuted into gold.

*

In November 1915, six months after the reopening of the Apollo Civic, Geare placed the Knickerbocker blueprints on Crandall's desk. If Crandall's earliest movie theaters had been palaces, the Knickerbocker would be a temple, a profane altar, designed to really make the fat cats reach for their wallets.

Coming down Columbia Road, you could see the neon letters out in the square: Crandall's Knickerbocker Theatre. The entrance was just round the corner, on 18th Street, under a concrete canopy with an illuminated sign announcing the showings. The floor was marble, the chandeliers crystal. A high-end sweet shop. There was a refreshment parlor on the ground floor and a balcony tearoom, so that patrons could prolong the experience before and after the movie. The cinema had a capacity of 1,700 and narrowed as it approached the stage; the acoustics were out of this world. Built-in Typhoon fans treated patrons to the caress of a gentle breeze on a summer evening drive with the top down. Even the smallest details oozed luxury; the chairs in the orchestra pit were upholstered in silk.

Meanwhile, the newspapers were keeping close track of Crandall's investments. The Knickerbocker's grand opening on October 13, 1917 was a memorable event, thanks in part to the movie stars hired by Crandall. He screened the romantic drama *Betsy Ross*, whose patriotic title character was said to have sewn the first American flag. Alice Brady, who played Betsy, graced the opening with her presence, accompanied by her beau of the hour, Carlyle Blackman. All 1,700 seats were sold out.

The next morning, the reviewers dubbed Reginald Geare the "architect of the silent film era." His career took off. Crandall and his golden boy Geare would work together on several other theaters, including the Metropolitan, the York and the Lincoln. At the height of his empire, Crandall owned no fewer than eighteen profitable theaters in D C and Virginia.

It is not improbable that on this very first night the steel trusses supporting the Knickerbocker's roof began their slow sag, which – combined with the mass of the snow four years later – would cause the fatal accident.

*

I knew beforehand that the Knickerbocker no longer existed. Yet its absence leaves more of a gap than I'd expected. After the rich architectural history of this site, the bank that stands there today forms a dismal coda. Since the 1970s, this uninspired structure has bricked over the stormy past of the location where it stands. The front has an indentation that looks vaguely like a stage, but it would strain the imagination to call that a historical allusion.

A year after the collapse in 1923, a new theater was built on the site of the Knickerbocker: the Ambassador, which did good business for decades. In the late 1960s, the cinema became a mecca for the hippie movement. Jimi Hendrix gave his first, legendary Washington concert there in 1967. Barely two years later, the owners were required to have it demolished. The site fell into the hands of a developer who sold the land to Sun-Trust Bank, and the square in front of the theater was renamed SunTrust Plaza. Today, 18th Street is the artery of the yuppie neighborhood Adams Morgan, home to a string of international eateries: an Italian restaurant, a McDonald's, Songbyrd Music House and Record Café, a barbecue joint, a pizzeria, a Swedish coffeehouse, a ramen bar, Turkish and Indian places, a Korean hole-in-the-wall doubling as a tattoo parlor, a falafel shop, a display of vintage clothing and another pizzeria.

*

Tucked away among these 18th Street restaurants, near the former site of the Knickerbocker, is the Idle Times bookstore: two floors and a landing stacked high with secondhand books. Every shelf lures you in with the promise of rare editions. The books give off the distinct sour whiff of old paper. At a bookcase in the remotest corner of the upper level, I scan the spines. On the topmost shelf, a brown strip of masking tape announces in felt tip, NON-FICTION. I seek out John McPhee for a consultation. My hope is to learn from him how to be less present in the book I'm trying to write. McPhee writes narrative nonfiction; he's the narrator, main character and camera, all in one, but never omniscient or radically documentary, and he's anything but a runaway extra blocking the view of his own subject matter. McPhee never shows the slightest inclination to put himself in the spotlight. He's more like some kind of disembodied voice. With apparent effortlessness he conveys a sense of himself as a flesh-and-blood man rooted both in his books and in the real world. He lends you his eyes and his mind, observes the object of his writing, absorbs the experience, and somehow expresses it as a set of irresistible conclusions. And all this with a bare minimum of narrative intervention. I pay $8.99 for *Oranges*, McPhee's "classic of reportage" about the titular fruit, and $12.99 for the complete works of Anne Sexton.

*

When Reggie Geare arrived at the Knickerbocker that fateful night, he reacted by warding off the image of the horror that had taken place there, as if his nervous system was trying to protect him from the police barricade, the stretchers, the mangled bodies, the shovelers like gravediggers clearing away the snow, the pickaxes and crowbars relentlessly attacking wood and stone, forcing their way in, the sirens, the shouts of the assembled crowd. In the midst of it all he saw the four walls of his building, still standing. What in the name of God could have happened when the walls were still standing, reaching up to heaven for a mercy forever denied him the moment his body registered the shock: the walls bore no roof.

Half-crazed, he pushed his way through the barricade to join the team of rescue workers. He knew that building inside and out. He had two arms.

But manpower alone was not enough. They needed machines: derricks, cranes and hydraulic jacks, crucial in the attempt to remove the debris as carefully as possible. Until late the next afternoon, they still cherished the hope of finding survivors among the crushed corpses and the terrible weight of the rubble.

*

In *The Last Poet*, a twenty-minute video essay by the American visual artist David Hartt, the camera explores an ill-defined neighborhood along the edge of a nameless East Coast city. A fleet of trucks. A wrecking yard. An aluminium telephone booth with no phone or receiver. A church. White plastic lawn chairs. A breath of wind. Row on row of identical prefab houses. A green shoot breaks through stone tiles. Someone runs across the street to catch a bus. The bridge in the distance is under construction. The river flowing under the bridge is a gray shade of brown. Over these images, Francis Fukuyama's voice says, "This deep historical sense where you want to preserve old things, ruins, we haven't gotten there. Americans still want to start all over again."

*

After the First World War Europe lies in ruins, but in the United States the 1920s bring an economic boom. A foreign policy of isolationism keeps other people's problems at bay, while the domestic market rides the new wave of capitalist fervor. Mass production causes an exponential leap in economic activity, which brings new prosperity – Ford Model Ts for everyone. This fever dream of wealth creates opportunities for personal development, though only for the middle and upper classes, and mainly for white Americans. In this climate, optimism spreads like an infectious disease, and Reggie Geare, like so many other Americans, sees life as a journey towards personal happiness and fulfilment.

Around the time of his first architectural triumph, he marries the gorgeous Dorothy Smallwood in St. Margaret's Episcopal Church in DC. In attendance are three bridesmaids: Marie Tunstall, Marguerite Weller and Lela Howard, all green with envy. Any one of them would stab her friend in the back without batting an eyelid if she thought she could steal away the young architect. He glitters with promise, youthful audacity and the mysterious, unfathomable aura of the artist.

A few years later, when Marie, Marguerite and Lela each receive the same phone call from their friend Dorothy, they are grateful, once the initial shock has passed, that it is not their husband who has all those deaths on his conscience.

*

At some point on January 29, 1922, it must have stopped snowing. Some time in the days that followed, it started to thaw. But none of that made any impression on Reggie Geare. After the collapse, he did not leave home for a week. He did not speak to anyone, not even his wife. He did not dress for work again until he was summoned to the hearing in the District Building. Eyewitnesses said he was as pale as death and his eyes had a haunted, stricken look.

He was questioned for eight days. Geare did not even presume his own innocence; he was as driven as the coroner's jury to find out what had happened and became an active, constructive participant in the inquest. He revisited every decision, redrew the plans and then redrew them again to make sure. Night after night, he rebuilt the theater from the ground up, stone by stone. What was he overlooking? Where did he go wrong? In his defence, he could not find the answer.

The exhausting examinations took a physical toll; he slouched farther and farther into the witness box. He could feel himself breaking.

Once Clyde Gearhart, Caroline Upshaw and Edward Williams were no longer in critical condition, the official death count was ninety-five. Hundreds of other people were severely wounded, many mutilated for life because of their night at the movies.

The jury concluded the victims had died as a direct result of faulty building design that could have been prevented by the architect. Reginald Geare was indicted for manslaughter. Even though he was never convicted, the charge was enough of a judgment. The public, and history, held him responsible.

*

There is every indication that one day failure will be obsolete. The whole Hegelian arc of human progress points in that direction. Each year there are new and improved techniques for becoming more intelligent, attractive, efficient, healthy, robust and generally long-lasting, for stretching beyond the limits of human existence. And yet. From minor mishaps, like the time I was so tired I dropped my cup of coffee and it smashed to pieces, to our inability to cure terminal illness, every form of failure calls the arc of progress into question. No wonder failure leads to existential anxiety; it casts doubt on the very way we move through time from past to future. And as usual, we try to soothe that anxiety with words. Learn from your mistakes. Fail forward. Lean in. What doesn't kill you makes you stronger. Apparently the only acceptable response to failure is to keep trying, harder than ever – to use the failure as a springboard to future success. Failure is fertile soil for new accomplishments.

Sometimes the days seem like a succession of goals, stepping stones on the road to fulfilment. Washing up is an achievement; writing a thousand words is an achievement; and just making it out of bed is an achievement in itself, because it means I'm accepting the challenge of the day, and after that day the next – that I'm leading my life in the right direction, with forward-moving energy.

Failure contradicts that current, giving an unpleasant push in the opposite direction – backwards, towards nonexistence. It is a trapdoor into the underlying void, a crack that reveals the hidden flaw. A terrifying sight.

Maybe it's a matter of perspective: if failure points towards nonexistence, then from life's perspective, death is the critical failure. From death's perspective, a failed life is the ultimate accomplishment. Not failing would mean the triumph of life, a victory over death. Maybe fulfilment and failure converge in suicide, in the very darkest way.

Of course, some philosophers, sociologists and psychologists say we are simply fundamentally imperfect creatures, groping and incomplete, that the chasm between who we are and who we dream of being is a gap that will always be present within us, and a good thing too, because that gap is the breeding ground of all ambitions. That gap contains the pursuits with which we keep ourselves standing.

For Reggie Geare, when the roof collapses, that gap is closed completely. No longer can he hope he will ever become something more than he already is: a fallible being whose fatal errors have cost many lives.

In the years that follow, he never recovers his inner drive. Not only must he learn to live with the deaths caused by his mistakes, but he is also in mourning for his own career: no one will work with him anymore. He is unable to reclaim any kind of professional status. His dream of building was crushed, along with the theater's audience, by that fallen roof. This is the truth that confronts Reggie Geare at the age of thirty-eight. At the same time, he sees the impossibility of changing fields. He remains an architect. Or do you have to do it in order to be it?

*

Geare dies in his home at 3047 Porter Street, just outside what is now the cosmopolitan Georgetown district of Northwest DC. He spends the day of his chosen death at the office. Five years after the collapse, he still goes in daily, even though no work awaits him. It keeps him going; as long as he has an office, he is an architect. Today, unlike most days, he knocks off early for a round of golf. He arrives home at the usual time, bearing a box of sweets for his wife, Dorothy. To her, Reggie seems relaxed, affectionate as always and out of reach, as he has been ever since that night.

After dinner he retires to the attic room where he has his office and a couch. When he stays up late drafting, he sometimes sleeps there so as not to wake Dorothy.

Although she hopes he will eventually pull himself together and find a different job, Dorothy does think it's brave of her husband to go on drafting. It's a fixed point in his personality, which gives her a sense of orientation, of recognizing the husband she used to have. That night she leaves him be. Reggie often tells her how grateful he is for the space she gives him. You can't rush these things, she tells herself; it's a lot for him to handle.

Before Reggie goes to sleep that night, he turns on the gas. The attic is anesthetized with coal gas, a cocktail of hydrogen, methane, ethylene, carbon monoxide and nitrogen. Asphyxiation is the gentlest of deaths. The lungs are still taking in air, so they don't squeeze shut in panic; it's just that the air has less and less oxygen in it; a thread in the chest stretches ever thinner until it breaks.

Only the next morning, when he doesn't show up at the breakfast table, does Dorothy start to feel uneasy. She knocks repeatedly on the door of his attic room, a little annoyed that she has to call him to the table like a child. And when on top of that he refuses to open the door, she curses him. She fumbles with the doorknob, kneels down to look through the keyhole, sees nothing – strange, there seems to be a piece of cloth stuffed into it – but before she can even think what that might mean, she catches a whiff of something. Gas. Although she doesn't yet know what he has done, she is in some primal way certain of it, because in a sense it's been going on for years. Dorothy rams the door down, bruising her right shoulder. Reggie is stretched out peacefully on the couch in his pyjamas. Dorothy shuts off the gas and tries to revive him, cursing even louder now. She calls an ambulance. The doctor arrives and pronounces him dead.

The medical examiner asks about warning signs. Dorothy replies that he was doing fairly well recently. Yes, he'd been worried about their financial situation, with no work coming in, but suicide? What does suicidal behavior look like? And how was she supposed to recognize it?

There was the recurring dream she would never know about, because Reggie had never told her. It was just too gruesome:

A boy, he can't be more than fifteen years old, is caught under a piece of rubble near the entrance to the theater. He came so close to escaping. The rubble has crushed everything from the waist down, leaving his upper body and head untouched. Despite his pain, the boy is not crying, not screaming, not groaning, not delirious. He is doing everything he can to help his rescuers. Blood runs from his dusty hair. Two doctors are administering first aid, while a dozen firemen are trying to lift the incredible weight from his lower body with hydraulic jacks.

"You are as courageous as any man in the trenches, my boy," says one of the doctors, who remembers from experience that courage in the trenches was always in spite of knowing you didn't have a chance.

At some point, the boy manages to sit up on his elbows. Ignoring his horrible, unimaginable pain, he props himself up to watch the rescue workers try to remove the weight. He is determined to make it out from under that weight. The boy in the dream is the same boy of which the *Washington Post* would write, the day after the collapse, "It was the American spirit intensified. It was the supreme splendor of the nation in the face of crisis. It was boyhood risen to man's estate."

Each night, the boy rises up on his elbows again in Reggie Geare's dream. Sometimes he lives through the dream from the boy's perspective, looking at the crushing weight on his lower body. Sometimes he is one of the rescuers, trying with all his might to lift the weight but never succeeding. He is never the doctor in the dream, who of course cannot save the boy either.

*

Harry Crandall is eventually crushed too, even though his initial response shows resilience. Soon after the collapse, he is advised to rebuild as soon as possible with a new architect. Crandall drops Geare and hires his rival, Thomas Lamb, who erects the Ambassador Theater in 1923, leaving the old cinema's surviving walls in place. While the new theater covers over the scars of the disaster, the trauma remains. The impact of what happened that January night will be felt for years to come. Crandall realizes he is as guilty as Geare in the eyes of the public. His glory days are behind him.

In 1927, he sells his empire to Warner Bros. Most of his cinematic palaces are now long gone. The Lincoln Theatre at 1215 U Street, one of Geare's designs, is still standing. It will later be registered as a historic site, but for its social rather than architectural significance; the Lincoln is the heart of Washington's "Black Broadway," built for African-American patrons barred from other theaters by racial segregation.

Fifteen years after the collapse, in 1937, Harry Crandall commits suicide. The former millionaire's estate consists of a diamond ring returned to him (value: $500), a wristwatch (value: $50), some clothing and furniture, and a few near-worthless shares. He leaves a note asking the newspapers that report his death not to be too hard on him. "Only it is I'm despondent," he writes, "and miss my theaters, oh so much."

*

In the days that followed the disaster, the building inspector's office was flooded with requests to look into the safety of homes and public buildings. Under the roofs of Washington, DC, the dominant mood was suddenly a very reasonable fear of collapse.

On January 31, 1922, the Bureau of Standards organized an investigating committee for the Knickerbocker. Officials took samples of the building materials and reviewed the safety regulations on the site. This investigation offered no consolation to the wounded or the families of the victims but performed the essential task of looking to the future. Its objective was not only to determine exactly what had happened and who should be held responsible, but also to contribute to the revision of the DC building code, which had proved to be quite out of date and no longer consistent with modern construction methods.

Alongside the official investigating committee, dozens of outside experts signed up to work on this catalogue of errors. They included Chicago's chief city architect and a representative of the American Society for Civil Engineers. The report on the investigation into the Knickerbocker disaster showed that there had, in fact, been a construction error: the main truss of the roof had come unseated at the north end, because of flaws in both its northernmost top gusset plate and the bottom chord where it rested on the wall.

The gusset plate, a half-inch thick, was the only source of lateral stiffness for the heavy top chord. The bottom chord rested directly on the wall without any reinforcement. Both were crushed and tilted by a combination of tension, compression and torsion.

The weight and pressure of the snow bent the main truss downwards. It had been designed to transfer most of the stress to the walls, but the trusses were not properly anchored to the walls. Furthermore, the cold, damp weather had made the walls expand, sliding away from under the roof. This outward movement of the walls and the downward bending of the trusses unanchored the roof.

The examination of Reggie Geare revealed that during construction, a last-minute switch had been made to lighter, cheaper material because the First World War had led to a shortage of steel, but also because the contractor, Crandall, thought the switch would speed up the building process. The architect agreed, but not before requesting approval from the Washington Building Department. Approval was granted, but it remained his responsibility to recalculate the load-bearing capacity. The responsibility for the error can be traced directly back to Geare, who succumbed to pressure from Crandall. On the other hand, the sheer weight of snow dropped by the snowstorm was exceptional. Could the architect really have anticipated that such a mass of snow might fall from the sky, let alone that the roof would have to bear it? In the fraught emotional aftermath of the collapse, there were even complaints that district employees had failed to clear the streets properly so that the emergency services could respond in time. If even the snow removers were held responsible, it is easy to imagine how much the public must have despised Geare.

After the investigation, the building code was revised, with a new emphasis on safety and prevention. A guiding principle was adopted that served as a warning to all architects and builders: "Safety first from foundation to capstone."

*

Near the Brookland metro station is the American Poetry Museum and Center for Poetic Thought, housed in a large industrial building with all sorts of start-ups. Through the museum's front window, which is really a display, I see an elderly man, slightly hunched, who beckons me inside. One look around and I've taken in the whole museum, a single small white gallery not much larger than my living room. On one wall hang four paintings. In the back are a modest bookcase and a microphone on a stand.

"Come in, but don't expect too much of me yet," the man says, after introducing himself as Reuben. "I'm still a tad bit undercaffeinated."

Then he sits back down at his laptop by the display window.

He reminds me a little of an animal in a zoo: the contemporary poet in his natural habitat, a small white room equipped with a MacBook, locked up behind glass. I think of Walter and his riddle about the museum guard and the empty room.

The paintings don't really speak to me, but as I run my eyes over the spines in the bookcase, I feel a thrill. Maybe they have a rare handwritten manuscript of John Ashbery's debut, or I can hold a first edition of William Carlos Williams's *Spring and All* in my own two hands, or study Elizabeth Bishop's diary entries, or leaf through the Pulitzer Prize–winning collected works of Wallace Stevens. But the collection does not live up to those expectations. It holds mainly themed anthologies and remaindered volumes.

"Do you like poetry?" I hear Reuben asking me.

I try to conceal my disappointment. "This isn't how I'd pictured America's national poetry museum."

"We scrape by. We're going through a downturn in the book market, especially for poetry. On a good night we draw an audience of twenty or thirty."

"It always seems to be a hard time for poetry," I quip.

Reuben says something sensitive about inner necessity and the transformative power of the poem. I respond with a speech about resonance, metrical violence and the will to live. We go on like that for a while, like two caricatures. Poets are great at finding phrases to express the importance of poetry; we get plenty of practice, since we constantly have to defend our line of work. Reuben stares at the ground as he searches for words, reinforcing the impression that he's dredging them up from some tender inner place. From similar discussions with other poets, I recall what this kind of conversation requires of me, and I do my best to deliver my lines with gusto. Neither of us seems especially passionate about the topic at the moment, but we owe it to our craft.

Reuben volunteers at the museum and is also the curator of the Smithsonian's Duke Ellington collection. Jazz is his life, but his first love – and you never forget your first, he adds – is poetry. In the 1990s, when he was still in college, his debut volume was a modest success. It opened the right doors and introduced him to the right people, but once the initial attention faded, he stopped.

"You should never write if you don't have anything to say. It took me almost thirty years before I had anything to put down on paper again. Now I'm getting old, and mortality is a rewarding theme," Reuben says with a hint of self-satisfaction.

"I admire you," I say, and hope it sounds as sincere as I intend it to be. Reuben had the courage to wait. That strikes me as the most honest thing an artist can do.

"Oh, well, my poems were never essential to my survival. If you're in inner crisis, you write a very different kind of poetry."

"Anne Sexton," I reply, but I could just as well name Sylvia Plath, Ingrid Jonker in South Africa, or Karin Boye in Sweden, or any one of the many whose poems could hardly save them. Each of those women poets left this world at a young age. I think of Anne Sexton's poem "Sylvia's Death," which she wrote when Plath died:

how did you crawl into,

crawl down alone
into the death I wanted so badly and for so long

the death we said we both outgrew,
the one we wore on our skinny breasts,

the one we talked of so often each time
we downed three extra dry martinis in Boston

As I make my way to Dulles Airport, it's snowing; it's been snowing since yesterday evening. Maybe it's because I'm not prepared for it, wasn't expecting snow until I reached the mountains of Colorado, or maybe it's because the Uber driver is focused, wordless, on the slippery road, and for a while there's nothing and no one to interrupt my thoughts, that I slowly become tangled up in them, or maybe it's the sky ahead, so dense and white, and the ground too, buried ever deeper, the cars, the highway, the guardrails, the road signs, the lamp posts, everything losing definition under the snow that is whiting out the world, and wasn't it Cioran who said, "To embrace a thing by a definition is to reject that thing, to render it insipid and superfluous, to annihilate it?"

Now everything is new, and it's clear in my mind that it makes so much more sense to leave all these stories untold, to wipe the whole thing blank. Already, in the white expanse through the car window, I can barely see a thing anymore, except for the road signs that flash past at intervals, orange letters screeching through the snowfall: "Caution."

XIII

KEMPF'S KINETIC SCULPTURE GARDEN (EST. 1978), COLORADO SPRINGS

STARR GIDEON KEMPF (1917–1995)

An FN Browning Challenger .22, manufactured in Belgium. Without waiting to be asked, Joshua Kempf lays the pistol with which his grandfather shot himself in the head in my hand.

This is the first time I've held a gun, and I feel like handing it back as quickly as possible, but since it obviously means a lot to Josh that he can show it to me, I let it rest there for a few admiring seconds. Tiny muscles in my hand contract; blood vessels open. I feel a burning desire not to be damaged.

"It was a clean shot." Josh lifts an illustrative hand to his left temple and cocks his head to the right. The shot propelled Starr Gideon Kempf's head into a piece of cardboard on the wall, smashing his skull and leaving a gory mess. Josh tells me he has that piece of blood-soaked cardboard lying around somewhere if I'd like to see it, but he'd have to hunt for it.

The Browning is more than just a keepsake. Josh and his ex-wife, the Hungarian one – well, actually, both his ex-wives are Hungarian – once took it out shooting. It's not really a powerful weapon, not special enough to justify the long trip to the shooting range, so they just strolled into the park across the road from the house and went partway up Cheyenne

Mountain. They tried it out for a while there, mostly on rocks, just to get a feel for how it handled.

*

The Kempf House is all the way at the top of Pine Grove Avenue in Colorado Springs. The street rises as it approaches Cheyenne Mountain. In the front yard are six kinetic bird sculptures several meters tall. When the wind blows, their wings and other parts rock, squeak and rotate into upward motion, as if their 3,000-kilogram forms could lift free of the earth. The giant birds are halfway between artistic feats of engineering and lawn ornaments.

Josh shows me *The Charger*, the first in this series of monumental sculptures to which architect and sculptor Starr Gideon Kempf devoted himself until his death in 1978. You can see it as a kind of telescopic fishing rod, or as a knight on horseback lifting his lance. The turning center of the work is an onion-shaped gadget.

"Birds nest in the wind turbine every year," Josh says, pointing at the onion. "By the time the chicks spread their wings, they think the world's a turntable. It's hopeless: as soon as they've taken off, they get dizzy and crash, one after another. It made my grandpa sick, used to ruin his whole day, the sight of those baby birds falling to the ground."

Kempf tended to show less empathy for his fellow human beings. The more he could rub other people up the wrong way, the more motivated he was to do exactly as he pleased. When he was told he couldn't do something, he went off and did it. Just like that, to see how it would turn out.

For years, Kempf's sculptures led to complaints in his residential street. Not only did they spoil the view of the mountains, but there were also practical issues. While working on *Sunrise*

Serenade, a 15-meter-tall ascending bird, he collected a shoebox full of official warnings, fine notices and court summonses. The bird was lying on its belly in the foundry. Because of its enormous length, its flamboyant phoenix tail stuck out of the front gate several meters into Pine Grove Avenue. It blocked traffic for months, an implacable presence.

"That's how he was," Josh says, "a grumpy old bastard, always blowing his top."

Once a woman in a Chevy Blazer truck made the mistake of turning into Pine Grove Avenue. She thought that at the end of the street she could turn around onto Cheyenne Boulevard and get back on track, but a huge steel structure, lying straight across the road, made her slam on her brakes. She got out to examine the obstacle, but in her surprise she forgot to put on the handbrake. The truck rolled into the sculpture. Before she could get a grip on the situation, a man came roaring out into the street, wielding a cutting torch. The woman just barely had time to get away.

*

In 1948, when Starr Kempf drove from Ohio with his wife and three children in a run-down pickup truck, Pine Grove Avenue was not yet what you might call a neighborhood. Colorado Springs, now a medium-sized city with 400,000 inhabitants, was then no more than a small settlement surrounded by acres of untilled farmland.

On the far edge of that land, at the foot of Cheyenne Mountain, and in the shadow of Pike's Peak, one of the highest mountain tops in the Colorado Rockies, Kempf bought himself a plot of land. He set off dynamite to blow chunks of rock out of the substrate for the split-level home he intended to build on the mountainside. The foundry was on the lowest level, then the studio, and finally the living areas.

For eight months, the family of five lived in the truck on that plot of land while Starr completed his first major project, the Kempf House. He already had a special fondness for robust materials. The house front is made of yellow brick with dark wood trim. The inside walls are 30 centimeters thick, the foundations 120 centimeters deep. He used a surprising amount of ironwork in the interior. A friend, David Supperstein, had a scrapyard, where Kempf often went to pick up discarded iron free of charge. He used rebar, most often found in reinforced concrete, to make all kinds of curlicued gates and fences, sconces and a shrine. The most peculiar parts of the house were the low ceilings. Kempf had a complex about his height; he was five foot five and didn't want to look short in his own home. By lowering the ceilings, he created an optical illusion he could live in.

*

Around the same time, Colorado Springs, with its picturesque location in the Rockies, began to attract new money. In no time at all, Pine Grove Avenue was lined with quirky detached houses, mostly mansions in neo-medieval styles and architects' self-designed homes. Kempf was dismayed to witness this upper-middle-class invasion and wanted nothing to do with it. He marked off the border of his property with a very conspicuous series of menacing aluminium rams' heads.

For about twenty years, the sculptures stood in his garden, until the night they were stolen. The next morning, Kempf started hammering a garden fence into the ground. His wife, Hedwig, still in her dressing gown, called out from the doorway, "What the hell's all that banging for? Where are the rams' heads?"

"The sixties are well and truly over, darling!" Kempf shouted back, without looking up.

*

Hedwig Roelen-Kempf was born in Aachen and fled to the Netherlands just before the Second World War. When the roundups of Jewish people began there too, she hid her savings in two antique wardrobes, forged a certificate from a fictional American buyer and accompanied the "artworks" on the ship to America.

When she reached Ellis Island, she didn't even have to pawn the wardrobes; she found a job as a nurse and could start right away. After a few weeks, she was offered a permanent position at Penrose Hospital in Colorado. The idea of going even farther west didn't bother her, as long as she could find a good pair of shoes.

And so it came to pass, one day in December 1941, that the young German beauty stepped into the only shoe shop in Colorado Springs in search of a pair of sturdy loafers. As the young clerk slipped her foot into a white moccasin, he could see, from his kneeling position, her nylon stocking rising under her skirt, far above her knee. Before standing up, he asked her out. Hedwig, having just embarked on a new life, appreciated his adventurous spirit and said yes. That evening, sitting alone in the restaurant, she would curse herself for it.

Starr hated his day job in the shoe shop. He had no interest in shoes or customer service, and work kept getting in the way of his plans. That very evening, for instance, he was told to stay late and stocktake. By the time he made it to the restaurant, dinnertime had come and gone, and so had Hedwig.

Starr didn't exactly feel he owed her an apology, but the

promise of those rising nylon stockings filled him with determination. He could already picture them puddled around her ankles.

The white moccasins were enough of a clue. He called the hospital and didn't have to do much explaining to get the home phone number of the new nurse from Germany.

Late that same evening, they met in the only place that was still open, the Navajo Hogan, an octagonal barn along the roadside where miners came to dance.

He sat across from her at one of the cafeteria tables, like a young Ernest Hemingway. Despite his small stature, his self-confidence and burly build made him an impressive sight. He didn't do a thing to put her at ease, not even striding over to the jukebox, as Hedwig had imagined American men did on dates. She soon learned that this shoe salesman was an artist, originally from Ohio. A strange path had brought him 2,000 kilometers to Colorado Springs.

*

Starr Gideon Kempf was born in Blufton, a small village of barely 1,000 inhabitants in northern Ohio. He grew up on a farm in an insular Mennonite community, where he had an exceptionally strict religious upbringing. His father and seven uncles trained him in carpentry and smithing, but also taught him about mechanics and engineering. What young Starr loved most was making wood carvings of the animals he saw around him.

At the age of sixteen, he escaped the community. Starr hopped aboard the first westbound train and continued that pattern for the next four years, moving ever farther west. It was as if his eyes were opening for the first time, letting in the light, scanning the horizon – and all the other fairy tales a young adventurer tells himself so it feels like he's going places instead of running away.

Now and then he stayed put for a while to earn a little money, however he could, for the next leg of his journey. He filleted fish by the pound for a restaurant in Salt Lake City, and in California he took care of the animals in a circus. The blissful impermanence of all this stood in stark contrast to the threat of eternal hellfire he'd grown up with among the Mennonites.

During his bumpy nights on cross-country freight trains, he spent a lot of time with people from all walks of life. In the narrow world of his childhood he'd never met a Black person, let alone spoken to one, but he soon had African-American friends and became enthralled with their culture. He especially loved spirituals and borrowed two titles for early murals: *Over Jordan* and *Swing Low, Sweet Chariot*.

In 1937, his interest in wall painting led him to Colorado, where an intriguing circle of artists had formed around the Canadian-American muralist Boardman Robinson. The young Starr Kempf showed him one of his drawings, a rural scene of a family with a nineteenth-century appearance and a horse-cart. Robinson was so impressed that he arranged a scholarship for the young man at the Fine Arts Center, where he was on the board.

The evening the scholarship was officially presented to Kempf, he was asked to say something about himself. He kept quiet about his childhood in the Mennonite community and let people think what they liked about his past.

His artistic genius came into full view during his education at the Fine Arts Center, although not in the way his bene-factors had expected. After enrolling there, he never drew another horsecart. Again and again, he portrayed the African-Americans he'd met on his wanderings. In the Midwest, then still a highly segregated region, this subject matter did not meet with a warm reception. One teacher ordered him to cut out the "Negro nonsense." As the story goes, Kempf gave him such a beating he almost ended up in the hospital.

Despite this incident, Kempf graduated with honors and went on to serve as an aviation technician in the Army Air Corps for two years. This was when the first symptoms of depression began to show themselves. He received an honorable discharge because of his "inner heaviness." Relieved to be free of responsibilities, he returned to taking undemanding jobs here and there, as he had during his travels, but now to support his artistic work. By the time Hedwig walked into that shoe shop, he had probably been working there for about two weeks.

Only eight days after they met, on January 6, 1942, Starr and Hedwig drove to Denver to get married. From the city hall, they drove without stopping to the region of Ohio he'd run away from. We can only guess what he was looking for there; reconciliation was not his bag. Still, they stayed for the first six years of their marriage and had their three children there, Madeline, Michael and Charlotte.

*

Josh orders me a portion of buffalo wings and a dirty Sanchez. The place where his grandparents went on their first date is now called Johnny's Navajo Hogan. Outside is the giant neon face of a Navajo man.

"Not really OK anymore, I know, but hey, it's a great place to eat," Josh says. For the first time I notice his lazy eye, on the left.

The Hogan borrows its name and design from the traditional Navajo dwellings built for the Colorado miners, who were mostly Navajos. The roadhouse consists of two octagonal areas, each domed over. "Built without a single nail. A true miracle of technology," Josh tells me. He's inherited his grandfather's enthusiasm for construction and architecture.

In the middle, where the two octagons meet, is the bar, surrounded with tables and leather sofas in the typical American diner style. On the stage behind the bar, a few veterans are taking turns singing karaoke. It's a sadder sight than they mean it to be.

"I want hot sauce with that," Josh tells the waiter serving the buffalo wings. "And I'm gonna need another cocktail."

Beforehand, I thought it would be hard to arrange an interview with a surviving family member of one of my architects, considering my interest in sensitive issues like their failure and their despair, but Josh is not the cautious type. In fact, he seems to feel an inner drive to tell me all he can about his grandfather's suicide, not because it's a trauma he needs to process – he hardly knew the man – but because it somehow gives his own life meaning. Before the event, he didn't have any special interests. Starr's well-aimed shot wrote him into a story in progress.

"We knew it was going to happen and couldn't do a thing about it. Once he couldn't work anymore, he didn't want to live. He'd been saying it for years. 'When I'm done, I'm done.' I think he'd have fought like a wildcat if we'd tried to stop him. Hell, he pointed a rifle at my dad, Michael, one time when he suggested an old people's home."

On top of that, his dead grandfather gives him something to do. Josh has only just settled in Colorado Springs after living in the UK. He first came back here to take care of some family business for Starr Enterprises, but he recently took on the renovation of the sculptures. It's a full-time job, to say the least – he spends up to sixteen hours a day on it. There's always something that needs to be fixed. The sculptures are severely tested by the local weather conditions. The latest damage is to the head of *Spirit Sunshine*, a bird with flapping wings, battered by a hailstorm. Josh has to repaint the sculptures every so often so they don't rust. His main project is the sculpture that Starr left unfinished in his studio, *Untitled*. Josh's dream is to complete it – more to have something of his own, I suspect, than out of devotion to his grandfather. He doesn't understand what Hedwig saw in that blowhard on that first night here in the Hogan. Though Josh talks about his grandmother as if she were a saint.

"Hedwig spent her whole life caring for people who were terminally ill. When Julie Penrose, the wife of hotel magnate Spencer Penrose, was sick, my grandmother went to her house to nurse her, alongside a full-time job at the hospital. On her deathbed, Mrs. Penrose said an angel came to lead her to the light. That angel was my grandma."

I nod. Whatever Hedwig saw in the surly figure of Starr Kempf, it was compelling enough for her to marry him eight days later, and it formed a solid basis for fifty-one years of marriage.

For their fiftieth anniversary, Starr installed a new piece in the front yard: a kinetic sculpture dedicated to Hedwig. *Peace Symbol* is a simple steel frame around a rotating peace symbol. Among the other sculptures, it stands out like a piece of cheap jewelry.

*

"Well, he finally did it," Hedwig said when she came home the day of Starr's death. She didn't shed many tears – not because she didn't grieve for him, but because she knew his decision had little to do with her. Once his body no longer permitted him to make art, he had no more use for it. *When I'm done, I'm done.* A narcissistic flare-up, a last stubborn assertion of self, or maybe just a healthy acknowledgment of mortality.

Starr Gideon Kempf was seventy-eight on April 7, 1995, when he shot himself in the head in his foundry. On that arbitrary day, his body refused to work. His knees were shot, his back a mess from dragging around scrap metal. He had rheumatism. An unreliable heart.

When he realized the time had come, he was in the foundry, at work on his last sculpture. *Untitled* lay on its stand, polished and assembled. All he had to do was paint it, but his fingers refused. He couldn't get a grip on that damn brush.

The next-to-last step. The final coat of paint. But any idiot could take care of that. What mattered to him, in the end, was not arriving at a finished product, but staying in charge of the process. So with the reassuring thought that he could leave the sculpture unfinished, he chose his own ending.

*

That shot was an autonomous, intentional act. I believe Kempf pulled the trigger with the intention of dying. That action must have mattered more to him than the result, than the idea of being dead.

If I'm being honest, I admire Kempf's irresponsible approach to life. By focusing all his attention on himself, he seems to have avoided ever facing the consequences of anything, simply because they never interested him.

As for me, I strain to work out the consequences of every action I take. It's probably because of that one illustration in my fourth-form history textbook: a picture of hell. In a series of explicit torture scenes, devils punished wicked souls for their sinful lives, and this went on for all eternity. Under the illustration was a caption: "Predestination in Calvinist doctrine." In the end, the picture did not put the fear of God into me, but for a long time I seriously asked myself, what if it's true?

As I was looking around Kempf's studio with Josh, my eyes fell on an etching, *The Furies*. A nude, muscular man representing God stands with his hammer raised over a human on an anvil. It's tempting to offer a psychological explanation: somewhere in a corner of his mind, his Mennonite upbringing was still eating away at him, condemning his choices.

But that's bullshit. And the proof is the bullet hole in the foot of the anvil. Kempf made this etching with the intention of shooting it. Nothing and no one was telling him how to live.

*

Sometime halfway through the 1970s, Starr Kempf, just past sixty, must have noticed that his rock-solid faith in his own genius was not matched by the reception of his work. If he thought it through, he could objectively conclude that he'd received little or no recognition so far.

This insight did not fill him with doubt or make him feel like a failure; on the contrary, it steeled his determination to create a work of art that could not be ignored. There would simply be no way of overlooking it.

He was already in Czechoslovakia by the time he called Hedwig to tell her where he'd gone. He'd be away for a few months, he said. He needed a better handle on a few techniques, so he'd signed on as an apprentice in a Czechoslovakian foundry.

A year after returning home, he started work on the monumental series of kinetic sculptures that would establish his reputation. Each one took two or three years to produce. Kempf did almost all the work himself, right through to the assembly with industrial cranes. From 1977 to 1995, he erected ten sculptures in his front yard in one continuous display of sheer artistic muscle.

In their ambition alone, the *Kinetic Sculptures* stand out from the rest of Kempf's body of work. Two houses. Seven plays, three produced in a California theater. An autobiography, which he destroyed without a trace. Ten etchings or so. Two murals. And a series of fifty-two coffee-table sculptures of stylized African figures – you might see them as curios in a faux-ethnic style or as a misguided attempt at cultural appropriation.

According to Kempf, the figures embodied his existential struggle and the quest for freedom.

Octave and Twelve, number 49 in the series, stands out for its fragile beauty. It represents a naked man and a pelican entangled in a harmonious dance. Its tactile quality is reminiscent of Rodin.

The bronzes were popular among collectors. Kempf produced each one in a limited edition, which was sometimes a full-time job in itself. The gutter in front of his studio was often filled with plaster impressions, tossed out of the window because of some imperfection in their shape. Some neighbors would pick them up and try to take them home, but nine times out of ten Kempf would charge outside and knock the sculpture out of their hands.

He eventually stopped making bronze sculptures because of his health. By then he already had serious symptoms: the whites of his eyes had turned yellow and his tongue tasted like iron. Long-term exposure to toxic fumes had given him the zinc shakes.

*

Despite his considerable success as a sculptor, Kempf felt that there were forces working against him: not only the incestuous

Denver art scene, but more than that, the general preference for modernism, which he despised.

For Kempf, art had to be personal, and above all robust: you should be able to throw a sculpture off a cliff, jump after it, and see when you land that it had survived without a scratch. The damage to the artist was immaterial – most of them were insufferable pricks anyhow. That was really the only reason he still went to their garden parties – to say as much to their faces.

*

A few houses down from the Kempfs' is a phenomenal residence, a skeleton of thin wood and glass, branching out from the center of the design, a majestic American oak. The house was the creation and the home of Elizabeth Wright Ingraham, granddaughter of the famous architect Frank Lloyd Wright. At the age of fourteen, she became an apprentice in her grandfather's studio; later, she continued her studies with Mies van der Rohe in Chicago.

In 1948, soon after receiving her architecture degree, she moved to Colorado Springs. The biggest attraction were the wide open spaces. The small town center was surrounded by vast tracts of unused land spread out like a blank sheet of drafting paper; the design potential was boundless. And there was no competition. Wright Ingraham made the most of her monopoly, designing no fewer than ninety homes in and around Colorado Springs.

Starr Kempf, despite seeing himself as a serious competitor, designed only one other house in his entire career, a modest dwelling opposite his own home. It was intended for his parents, as soon as they were ready to leave their Mennonite community. They never moved in.

*

"The olives are disgusting."

"No, they're nice," Hedwig corrects him, suspecting that when Starr says "olives," he means the Wright Ingrahams.

Elizabeth and her husband, Gordon, throw frequent back-yard cocktail parties, which, like everything else about them, express a clear aesthetic: an offshoot of Lloyd Wright's prairie style. In other words, third-rate ambition, Starr thinks, but he keeps it to himself.

The backyard is covered with bark chips and surrounded by beeches, like a clearing in the woods. Bossa nova in the back-ground. Lights hang between the low branches like twinkling fairies. Starr scrutinizes the strings of bulbs, wondering where Gordon hid his generator. Before he can figure it out, he's dis-tracted by the obnoxious crunch of the bark underfoot. Real American architecture begins with a lawn, he thinks. Now that would be a groundbreaking transformation of the landscape. Cocktail parties are not among the things Starr likes about the sixties, but he goes to them anyway – partly because he knows the neighbors don't like to see him there, and partly because Hedwig believes in community spirit. If it makes her happy . . .

The dentist from 2010 Pine Grove Avenue, very probably the most tedious man in the whole state of Colorado, comes walking their way.

"Be nice?" Hedwig says, as if it's not an order but a suggestion.

"As long as he pulls that stick out of his ass," Starr promises.

"Hey, buddy!" the dentist shouts. "What a garden, huh? This is really some world-class architecture here."

Starr coughs up a mouthful of phlegm.

"By the by, I saw one of your African numbers in the *Springs Gazette*," the dentist continues. "The one with the pelican. Pretty impressive piece of bronze, very modern."

Modern? Who the hell does that sadist think he's talking to,

Jackson Pollock? The lazy dripper. Starr can just picture him, dancing around with a wet paintbrush like he's at a powwow. He slings paint to the left, he slings paint to the right, and before you know it, idiots like Sigmund Freud are gushing about it – so modern! Modern art! Intuition, my ass! That paint-slinging's enough to make a person puke!

Starr spits out the phlegm in front of the dentist's feet: two astonished white hospital clogs. Hedwig nips at her dry martini, using the glass to hide her smile.

*

County Road 62 turns out to be a winding mountain path. At this altitude, the snow is 20 centimeters thick. Fortunately, an earlier driver has left tracks for me so that I can see where to go, but it's hard to steer, even with snow chains. As if that weren't bad enough, the white surface reflects the sun and dazzles me; I can't see my hand in front of my face. The road is a slippery, blinding, unpredictable place that draws me in so it can wipe me out.

Past the fifth bend lies the Rocky Mountain Mennonite Camp. After that, the bends become shorter and steeper. The road leads to Crags Trail, a hike up to a height of 4,267 meters. At the visitor parking lot, Fourmile Creek veers to the left and the road ends. On the slippery slope up to the trailhead, I see a man furiously waving his arms over his head, his face bright red with cold. Farther up, in a ditch alongside the road, is a black BMW.

"Thank God!" he exclaims. He's been stuck up on the mountain for two hours, he tells me.

"I should never have come up here. I'm such a dumb shit. Why did I come up here? I should just kill myself. Thank God you're here."

He gets in the ditch and tries to push the BMW out while I hit the accelerator in an attempt to tow it out. After a while we switch places. I can't get enough leverage; I'm sinking into the snow; it's up to my knees. After a few attempts, the spinning wheels of the car have buried it still deeper in the snow. I throw all my weight against the boot, but it barely moves. This is not going to work. The man honks the horn in frustration and the sound rips through the silent landscape. For a second, I'm scared he'll wake some ancient being living on the land.

"Calm down!" I shout over the horn. "Why don't I drive you down the mountain so you can get help?" He bangs his head into the wheel, three, four times.

"You can't help me," he says, and slams the door.

Three hours later, when I return to the parking lot after my hike on Crags Mountain, the car is still lying in the ditch. If the man left footprints, the snow has wiped them out in the meantime.

*

The next day, Josh takes me to the foundry in the basement of the house. He lets me go first down the rickety spiral staircase, a descent into a black hole. Wet wood. Iron filings. Dust. Rust. Matches. What am I smelling? I've just reached the damp, pitch-black bottom of the steps when an arm slides across my chest. With the force of a punch in the ribs, a soundless gasp, my chest caves in, and for a few suffocating seconds I can't breathe. I try to scream, but my mouth is full of liquid, as if the arm is holding me underwater, as if I'm trapped under the mat again with the fat boy from my class still sitting on top. Who will ever believe that I drowned here?

Josh apologizes for brushing against me and reaches past me to switch on the light. We're in the foundry, a long, deep room extending some 12 meters to the street side, packed to the ceiling with tools, all kinds of little machines, old pieces of iron, sheets of aluminium, hundreds of loose screws and bolts. It all seems to have been thrown on the shelves willy-nilly, in a frenzy of activity. Your first time in this room, you'd have trouble even finding a screwdriver – and on top of that, you have to watch where you walk. The floor is a tangle of loosely rolled-up cables and power cords.

But there's no life in this snake pit now, twenty-three years after Kempf shed his skin and slid on to the next world. Since his death, the workshop has gone unoccupied; his tools lie untouched where he left them. Even his last sculpture, *Untitled*, is still laid out on six trestles in the middle of the foundry.

"Here it is," Josh says.

We stare solemnly at the sculpture on its bier, longer than I can stay interested. An oar, several meters long. A giant butter knife. A long, thin form. Austere, compared to the ingenious turbine-birds in the front yard.

Josh once again brings up his plans to finish and install the sculpture.

I nod. My eyes wander up to the rafters, where dozens of license plates are nailed to the wood.

"Those were all rust buckets that Starr fixed up into race-horses," Josh explains. "They came from the scrap heap, but boy, those were some sweet rides. This one comes from a mint green '57 Cadillac Eldorado, and that one's from his white Harley-Davidson. He took Michael, my dad, for a ride with him on the Harley once for his ninth birthday. Starr was lost in a daydream at a red light that turned green on Uintah Street when the car behind him decided to pass him. Starr tore down the street after it, pulled in front of the car and forced it to pull over. Then he dragged the driver out of the car and beat the living shit out of him. My dad was nine years old. He survived his upbringing without too much damage, but that was no thanks to Starr. You know what the thing is? My dad's this rugged, handsome guy, always has been − six foot two, broad shoulders. The opposite of Starr. The man was constantly competing with his own son. Who would do a thing like that? It left a lot of bitterness. To be honest, I hardly knew him."

*

After Starr's death, Michael Kempf made no objection when his sister Charlotte asked if she could live in the house. Michael had lived in the UK for years, at a safe distance from his complicated relationship with his father, and he still didn't want to have to think about the sculptures. Their elder sister, Madeline, had her own life in Lafayette, Louisiana. Besides, if Charlotte lived in the house she could care for their mother, Hedwig, who was getting old.

Charlotte "Lottie" Kempf was forty-eight years old when she lost her father. She was unmarried and very attached to her parents; not a day passed that she didn't stop by the house.

When Charlotte discovered her father slumped against the wall of his studio on April 7, his face half blown off, she saw it as the fulfilment of her mission in life: of his three children, she was the one who found him. His palms were opened upward, as if to grant her this gift.

The blood hardly showed − dried up, it was a shade darker than the red of his sweater, which he normally wore only when he went out, so that he would stand out in the crowd if a photographer happened to be at work somewhere. But there was no one else competing for attention in the final photo.

After the body was found, Lottie went across the street. Their neighbor Jeff, who had often helped Starr move big pieces of metal, helped her scrape him off the wall and clean him up. By the time Hedwig got home, around noon, Lottie had wound a cloth around his mutilated head and laid him out on the bed. He looked like one of the lovers in Magritte's *Les Amants*.

Soon after the funeral, Lottie began offering commercial tours of the house and grounds. She opened up the foundry, the studio and the sculpture garden to the public. Hordes of tourists paid to see them, sometimes as many as eight busloads a day. Art lovers from all over the world came to marvel at Kempf's kinetic wind sculptures against the sublime backdrop of the Rocky Mountains.

*

Before long, Pine Grove Avenue was clogged with traffic. Parked vehicles lined both sides of the street, blocking some driveways. Rental cars ran over several cats belonging to the neighbors, such as Mrs. Winemiller of 1923 Pine Grove Avenue, who felt she had no choice but to circulate a petition for the welfare of Pine Grove's feline residents. Cats who had once sashayed their way across the residential street now had to run for their lives to dodge the visitors' speeding wheels. Enough is enough, said Mrs. Winemiller, who collected 800 signatures.

After Mrs. Winemiller's successful campaign, a group of neighbors teamed up and collected other complaints. Seven years later, their ingenious scrutiny of the zoning laws paid off: they were able to prove that the sculptures in the yard were noncompliant. The Kempfs owed fines totaling some $72,000.

Lottie's reaction was to stop opening the mail. Josh was the first to grasp how serious the situation was, when his father in England began receiving warning letters about the fines.

In 2002, the courts presented the Kempf family with an

ultimatum: if Lottie did not stop the tours, the sculptures would be removed by court order. Six of the ten were in violation of zoning regulations.

Josh went to Colorado to mediate the proceedings. When he arrived, he found a confused Hedwig locked up in the pantry, while Lottie gave a tour to a group of retired visitors in the front yard.

"Don't waste your breath, kiddo, we have a patent for this land. The zoning regulations don't apply to us," Lottie said.

Josh showed her the summons and explained that the city had the authority to remove the sculptures. Lottie launched into a rant, saying she had long suspected Josh of conspiring with the city of Colorado Springs to bring her down. They weren't the only ones, she added: she also had evidence Kofi Annan was out to destroy her . . .

*

The next morning, Hedwig had disappeared. With the help of a private detective, Josh found his grandmother two days later in a fleabag motel with no air-conditioning. She showed signs of dehydration; a doctor diagnosed her with late-stage dementia. Hedwig couldn't remember how she had ended up in the hotel room or who had locked the door from the outside.

One morning a few days later, in early June of 2003, neighbors clustered outside the Kempfs' garden gate. Some were in dressing gowns, holding their collars shut, while others had come from farther away and dressed first, in anticipation of what they would witness.

The first family member to arrive was Josh Kempf, escorted by two police cars with their blue lights on but no sirens. Lottie was waiting sleeplessly at the window. When she saw one of the police officers forcing the gate, she ran outside, shouting,

"You are trespassing on private property. You have no warrant. He has to go away. We have a patent for this land. He has to go away."

Lottie cut short her tirade when she saw the cranes approaching from the distance. She tried to shoulder her way through the officers to Josh, cursing and swearing. As she reached him, she shouted that she would kill him. Remove the sculptures? Over her dead body!

The agents arrested her when she started biting them. Josh opened the gate so that the crane could drive in. Hedwig was standing in the doorway, bewildered.

"Where are the aluminum rams' heads? Why are those cranes here? Starr?"

She started to wail, cramming a handkerchief into her mouth to muffle the noise. Josh put his arm around his ninety-year-old grandmother, whose bones showed sharp through her dressing gown, her dismayed figure creaking with each racking sob.

Lottie was pushed into the back of the police car. Most of the neighbors stayed at the gate all day, until the cranes were done.

*

Last December, three weeks before I was scheduled to arrive in Colorado Springs, Charlotte "Lottie" Kempf died at the age of seventy-two, alone and isolated in an old people's home.

"I'm sorry for your loss," I say to Josh in the foundry.

"The woman who threatened to kill me, more than once? I'm not sorry she checked out," Josh assures me. "But ever since Grandma died, I miss her like crazy."

Josh runs his hand over the metal of the sculpture on the stands. It's barely even a caress, yet for a second he looks completely alone in the world.

Untitled regards us from its perch with an undefined expression. I am starting to think this sculpture wants nothing from its viewers, not even a name or a finished form. Who's to say it was ever meant to be completed? Maybe Josh knows well enough there's nothing for him to finish. Kempf's choice to leave it incomplete suddenly strikes me as heroic.

"Are you nervous about getting started?" I don't know if it's Josh who asks me, or if I ask Josh, but in any case, neither of us tries to give an honest answer. There's a damp spot on one wall, I notice. Is that where Starr's head hit it, after the shot?

Something's dripping. I wasn't going to say anything, but now that I see I'm standing in a puddle, I feel obliged to comment after all.

"You have a leak," I say.

"No, it's just that the foundry's below street level. When it rains, we get water in here."

"But it hasn't rained."

"Sure it has. The whole month of July it rained without stopping."

Perhaps he's right. The lowest shelves on the wall of tools are moldy, and the machines have spots of green and black corrosion. Still, I don't feel entirely reassured; already the water is covering the floor. The cables – some are still plugged in.

"Didn't cause a short circuit, but it did do a lot of damage."

The water's rising fast, but Josh seems to be right: we aren't being electrocuted. Water is now gushing through the crevice between the walls and the ceiling in several places. Before I know it, it's up to my waist. Josh doesn't seem to be in any hurry to leave. He gazes at the sculpture, lost in thought, and because he isn't moving, I stay there too. After all, there's no longer anywhere else I have to go.

"How long did it go on raining, then?" I ask, a little concerned, as the mass of rising water lifts the sculpture from the stands and swallows it up in its now-considerable depths. Before Josh can reply, the water has reached our lips. I stand on tiptoe and, just above water, cough up what I swallowed. The water tastes like chlorine; if I swallow much more, it may just swallow me. The whole foundry is full now, right up to the rafters. I try to keep my eyes open underwater so I can see where Josh is, but the chlorine stings.

How long can I hold my breath? Not much longer, because across the diameter of my skull I can feel a thin thread of oxygen pulled taut, and I have to hold on to it, that much I remember: if I don't want to drown, I have to hold on to the thin thread of pinched oxygen I feel running through my head. I manage to go on clinging to it until the mass of water puts so much pressure on the walls that the entrance on the street side bursts open. The water floods outside, spewing the tools and machines out into the street. I ride the current out with them, like a fish spilling out of its broken bowl. All the water I've breathed in sends me into a coughing fit.

As I stand there, still reeling from the experience of drowning, I see Starr Gideon Kempf standing at the entrance to his workshop, wearing a red jumper and smoking a cigarette. He's just made a quick call to his lawyer, Mr. Grouse, for a business update. As he flicks away the butt, his neighbor from across the street, Jeff, comes driving up in his maroon truck.

"Went hunting up on Cheyenne, but I didn't bag anything," Jeff calls out from his driveway, pulling his rifle out of the back.

"Whaddaya got there, a Marlin?" Starr asks.

"Classic Marlin, all right," Jeff replies.

"Nice. I used to have a Remington, now all I got's a Baby Browning."

"What does a sculptor need a pistol for?"

"No one remembers an artist who dies in his sleep."

ACKNOWLEDGMENTS

Preliminary versions of several chapters of this book were written as part of my master's thesis at the Royal Conservatoire in Antwerp. My thanks to my mentor, Lucas Vandervost, and my supervisor, Ilja Leonard Pfeijffer, for the care and attention they devoted to these writings in their earliest, fragile state.

My thanks to the Association des Clochers Tors d'Europe, the mayor of Verchin, the mayor of Turnhout, Koen Broucke (who, I should add, took the photo of San Carlino and introduced me to the work of L. S. Lowry), Koen Peeters, Koen Van Synghel, Dirk Beirens, Marc Dubois, the Liberas archives in Ghent, Werner Van Hoeydonck, David and Hilde Maenaut, the Architekturzentrum Wien, St. John's Library, Pasquale M., Mrs. Cairns, the Library of Congress, Thomas MacWood, Catherine Rashid and Joshua Kempf.

My thanks to Els Snick, who offered me a place to stay in Ostend, so that I could do my writing with a view of Lowry's *Seascape*.

My thanks to my dear friends Juicy, Eli, Harm, Jonas in the tower room, Eliene, Anouk and the quadruplets for traveling with me, conversing with me, reading and commenting on my work and sticking close to me as I explored this dangerous topic.

My thanks to my editor, Peter, my agent, Michaël, and my designer, Steven, for the direction, space and shape within and thanks to which this book could grow.

My thanks to my translator, David McKay, for his meticulous work on the translation and his loving attention to the original text.

My thanks to my love, my traveling companion, Wouter. For everything that happened in and around this book.

CHARLOTTE VAN DEN BROECK has published two collections of poetry. Her debut collection, *Chameleon*, was awarded the Herman de Coninck debut prize for poetry. For her second collection, *Nachtroer*, she received the triannual Paul Snoek Prize for the best collection of poetry in Dutch. Her poetry has been translated into German, French, Spanish, Afrikaans, Serbian, and English. *Bold Ventures* was a Dutch bestseller and won the Confituur Boekhandels Prize, the Dr. Wijnaendts Francken Prize, and was short-listed for the Boekenbon Literature Prize and the Jan Hanlo Essay Prize.

DAVID MCKAY's translation work has been described as "dazzlingly lyrical" (Neel Mukherjee, *The Guardian*). He received the Vondel Translation Prize for *War and Turpentine* by Stefan Hertmans, which was also nominated for the 2017 Man Booker International Prize and short-listed for the Best Translated Book Award. His co-translation with Ina Rilke of the classic nineteenth-century novel *Max Havelaar* was short-listed for the 2020 Oxford–Weidenfeld Prize, and in 2021 he was the ALTA Dutch-English mentor.